The Faces of Intellectual Disability

The Faces of Intellectual Disability

Philosophical Reflections

Licia Carlson

Indiana University Press
Bloomington and Indianapolis

This book is a publication of

Indiana University Press
601 North Morton Street
Bloomington, IN 47404-3797 USA

http://iupress.indiana.edu

Telephone orders   800-842-6796
Fax orders   812-855-7931
Orders by e-mail   iuporder@indiana.edu

∞The paper used in this publication meets the minimum requirements
of the American National Standard for Information Sciences—Perma-
nence of Paper for Printed Library Materials, ANSI Z39.48-1992.

Manufactured in the United States of America

Library of Congress Cataloging-in-Publication Data

Carlson, Licia, date
 The faces of intellectual disability : philosophical reflections / Licia
Carlson.
    p. ; cm.
 Includes bibliographical references and index.
 ISBN 978-0-253-35421-1 (cloth : alk. paper) — ISBN 978-0-253-22157-5
(pbk. : alk. paper) 1. Mental retardation—Philosophy. 2. Mental retarda-
tion—Social aspects. I. Title.
 [DNLM: 1. Mentally Disabled Persons. 2. Ethics. 3. Mental Retardation.
4. Philosophy. WM 300 C284f 2009]
 RC570.2.C37 2010
 616.85'88—dc22
                                                            2009022454

1 2 3 4 5 15 14 13 12 11 10

To my parents
And to the memory of my beloved grandparents

There is no sovereign philosophy, it's true, but a philosophy or rather philosophy in activity. The movement by which, not without effort and uncertainty, dreams and illusions, one detaches oneself from what is accepted as true and seeks other rules—that is philosophy. The displacement and transformation of frameworks of thinking, the changing of received values and all the work that has been done to think otherwise, to do something else, to become other than what one is—that, too, is philosophy.

Michel Foucault, "The Masked Philosopher"

Contents

Acknowledgments

This book has gone through many incarnations, and I am deeply grateful to so many who have generously shared their insights, questions, and voices along the way. This book would not exist were it not for the amazing individuals I met at the Rehabilitation School in Poughkeepsie, New York, and the philosophical inspiration and support I received as an undergraduate from Mitch Miller, Douglas Winblad, Uma Narayan, and Michael McCarthy. As I began to develop these early ideas in graduate school, my colleagues and mentors at the University of Toronto—especially Kathryn Morgan, Amy Mullin, and André Gombay—provided a rich environment in which to nourish my thoughts about philosophy and disability. To the incomparable Ian Hacking: I thank you for your unwavering support of this project through its many stages, and for the innumerable ways you have shaped, expanded, inspired, and challenged my philosophical work.

My understanding of disability, both as lived experience and as an area of academic inquiry, has been greatly enhanced though an interdisciplinary dialogue with others within and beyond philosophy. I thank Paul Longmore and Rosemarie Garland Thomson for inviting me to participate in a summer NEH seminary on disability studies in the summer of 2000, as well as all the participants and presenters whose passion for these issues continues to sustain me. My ideas and arguments have also benefited from the enormously helpful feedback I have received in presenting parts of my work at the American Philosophical Association, the World Congress of Bioethics, FEAST, the Society for Disability Studies, the annual philosophy conference at Seattle University, the Bioethics

Center at the Brigham and Women's Hospital, Smith College, and the Workshop on Gender and Philosophy at MIT. I am particularly grateful to Eva Kittay for inviting me to organize a conference on cognitive disability and moral philosophy at Stony Brook University in the fall of 2008, and to Jennifer Clegg for including me in Counterpoint: A Roundtable on Intellectual Disability in Nottingham, UK, in April 2009. The enormously rich ideas and conversations at these meetings have broadened my philosophical horizons and have given me a new critical perspective on my work.

This book has been immeasurably improved thanks to the close and thoughtful consideration of a number of people, including Anita Silvers, Sophia Wong, Shelley Tremain, Hilde Lindemann, Lisa Dietrich, and the many anonymous reviewers and editors who reviewed earlier versions of this work. The material in chapter one first appeared in *Foucault and the Government of Disability,* ed. Shelley Tremain (Ann Arbor: University of Michigan Press, 2005), and chapter two is an extended version of "Cognitive Ableism and Disability Studies: Feminist Reflections on the History of Mental Retardation," published in *Hypatia: Special Issue on Feminism and Disability,* part 1, vol. 16, no. 4 (fall 2001). I am particularly grateful to Eva Kittay for taking such care with my words and ideas, for the depth and wisdom of her own work on this topic, for introducing me to her beautiful Sesha and the Center for Discovery, and for inviting me to collaborate with her on such important work. Finally, I am deeply indebted to my wonderful editor, Dee Mortensen, for her enthusiasm and support for this project, to Laura MacLeod, and to Chrisona Schmidt, who has given shape and clarity to my thoughts and words.

I am fortunate to have found welcoming intellectual homes at Seattle University and the Harvard Writing Program. I am grateful to both departments and universities for funding much of my research, to my students for partaking in philosophy with me, and I am deeply fond of my wonderfully generous colleagues with whom I have shared ideas, friendship, and good wine. I am also tremendously lucky to count among my closest friends philosophers who have helped me flourish in so many ways: Mark Clamen, Corinne Painter, Christian Lotz, Michael Eskin, and Kathrin Stengel.

To all my dear friends and my beautiful family, this book gives voice to ideas and convictions that I learned from my wise and loving parents, and that I have come to appreciate in sharing my life with you: the belief in the beauty and dignity of human beings, the importance of empathy, kindness, and respect, the value of loving relationships, and the possibility of hope and change. To my parents, thank you for reading every word I've written and for encouraging me to follow this path. To my sweet Jeremiah, I cannot thank you enough for your patience, love, dedication, and the innumerable gifts you have given me (including a willingness to hear me talk endlessly about the history of idiocy). And to my precious Julian: thank you for being a part of my world and for making so many other worlds possible.

A Note on Terminology

In this volume I have chosen to use the term "intellectual disability" to refer to the general conditions traditionally associated with mental retardation. I prefer this more general term, in part because it reflects the recent shift (both professional and political) away from "mental retardation." However, I will use the term "mental retardation" when I wish to speak about this category specifically (in the context of a particular argument, professional use, or historical period). Similarly, when I use other terminology from the past, it should be understood that I am referring to historically defined conditions (e.g., idiocy, feeblemindedness, mental deficiency). When speaking about actual individuals, I prefer to use the phrase "persons with intellectual disabilities," as opposed to "the intellectually disabled." However, when appropriate, I will preserve the terminology used in specific contexts (e.g., idiots, imbeciles, morons, the feebleminded, the mentally retarded, the intellectually disabled). For the sake of clarity I will forgo placing these terms in quotation marks, but it should be understood that I do not take them to be self-evident "natural kinds" or unproblematic terms.

The Faces of Intellectual Disability

Introduction:
The Philosopher's Nightmare

> Curiosity . . . it evokes "concern"; it evokes the care one takes
> for what exists and could exist; a readiness to find strange
> and singular what surrounds us; a certain relentlessness to
> break up our familiarities and to regard otherwise the same
> things; a fervor to grasp what is happening and what passes; a
> casualness in regard to the traditional hierarchies of the im-
> portant and the essential. I dream of a new age of curiosity.
>
> —MICHEL FOUCAULT

> [The intellectual] must first tend to his own garden.
> For the intellectual's project is to engage in a struggle
> against the mechanisms of power as they extend and
> reproduce themselves through his or her disciplin-
> ary critical, teaching and scholarly activity.
>
> —PAUL BOVÉ

This book is born of the kind of curiosity that Foucault imagined. It traces a philosophical journey of sorts that began with Plato—hardly an original start-ing point. I was an undergraduate in a seminar on the Platonic dialogues. This three-hour class happened to be held immediately after a weekly volunteer job I had working with children who, despite the broad age range (from 5 to 18), were in the same classroom because they were labeled "multiply handicapped." On an unremarkable day in the late 1980s, I was struck by a question during my Plato class: what do philosophers have to say about this group of individuals, these persons who appear to so many as strange and yet had become beautifully singular to me in their familiarity? As I began to look for an answer, I found relative silence, or worse. Plato decreed that "defective babies" should be left to die. Locke and Kant defined those who lack reason as less than human. And most troubling of all, when I looked for contemporary discussions about this group, most of the references I found were in discussions of animal rights, asking pointedly whether the severely mentally retarded can be distinguished from non-human animals in any meaningful sense. The first book I encountered that seemed to present a different portrait, not of intellectual disability but of its close and more philosophically attractive cousin, was Michel Foucault's *History of Madness*. I owe a great debt to my first encounter with this book, with its passionate commitment to expose "Reason's monologue" in the face of a silenced other. My excitement at finding a philosophical home in Foucault's pages where I can make sense of philosophy's treatment of intellectual disability has not waned.

This book is not a personal narrative, but I cannot leave the autobiographical behind without mentioning a recurrent theme I encountered while working in this rather anomalous philosophical field. One of the first questions I am often asked by other philosophers when I tell them about my interest in intellectual disability is, "Oh, do you have a disabled family member?" This question might not have struck me as particularly odd had it not been asked so consistently. I became increasingly irritated by the assumption that seemed embedded in the question (though I don't mean to suggest that everyone who asked me necessarily subscribed to this): the only reason I would have an interest in this topic is because someone in my family has an intellectual disability. As I have delved deeper into the margins of philosophy, this relatively benign question has come to represent far more troubling beliefs that I have encountered. First, the intellectually disabled are not persons. They are owed respect and justice only by virtue of their relationship to non-disabled family members who *are* persons. Second, this realm of inquiry is justifiably marginal since concerns about intellectual disability are remote, and, third, those who *do* have close personal ties to persons with intellectual disabilities are unable to achieve the distance required for objective and reasonable moral considerations. So in an effort to head the question off at the pass and to betray my own location, I will identify myself as a non-disabled philosopher who, though not entirely personally distant from the issue, fervently believes that the philosophical questions that emerge in connection with intellectual disability are matters that not only are worthy of scholarly interest but speak to the deepest problems of exclusion, oppression, and dehumanization; and that one's proximity to persons with intellectual disabilities should be neither assumed as a basis for participation in this conversation nor grounds for disqualification when speaking philosophically about this topic.

Much has changed, both in philosophy and beyond, since my early encounters with Plato, Foucault, and the children in the Rehabilitation School in Poughkeepsie, New York. The presence of disability in philosophy and other academic disciplines is notably greater. There is a vocal and robust disability rights movement that has led to legislative and social changes. And there is a rich body of philosophical literature that is now grappling with many of the questions that I asked myself when I first began to consider this topic, with prominent, mainstream philosophers weighing in.[1] At the same time, prenatal testing for Down syndrome and other genetic and chromosomal abnormalities linked with intellectual disabilities has become standard practice. The increasing intersection between bioethics and clinical practice has offered philosophers a venue for speaking about and making concrete recommendations in regard to persons with intellectual disabilities. The case of Ashley X is a good example of this. The parents of a severely disabled girl authorized growth attenuation therapies (removing her breast buds and sex organs and giving her hormone injections) to keep her body in a state of perpetual childhood. Their actions attracted the media spotlight, with prominent philosophers like Peter Singer responding in the press.[2]

Despite these changes, intellectual disability remains relatively marginal within philosophical discourse. One worthy project would be to map the exclusion of intellectual disability from the philosophical scene, something like the "archaeology of silence" Foucault hoped to achieve in *The History of Madness*. However, this book has a different goal: it focuses on the philosophers who *have* spoken about this topic. In *The History of Disability*, French historian Henri Stiker argues that to examine the *integration* of persons with disabilities into society is "a method more critical, even more militant, than to address [disability] in terms of exclusion. The motives and factors that lead to rejection, even when such rejection is hidden and subtle, are fairly obvious to the attentive. Integration passes more unnoticed."[3] In a theoretical context, the traces of intellectual disability in philosophical literature raise critical questions. Why and how do philosophers integrate the "intellectually disabled" into their work?

Question

By what mechanisms do they do so, and what is behind their intentions? Stiker concludes that the project of integration bespeaks a desire to assimilate, to normalize, to erase difference and make the disabled fit a celebrated vision of sameness. However, we find a very different picture in philosophical discourse. Rather than promoting goals of assimilation and normalization, many who bring the intellectually disabled into the philosophical fold mark this group out according to its departure from the normal and highlight its profound otherness, its radical alterity.

In her fascinating exploration of blindness, *Sight Unseen,* Georgina Kleege critiques the representation of blind characters in Hollywood films. "While Hollywood did not invent these stereotypes, the repetition and intricacy of these images seems to reveal something disturbing about the filmmakers' vision of the world. The blind are a filmmaker's worst nightmare. They can never be viewers, can never be enlightened and dazzled by the filmmaker's artistry. So filmmakers treat the blind the way we all deal with nightmares: they belittle them, expose their weakness, make them at best pitiable, at worst somewhat unsavory."[4] If we move from the filmmaker's worldview to the ones articulated by many philosophers, we find characterizations of intellectual disability that suggest it is a philosopher's worst nightmare. In many ways this book is an attempt to make sense of this phenomenon, to uncover the faces of intellectual disability that haunt philosophy.

A Changing Landscape

Question

Why focus on philosophy and intellectual disability? The convergence of these two areas comes at an exciting time in both fields. Both politically and theoretically, there have been significant changes in the ways that disability, generally, is addressed. In the wake of the 1990 Americans with Disabilities Act and the disability rights movement that gave rise to it, the emergence of disability studies as an area of academic inquiry has defined disability as a central lens of analysis and brought considerations that were once marginalized to the foreground in numerous disciplines. And though philosophy has been somewhat slower than other disciplines to take up questions surrounding disability, there is a growing body of literature that focuses on ethical, epistemological, political, and conceptual dimensions of disability as a category and an embodied identity.

One way to map these changes is to examine the evolution of two models of disability that have emerged in response to the dominant conceptualization of disability as a pathology and a tragedy. Historically, disability has been defined according to the medical model—viewed as a particular trait in the individual departing from what might be called *normal species functioning*. As many disability theorists point out, this model has been responsible for numerous beliefs and practices surrounding disability and the disabled. The view that disability is objectively abnormal and thus undesirable gives rise to a related constellation of assumptions that have been termed the "personal tragedy model": that disability is objectively bad, and thus something to be pitied, a personal tragedy for both the individual and her family, something to be prevented and, if possible, cured. That notion that disability constitutes a blemish on the rosy face of medical science and societal well-being explains many of the practices associated with it, ranging from involuntary sterilization, institutionalization, and forced rehabilitation to social marginalization, euthanasia, and "mercy killing."

Most philosophers and disability theorists do not globally reject the advances and benefits of medical and rehabilitative practices. However, many subject the assumptions and consequences of the medical model and the accompanying personal tragedy model of disability—which views disability as something inherently bad, objectively devalued, and worthy of pity, charity, and sorrow—to close scrutiny.[5] As a simultaneous rejection of and response to the devaluation of disability both implicit and explicit in the medical model, the social model of disability proposes an alternate definition of disability. According to this model, having an impairment (a particular biological, physiological, psychological condition or trait) is distinct from being disabled because the latter reflects the interaction between the individual and his or her environment. "Disability" is no longer located within the individual, as a particular static trait, but is a relational term. The social model of disability maintains that many of the disadvantages experienced by persons with disabilities are a result of social inequalities, barriers (physical and ideological) to opportunities, negative stereotypes and prejudices, discrimination, insufficient support systems, and general societal attitudes. Proponents of the social model argue that there is a more complicated story to be told than the medical model would have us believe, and they call for the abandonment of the individual/pathological/personal tragedy models of disability.

The adoption of the social model of disability is widely evident in disability memoirs, academic texts, expressions of disability culture in the media and the arts, grassroots political movements such as the independent living movement and the self-advocacy movement, and legal and clinical discourse.[6] For example, the Americans with Disabilities Act (ADA), the 1990 U.S. federal law that protects persons with physical and mental disabilities from discrimination, is legislative evidence of this shift. Anita Silvers argues that it "represents a reconceptualization of the meaning of 'disability'" that discards the medical model, and understands that "a disabling condition is a state of society itself, not a physical or mental state of a minority of society's members, and that it is the way society is organized rather than personal deficits which disadvantages this minority."[7] In a broader international context, this change is evident as well: "A major report commissioned by UNESCO for the World Summit on Social Development, Disability Awareness in Action redefined disability as follows: 'The term disability is now used by many disabled people to represent a complex system of social restrictions imposed on people with impairments by a highly discriminatory society. Disability, therefore, is a concept distinct from any particular medical condition. It is a social construct that varies across cultures and through time, in the same way, for example, as gender, class or caste."[8]

The social model has clear relevance for intellectual disability specifically. The departure from the traditional medical or individual trait model can be seen in the latest definition proposed by the American Association on Intellectual and Developmental Disabilities (AAIDD), the oldest American professional organization devoted to the study of mental retardation.[9] The notion that we should radically alter our conception of intellectual disability is borne out by the professional organization that was central to its inception. The 1992 edition of its system of classification changed its definition of mental retardation, a shift that reflects the adoption of the social rather than medical model of disability. It boasts a "paradigm shift from a view of mental retardation as an absolute trait expressed solely by an individual to an expression of the interaction between the person with limited intellectual functioning and the environment."[10] It defines mental retardation as follows: "Mental retardation refers to substantial limitations in present functioning. It is characterized by significantly subaverage intellectual functioning, existing concurrently with related limitations in two or more of the following applicable adaptive skill areas: communication, self-care, home living, social skills, community use, self-direction, heath and safety, functional academics, leisure, and work. Mental retardation manifests before age 18."[11] According to this new functional definition, "if intellectual limitations have no real effect on functioning, then the person does not have mental retardation."[12] It replaced the traditional subclassifications of mild, moderate, severe, and profound retardation with subclassifications based on "the intensities and patterns of supports systems: intermittent, limited, extensive, and pervasive."[13] And the latest definition (the 2002 revision remains faithful to the social model) confirms that its approach is rooted in a social model of disability: "Limitations in present functioning must be considered within the context of community environments typical of the individual's age, peers, and culture," and "valid assessment considers cultural and linguistic diversity as well as differences in communication, sensory motor, and behavioral factors."[14]

These conceptual changes come on the heels of significant social and political changes that have taken place in the last half century. The 1960s and 1970s witnessed a vigorous parent's advocacy movement, government attention to the violation of civil rights, and the beginning of the deinstitutionalization movement,[15] and led to a self-advocacy movement that is still active and thriving today.[16] In numerous contexts, then, intellectual disability has been reconceptualized by the social model of disability, suggesting that a shift away from the individual trait/medical model (at least in *some* disciplines) has occurred.

Yet there are also important and distinct questions that intellectual disability, as a category, raises for both the medical and social models and the tension between them. What are the implications of the emergence of genetically based forms of intellectual disability (e.g., fragile X syndrome) for mental retardation *as a category,* and is it desirable or even possible to do away with the medical model altogether, given this growing area of research? [17] While many critiques of the deleterious effects of the medical model are certainly applicable in the case of intellectual disability, it remains a category that is firmly rooted in biomedical and genetic discourse, a fact that disability theorists and philosophers cannot afford to ignore. The challenges posed by some theorists that certain features of intellectual disability (e.g., acquiescence bias and incompetence) are socially constructed must be considered in tandem with the dominance that the medical model continues to enjoy in defining some kinds of mental retardation.[18] Finally, one cannot assume that the personal tragedy model of disability that accompanies the medical model is articulated in the same ways for intellectual disability as it is for other disabilities. As we shall see, the notions of suffering and tragedy often assume a different hue relative to persons with severe intellectual disabilities. For example, in some cases the primary emphasis on suffering *beyond* the severely disabled individual—experienced by family members and society at large, and *not* by the person with the disability— suggests that the personal tragedy model cannot be assumed to function in identical ways for all persons with disabilities.

In terms of the intricacies of the social model itself, and the distinction it makes between impairment and disability, we must ask, What is the underlying impairment on which intellectual disability is based? A particular genetic impairment (e.g., chromosomal abnormality) may be involved in some cases, but in others the underlying fixed pathology is unclear or unknown. It is worth noting that "for 75% of children with mild symptoms and 30–40% with severe symptoms, no specific cause is apparent."[19] Moreover, debates about the significance and reification of IQ scores (which remain a cornerstone of the DSM-IV definition of mental retardation) highlight further ambiguities in identifying the precise locus of impairment in many cases.[20] Finally, one must ask whether it is possible to speak in any coherent, unified way about the modes by which intellectual disabilities are produced, given the wide range of abilities and conditions that are encompassed by such broad categories as mental retardation and intellectual disability.

These concerns underlie the development of a model that further disrupts the very category of disability: the postmodern model. Like the elusiveness of the term "postmodernity" itself, postmodern models of disability cannot be described univocally. However, there are a number of features of the postmodern model of disability that are particularly significant for a philosophical analysis of intellectual disability.

Many postmodern disability theorists are challenging the very concept of impairment, defined by the social model as that fixed point on which disability as a disadvantage is socially constituted. Drawing on postmodern theories of the instability of the body and identity, some argue that a definition of disability must expose the dynamic and constructed nature of impaired bodies and minds in order to adequately capture the way in which disabilities and disabled identities are created.[21] The postmodern turn in disability theory is at once critical/deconstructive and positive/constructive, insofar as the conceptual tools of postmodernity are used not only to critique existing conceptions and models of disability, but also to reconsider disability as the postmodern identity or category par excellence. Lennard Davis, for example, argues that disability is an unstable category that mirrors the instability of identity itself, defining disability as *the* quintessential postmodern identity because "it is impossible to essentialize it the way one can the categories of gender and ethnicity."[22] Insofar as Davis defines his project as a "dismodernist ethics of the body," however, his project, like many others, focuses primarily on questions of disability and embodiment. Thus we must consider the viability of a postmodern model of disability for a category like mental retardation. What does it mean to deconstruct impairment in the case of intellectual disability? Are particular cognitive impairments *themselves* social constructs, and if so what would this mean?[23] What does it mean to talk about "disability" as the quintessential postmodern category in the context of intellectual disabilities? How are formulations of the instability and fluidity of disability as an identity relevant to an understanding of intellectual disability? From a political perspective, can this model adequately address the power relations that affect the ways that persons with intellectual disabilities can partake in disability advocacy? What place do persons with severe intellectual disabilities have within this discourse, and how can their interests be addressed in ways that don't perpetuate certain forms of oppression and marginalization?

Insofar as the social model and the more recent postmodern model of disability challenge entrenched assumptions and practices associated with persons with disabilities, they provide fodder for a new critical approach to disability. Yet the category of "intellectual disability" also poses critical questions for these models, and for the "mentally accelerated" theorists (to borrow a phrase from James Trent) who articulate them. One important task, then, is to consider what these three models—medical, social, and postmodern—contribute to an understanding of intellectual disability as a classification, and how its inclusion in discussions of disability can engage, challenge, and refine these models. Yet they also provide an important backdrop against which one can critically explore the inclusion of intellectual disability in philosophical discourse. To what extent have philosophers unwittingly or deliberately subscribed to and challenged these models? Within philosophy specifically, how has intellectual disability been understood and discussed?

Mapping the Philosophical Terrain

The topic of intellectual disability may be unfamiliar to many philosophers and is certainly not included among what might be considered canonical philosophical problems. However, the intellectually disabled do appear in numerous places within philosophical discourse in the past half century, and these discussions reflect two general approaches to the topic. I will refer to the first as the "traditional" (for lack of a better term) approach, found primarily in ethical and bioethical literature, and to the second as a critical disability approach, found in both ethics and bioethics, as well as in other areas of philosophy and disability theory.

In the traditional approach, intellectual disability is discussed in two ways: as an object of ethical discourse in its own right, and as a conceptual tool that serves to clarify or highlight a different philosophical problem or question. In the former case, philosophers focus on numerous ethical problems. Some address the moral status of individuals with intellectual disabilities and ask, Are they persons? How are the distinctions between mild/severe morally relevant? Are the severely intellectually disabled distinct from non-human animals? Others consider the challenges that intellectual disability poses to existing moral theories and concepts. Here the severely intellectually disabled provide a marginal case, a means by which to explore the nature and limits of concepts like justice, rights, respect, and responsibility. There are also inquiries of a more practical nature, which combine theoretical reflections and questions regarding how persons with intellectual disabilities should be treated. Topics can range from ethical issues like autonomy, self-determination, and proxy decision making, to specific bioethical debates regarding topics like involuntary sterilization, access to health care, and preventative practices such as prenatal testing and selective abortion.

This traditional approach has a number of distinctive features. First, intellectual disability is taken to be an unproblematic "natural kind," a definable and recognizable group of individuals typically characterized by deficits in cognitive capacity. Some philosophers explicitly define what they mean by the "mentally retarded" or the "intellectually disabled," but many assume that readers all share a common understanding of what is meant by a "severely intellectually disabled person" (or an "idiot" or "imbecile," language left behind in the early twentieth century but still used by some philosophers). Second, there is a normative assumption that intellectual disability is objectively undesirable, bad, and/or tragic. This devaluation may be explicitly stated, as Robert Veatch does: "Mental retardation . . . is a serious condition, one that any reasonable person would rather not have. In our terms, the disvalue is objective. This means that we cannot cope with the problem of stigma simply by trying to re-educate people into thinking the condition is not inherently bad. Retardation is not like race or gender stigma. Even the most dedicated and sympathetic advocate for the retarded acknowledges that it is a serious problem. . . . The problem is real. It is so clearly a bad thing to have that we can act as if it were objectively a bad condition."[24] The devaluation of intellectual disability can also be implicitly evident in the ways that persons with intellectual disabilities are characterized and discussed (e.g., the assumption that a life with a profound cognitive impairment is not worth living).

Third, the intellectually disabled are discussed in a way that is ahistorical; references to the history of this classification are either absent or considered irrelevant to the philosophical questions at hand. Intellectual disability is considered a case study with respect to concepts like personhood and justice, and members of this group are discussed in the abstract, rather than through an examination of concrete practices and the social and political context in which this group is situated. In traditional approaches that explicitly address intellectual disability, then, it is taken to be an unproblematic, self-evident, and undesirable *kind* of individual, about whom ethical and bioethical questions can be posed without reference to any historical, political, or social factors that might affect the nature or status of this group of individuals.

This traditional style of addressing mental retardation, as well as intellectual disability more generally, is also found in philosophical literature that does not examine intellectual disability per se but invokes examples to assist in making other philosophical arguments. A clear case can be found in arguments against speciesism. Animal rights literature is littered with references to the severely intellectually disabled, a group of individuals that serves to bolster the case for animal rights. For example, Peter Singer notably argues that to grant human beings higher moral status than non-human animals with comparable intellectual ability is arbitrary and unjustified and thus constitutes speciesism, a form of discrimination as morally problematic as racism and sexism. Here again we find that intellectual disability is assumed to be a self-evident category of individuals about whom philosophical analogies and comparisons can be made. Though the history of abuses to non-human animals is explicitly chronicled, there is no mention of the historical and political context in which intellectual disability emerged as a classification, or the history of abuses and oppression of people labeled as such.

There are numerous other instances where the intellectually disabled appear in moral discourse, as philosophical examples that provide support for arguments that are not directly applicable to persons with disabilities. In both examples of the traditional approach—direct or indirect philosophical discourse about intellectual disability—the mentally retarded or intellectually disabled serve as disembodied thought experiments through which philosophers may tease out the intricacies of their conceptual and normative positions.

The second philosophical approach to intellectual disability does not necessarily move far afield from the ethical and bioethical topics addressed by the traditional approach. Rather, a critical disability approach signals a change in orientation, a difference in *how* ethical, bioethical, and other philosophical questions are posed. While the same questions of autonomy, care, rights, moral status, justice, and treatment are often addressed, the critical disability approach is distinctive insofar as it problematizes the category of disability itself and poses critical questions regarding the nature, status, and treatment of persons with disabilities in both political and academic settings. In part, this shift in the mode of questioning and scope of analysis is symptomatic of broader changes on the disability landscape over the past few decades. Here we find the social and postmodern models of disability, and a growing body of philosophical work that critically interrogates the category of disability in a variety of contexts, including ethical and bioethical literature, as well as in the philosophy of science, political philosophy, feminist philosophy, and postmodern thought.

These critical philosophies of disability can be seen in many ways as a corrective to the traditional approach defined above. First, the very nature and status of disability as a category is being challenged by philosophers who refuse to accept it as a self-evident and unproblematic "natural kind." Second, in response to the ahistorical approach to disability found in so much philosophical literature, some philosophers are exploring the social, political, and historical foundations of the oppression of persons with disabilities. Finally, critical disability theorists are exposing the discriminatory and erroneous assumptions that underlie certain philosophical treatments of disability. For example, Anita Silvers calls into question the intrinsic "badness" of disability, Eva Feder Kittay explores the devaluation of dependence and caregiving, Ron Amundson exposes the fallacy in reifying the categories of normal and abnormal function, and Susan Wendell critiques the myth of control that supports the devaluation of disabled lives.[25]

While many of these philosophers pose the same ethical questions in the context of disability that are found in the traditional approach (e.g., questions regarding justice, autonomy, rights, respect), they are at once challenging the normative claims and assumptions built into this more dominant philosophical approach to disability. For example, they ask, Why is having a disability considered to be objectively bad and why are disabled lives devalued? How has the definition of disability as a marginal case limited the possibility of considering justice for persons with disabilities? And in what ways is the category of disability itself, as well as the experience of disability, socially constructed?[26]

Within this critical approach to disability, however, intellectual disability remains overshadowed by questions regarding physical disabilities and discussions of disability generally. Just as the three models of disability can be critically interrogated in the context of intellectual disability, there is room to engage with both traditional and critical disability approaches in order to give intellectual disability a more prominent place in this changing philosophical and political landscape. Yet my goal is not to simply transpose the three models of disability into a new key so that they reflect the specifics of intellectual disability, nor is it to bring these concerns to light within the confines of the two philosophical approaches (traditional and critical) that I have outlined. While I remain firmly rooted in a critical disability stance, I hope to uncover new ways of philosophizing about intellectual disability in dialogue with these various approaches and models.

Unmasking: A Foucauldian Prelude

This book has two main objectives: (1) to ground the philosophical conversation more explicitly in the history of intellectual disability and (2) to uncover certain features of contemporary philosophical discourse about the intellectually disabled. Thus part 1 explores the ways that intellectual disability in its various forms was constituted as an object of knowledge between the mid-nineteenth century and the early decades of the twentieth century. These historical investigations will yield a theoretical framework for addressing the complexities of this category, both past and present. Putting these analytic tools to work, part 2 unmasks four faces we find in contemporary philosophical discussions about intellectual disability: the face of authority, the face of the beast, the face of suffering, and the face of the mirror.

In using the term "unmasking" I have Ian Hacking's discussion of it in mind. Drawing from Karl Mannheim's original use of the term, he explains that unmasking "does not seek to refute the ideas but to undermine them by exposing the function they serve. . . . The notion is that once one sees the '*extra-theoretical function*' [Mannheim's emphasis] of an idea, it will lose its 'practical effectiveness.' We unmask an idea not so much to 'disintegrate' it as to strip it of false appeal or authority."[27] He goes on to clarify the distinction between refuting and unmasking: "Mannheim distinguished refuting from unmasking. Refuting a thesis works at the level of the thesis itself by showing it to be false. Unmasking undermines a thesis, by displaying its extra-theoretical function. . . . Talk of unmasking tends to undermine the authority of knowledge and categorization. It challenges complacent assumptions about the inevitability of what we have found out or our present ways of doing things—not by refuting or proposing a better way, but by 'unmasking.'"[28] Specifically, the chapters in part 2 unmask ways in which philosophers have laid claims to knowledge about intellectual disability, the associations between the intellectually disabled and non-human animals, the construction of prototypical cases of intellectual disability based on the concept of suffering, and the ways that the intellectually disabled function as mirrors for the non-disabled. Yet in addition to exposing the extra-theoretical function that these philosophical moves serve, I refute a number of assumptions and claims on which these arguments rest, and argue that we must critically rethink philosophies of intellectual disability in light of these.

In challenging certain philosophical approaches and uncovering others, however, this book is not intended to provide *a* theory or *the* doctrine that should be used in philosophizing about intellectual disability. Rather, in retracing these historical and philosophical steps, I am engaging in something akin to what Michel Foucault has called "historical ontology." In "What Is Enlightenment?" Foucault argues that we must adopt a "historico-critical" attitude in order to undertake what he calls a "historical ontology of ourselves." More recently, Ian Hacking has characterized his own work in this vein, describing historical ontology as an exploration of "the ways in which the possibilities for choice, and for being, arise in history. It is not to be practiced in terms of grand abstractions, but in terms of the explicit formations in which we can constitute ourselves."[29] This book, then, moves between two tasks that Foucault outlines in characterizing this historico-critical attitude: "this work done at the limits of ourselves must, on the one hand, open up a realm of historical inquiry, and on the other hand, put itself to the test of reality, of contemporary reality, both to grasp the points where change is possible and desirable, and to determine the precise form this change should take."[30] Parts 1–2—the historical and philosophical worlds of intellectual disability—mirror this dual task, and can thus be heard in this Foucauldian key.

The historical analyses that comprise part 1 serve a number of purposes. First, they provide the occasion to define and apply my theoretical approach to classification. Second, an exploration of this history creates a backdrop for the subsequent discussion of the philosophical world of intellectual disability. It will become evident in part 2 that many philosophers neither address the history of intellectual disability nor escape it. In many respects, contemporary philosophical discourse about persons with intellectual disabilities is closer to this historical world than to the contemporary reality reflected in other disciplines (e.g., psychology, sociology, and special education) and in the lived experiences of persons with intellectual disabilities and their families. Finally, I do not pretend to be a historian of intellectual disability, and much of this work draws on the critical and comprehensive historical studies done by historians in the field. However, by exploring this history from Foucauldian and feminist perspectives, I hope to add to the discussion by highlighting certain aspects that have not been explicitly discussed: the existence and effects of tensions internal to the classification, the ways in which these apparent contradictions served to shape and fuel the development of this new object of knowledge, how disabled *and* non-disabled women figure into this history, and how intellectual disability emerged as a gendered object of knowledge.

Foucault argues that critical ontology must be articulated along three axes— knowledge, power, and ethics—that are captured in the following questions: "How are we constituted as subjects of our own knowledge? How are we constituted as subjects who exercise or submit to power relations? How are we constituted as moral subjects of our own actions?"[31] My examination of intellectual disability in both the historical and philosophical worlds, then, moves along these three axes, "whose specificity and whose interconnections have to be analyzed."[32] So in bringing these preliminary remarks to a close, I will give a brief preview of how these axes infuse and motivate the chapters that follow.

Many experts have defined intellectual disability as an object of knowledge, philosophers among them; yet less philosophical attention has been paid to persons with intellectual disabilities as *knowing subjects* in their own right. As mentioned above, part 1 will closely examine how intellectual disability emerged as a complex and contested, gendered object of knowledge. Yet questions of epistemic authority pervade both parts of this book. As we shall see, there is a very interesting story to be told regarding the multiple positions women occupy in this history, and the ways in which they engaged in the production of knowledge about intellectual disability. In the context of contemporary philosophical discourse, there are equally important questions regarding claims to epistemic and moral authority, and good reason to problematize both the language and definitions that are often employed in discussions of intellectual disability. The role of the gatekeeper with respect to what kind of knowledge counts and whose voices are included is central to an understanding of mental retardation as a classification, both past and present, and this requires a close examination of local forms of knowledge and specific discursive and institutional practices through which they are produced.

As Foucault has taught us, discussions of knowledge inevitably raise questions of power, and in my analysis of historical and philosophical discourse about mental retardation, the problem of power is ever-present. Foucault defines power in terms of action: the exercise of power "is a way in which certain actions may structure the field of other possible actions."[33] Power is a relational term, a relation between two agents capable of action, where one agent affects the possibilities of another's actions. Thus every social relation involves power, not necessarily in the sense of domination but rather insofar as our actions are constantly shaped by various individuals and institutions. For Foucault, "a society without power relations can only be an abstraction."[34] In remaining faithful to Foucault's conviction that power must be analyzed in terms of its exercise, part 1 addresses specific modes of power as they occur within the history of intellectual disability (e.g., certain forms of disciplinary and psychiatric power in the first chapter, and complex gendered power relations in the second). Part 2 turns to the power relations established between the philosopher-expert, her objects of knowledge, and other voices that have been left out of the conversation. I find Foucault's approach compelling because it guards against a limited vision of power (as either localized in an individual, one institution, or a particular motive) and thus offers a more comprehensive analytical framework. Another important feature of Foucault's definition of power is the possibility for resistance: where there are multiple points of power, there can be multiple points of resistance.[35] While the historical chapters in this book do not focus explicitly on instances of resistance, the reflections in part 2 are intended to serve as a prelude to forms of practical and conceptual resistance that might emerge from this critical project.

The notion of resistance points to the final axis—ethics—which constitutes the basis of part 2. The purpose of unmasking philosophical faces of intellectual disability in contemporary moral discourse is to call into question the ways in which "we" (the non–intellectually disabled) define ourselves as moral subjects in contrast to those individuals who are perceived to be at the margins of personhood and moral consideration. This work is more archaeological and genealogical than normative, however. Foucault describes historical ontology as archaeological insofar as it seeks to "treat instances of discourse that articulate what we think, say and do as so many historical events"; and it is genealogical "in the sense that it . . . will separate out, from the contingency that has made us what we are, the possibility of no longer being, doing, or thinking what we are . . . it is seeking to give new impetus, as far and wide as possible, to the undefined work of freedom."[36] In situating contemporary incarnations of intellectual disability in philosophical discourse alongside this historical world, I hope to reveal how we can view this discourse as historically contingent, and go on to imagine what thinking otherwise about intellectual disability might mean in an ethical context. This involves challenging the close associations between the severely intellectually disabled and non-human animals and the concomitant danger of dehumanization, as well as the conflation of suffering with disability and the representation of the intellectually disabled individual primarily as one who is both the victim and cause (to those around her) of profound suffering. Problematizing the modes of exclusion that underlie attempts to delineate the boundaries of the moral universe, as well as the suspect means by which "we" constitute or dismiss certain others as moral subjects, is a step toward "the possibility of no longer being, doing, or thinking what we are."

Foucault acknowledges the necessity of historical analysis; in the case of intellectual disability, I believe that a discussion of this category of individuals must be grounded in the history of this classification. Hence the inclusion in part 1 of a series of historical analyses regarding the emergence, development, and persistence of this classification. Yet this historical analysis is not simply necessary for its own sake; if that were the case I would leave the work to historians who are far better equipped to do the necessary archival and interpretive work to tell a more robust history of mental retardation. As Foucault suggests in the above statement, historical analyses serve to illuminate the limits imposed on us. In the case of intellectual disability this amounts to exploring the ways that certain kinds of questions and forms of discourse were made possible, and others discounted or excluded. I will also critically interrogate the limits placed on the very conception of humanness and personhood, and begin to explain why some philosophical discourse about intellectual disability bears the mark of late-nineteenth- and early-twentieth-century conceptions of deviance and defect.

But Foucault's characterization of historical ontology is not simply a form of critique in the negative sense; it suggests that through this labor we may imagine ourselves to be other than we are, to move beyond certain limits unmasked by these inquiries. The chapters in part 2 consider what it might mean for those of us who fall outside the boundaries of this category to re-imagine intellectual disability and its relation to conceptions of normalcy and humanity.

My call for a philosophical reorientation with respect to intellectual disability is a call to rethink certain philosophical attitudes, to confront the "ethos," in Foucault's sense of the term, that is embodied in the practice of philosophy. More work is needed in this area, but I hope that these reflections will reveal new spaces for posing philosophical questions about intellectual disability, and will allow a fuller portrait of persons with intellectual disabilities as human *subjects* to emerge.

Nightmares and Dreams

The madman has long haunted philosophy; perhaps madness also constitutes one of its nightmares. In *The History of Madness,* Foucault masterfully exposes Descartes's uneasy relationship to the madman when he claims in the first meditation, "I would be thought equally mad if I took anything from them as a model for myself." Foucault sees this as a decisive moment in the history of madness, the moment when philosophy excluded the possibility of madness from its epistemological project. As Foucault writes in the original passage in *Histoire de la Folie: "La folie est exclue par le suject qui doute."*[37] As readers and inheritors of the Cartesian legacy, we are forced to ask ourselves, What prevents the madman from undertaking the Cartesian meditative project and ensures our participation in it? What separates us (rational, doubting subjects) from madness?

Whether philosophy has recovered madness from this decisive moment of exclusion is up for interpretation (as is Foucault's interpretation of this Cartesian move). Madness has held a certain fascination for philosophers from Plato to Nietzsche and, Descartes's *Meditations* aside, the madman has been accorded a far more prominent (though not always more humane) place in philosophical discourse than the idiot or the mentally retarded. As Roy Porter has said, "Madness continues to exercise its magic, but mindlessness holds no mystique."[38] Madness may be a bad Cartesian dream, but as I have become better acquainted with the faces of the intellectually disabled found in philosophy, I wonder whether intellectual disability is an even more frightening nightmare that begs for explanation and the promise of a new day.

As I embark on this project, however, I carry Foucault's optimism with me: "All of my investigations rest on a postulate of absolute optimism. I do not conduct my analyses in order to say: this is how things are, look how trapped you are. I say certain things only to the extent to which I see them as capable of permitting the transformation of reality."[39]

Part One

The Institutional World of Intellectual Disability

1

Twin Brothers: The "Idiot" and the Institution

In this chapter, I explore the world of institutions for the "feebleminded" that emerged in mid-nineteenth-century America. There is a vast and rapidly growing body of literature on the history of intellectual disability, much of which focuses on the fascinating story of these institutions and examines the complex evolution of the concept of intellectual disability.[1] Given the extensive scholarship in this area and the fact that I am not a historian by training, I want to briefly speak to how and why I decided to revisit these institutions and the discourse to which they gave rise.

In large part, my interest in the history of intellectual disability has been inspired by Foucault's institutional histories, specifically his account of the birth of the clinic, the modern prison, and the asylum.[2] I begin, then, with a series of broad Foucauldian questions in mind: What distinctive shifts occurred that transformed the ways in which knowledge about intellectual disability was gathered and produced? What forms of discourse and practice have shaped the definition and perpetuation of this category? What underlying continuities or discontinuities can be found? What forms of power can be found in the institutional techniques, and how are they related to the expert knowledge produced? Although a comprehensive Foucauldian history of intellectual disability would certainly be a worthy project, my aim here is far more limited: I will focus on the emergence of "feeblemindedness" as a new object of knowledge, the relationship between specific techniques and the distinct *kinds* they produce, and the persistence of certain conceptual tensions that underlie what might appear to be a discontinuous history of shifts and contestations.[3]

In *The Birth of the Clinic*, Michel Foucault writes that the nineteenth-century clinic "is a reorganization of the very possibility of a discourse about disease. . . . The clinic appears . . . as a new outline of the perceptible and statable."[4] Similarly, the birth of institutions specifically for "idiots" and the application of IQ tests to this population shaped what could be observed and said about intellectual disability. Thus between the time the first institutions opened their doors in the late 1840s to the publication of H. H. Goddard's book *The Kallikak Family* in 1912 and the dawn of mental testing, we find the creation of a distinctly new object of knowledge. Within the complex institutional world, intellectual disability was both found and made, knowledge was remade and reported, patterns were recognized, invented, imposed.

What allowed for this new object of knowledge to emerge? Here we must look to institutional practices and expert discourse. In *Discipline and Punish: The Birth of the Prison*, Foucault offers the following description of the relationship between penitentiary technique and the delinquent: "The penitentiary technique and the delinquent are in a sense twin brothers. It is not true that it was the discovery of the delinquent through a scientific rationality that introduced into our old prisons the refinement of penitentiary techniques. Nor is it true that the internal elaboration of penitentiary methods has finally brought to light the 'objective' existence of a delinquency. . . . They appeared together, the one extending from the other, as a technological ensemble that forms and fragments the object to which it applies its instruments."[5] One might say that a similar phenomenon occurred within institutions for the "feebleminded." The various instruments and techniques that were applied to the individuals within these facilities (called "schools," "asylums," "institutions") generated new typologies and classification schemas from which the "idiot, " "imbecile, " and "moral imbecile" emerged as distinct kinds. With the birth of mental testing in the early twentieth century, the understanding of "feeblemindedness" changed again, and the "moron" emerged in connection with this new way of gathering and organizing knowledge. Far from being discovered as scientific, objective kinds, the comprehension and creation of these classes of feeblemindedness as both objects and subjects went hand in hand.[6]

The creation of institutions for the feebleminded that began in the mid-nineteenth century and Goddard's introduction of Alfred Binet's IQ test to America mark two distinct moments in the history of intellectual disability. New ways of describing, defining, and treating feeblemindedness came into being.

Many historians point to other discontinuities as well. Some, for example, divide this historical period into three distinct eras. The period from 1850 to 1880 is generally considered a period of optimistic institution building, with the aim of "making the deviant undeviant." From 1880 to 1900 there was growing pessimism, a shift to custodialism, to "sheltering the deviant from society," and from 1900 to 1920 there was an attempt to "protect society from deviancy," and the view of mental retardation as a menace.[7] However, this history also includes elements that persisted throughout. Philip Ferguson's history of the "severely retarded," *Abandoned to Their Fate,* argues that for the most severely disabled groups, the hope for education or training was eclipsed by the sentence of incurability. The notion of "chronicity . . . the general social status of being judged somehow 'unfixable'," was firmly entrenched in the conceptions and practices surrounding mental retardation.[8] If one looks at this subgroup, the discontinuous moments disappear. For example, the historical shift from education to custodialism does not apply: "The eventual triumph of a policy of custodialism for mildly and moderately retarded people was, in reality, merely an expansion of the custodial approach that long applied to the most severely retarded population."[9]

Foucault has written, "To one set of difficulties, several responses can be made. And most of the time different responses actually are proposed. But what has to be understood is what makes them simultaneously possible: it is the point in which their simultaneity is rooted; it is the soil that can nourish them in all their diversity and sometimes in spite of their contradictions."[10] In the reflections that follow, I explore a series of internal, unresolved tensions or contradictions that have defined intellectual disability as an object of knowledge. These conceptual pairs, as I will call them, have provided simultaneous but very different portraits of the nature of intellectual disability and have directly and indirectly influenced the treatment that individuals received. I maintain that the existence of these pairs—qualitative/quantitative, organic/non-organic, static/dynamic, and visible/invisible—explains why the classifications of intellectual disability, which seem transient and unstable, have proved to be so stable and persistent. (As we will see in part 2, they can be found in contemporary philosophical discourse about intellectual disability as well.) The persistence of these underlying oppositions can help us better understand the surface changes that give the impression that the history of intellectual disability has been one of discontinuous moments and reform. Before looking at these conceptual pairs, however, we need a bit of background.

The Birth of the Institution

Historically, individuals who were believed to suffer from idiocy have been thought of in a number of different ways: viewed as objects of pity, demon-possessed, holy innocents, eternal children, and diseased organisms.[11] Originating from the Greek word *idios*, which means "private person," the term "idiot" dates back to the fourteenth century. Beginning in the Enlightenment, the interest in idiocy was often articulated in connection with other disabilities. For example, John Locke, in his *Essay Concerning Human Understanding*, made the following distinction: "Madmen put wrong ideas together, and so make wrong propositions, but argue and reason right from them; but idiots make very few or no propositions, and reason scarce at all."[12] The definition of idiocy as *lack*, as opposed to the *error* found in madness, persisted well into the nineteenth and twentieth centuries, and the complex relationship between these two categories continues to play a role in the discourse surrounding the classification of intellectual disability.[13] A comprehensive history of intellectual disability would be incomplete without recognizing the multifaceted ways that conceptions of idiocy were interwoven with theories regarding the deaf, dumb, and the "savage children" who served as objects of philosophical and scientific interest that began in the Enlightenment.[14] These overlaps are also evident in institutional practice; for many years idiots were housed in institutions for the deaf, dumb, and blind.

Yet in the first half of the nineteenth century, a process of differentiation took place that constituted idiocy as a distinct condition worthy of separate consideration; from this point on, idiocy is no longer viewed as a species of madness.[15] In the United States, the shift was given concrete form in the call for drastic institutional reform. A humanitarian and legislative campaign to separate idiots from other social outcasts, both conceptually and physically, began to gain force. In 1824 the New York secretary of state surveyed poor relief and reported that "idiots and lunatics do not receive sufficient care and attention in towns, where no suitable asylums for their reception are established."[16] Humanitarian appeals from reformers like Dorothea Dix argued against both the abominable conditions in which "idiots and the insane" were living, and the fact that they had been wrongfully grouped with paupers and criminals: "I come as the advocate of helpless, forgotten, insane, and idiotic men and women; of beings sunk to a condition from which the most unconcerned would start with real horror; of beings wretched in our prisons, more wretched in our almshouses. . . . I cannot but assert that most of the idiotic subjects in the prisons in Massachusetts are unjustly committed, being wholly incapable of doing harm, and none manifesting any disposition either to injure others or to exercise mischievous propensities."[17]

The words of Dorothea Dix echoed the general spirit of reform that permeated New England in mid-century. By 1846, a commission was appointed in Massachusetts to investigate the treatment of idiots.[18] Samuel Gridley Howe, a doctor who was working with three blind children believed to be idiots at the Perkins Institution for the Blind, was chairman of the commission. In 1848, under his direction, an experimental school for idiots opened in South Boston, later named the Massachusetts School for Idiotic and Feeble-minded Youth.[19] In that same year, a private school for idiots had been opened by Dr. Hervey B. Wilbur in Barre, Massachusetts. In the forty years that followed, institutions would open in New York, Pennsylvania, Iowa, Connecticut, Ohio, Minnesota, Indiana, California, Michigan, Maryland, and Nebraska, making a total of four thousand residents by 1888.[20]

If we consider these new American institutions through a Foucauldian lens, a number of interesting features emerge. For the first time, causes, definitions, descriptions, and treatments of idiocy were being discussed and practiced within an organized structure. In *Discipline and Punish*, Foucault describes the Panopticon as a laboratory of sorts, a "museum of human nature" that houses various species and kinds.[21] In a similar way, the schools for the feebleminded created a new space for the study of intellectual disability in its various incarnations. Thus the superintendents of these schools generated new typologies of idiocy that differentiated between individuals who had previously been carelessly housed with many other kinds of others. The French educator and psychologist Edouard Seguin, whose work at Bicêtre and the Salpétriere in France inspired the first educational facilities for idiots in the United States,[22] wrote in his treatise *Idiocy, and Its Treatment by the Physiological Method* (1846), "Since idiocy is ascribed to so many circumstances, taking place at such different periods of the formation of the child, it is not to be expected that it should assume an identical appearance; in fact, on entering a school, the idea of similarity is soon dispelled by the heterogeneous features of the inmates; therefore the same drawing cannot represent them but as a type, after a practical study of the varieties."[23] By 1848 Dr. Howe, influenced by Seguin's work, divided idiocy (which at the time was both the general term for all forms of mental deficiency as well as a subclassification) into three subgroups: idiots, fools ("a higher class of idiots"), and simpletons ("the highest class of idiots").[24] Thus the institution served as a school for not only the residents but the superintendents as well. In Seguin's words, it performed "the triple work of improving idiots, of studying human nature from its lowest to its highest manifestations, and of testing on idiots the true physiological means of elevating mankind by education."[25] In reflecting on the accomplishments of these institutions forty years after the first was opened, Charles T. Wilbur (superintendent of the Illinois Institution for the Education of Feebleminded Children and brother of the famous Hervey B. Wilbur, who was responsible for opening the first private school for idiots) counts among the institution's important contributions: "A large amount of valuable statistical information has been gathered in relation to [idiots] . . . a plan of organization of institutions and methods and a system of education, have been developed for them. . . . The causes and prevention of idiocy are being studied and reflected upon, with the hope that society may be benefited thereby."[26]

Within these institutional walls, a new expert was born: the superintendent. The male physicians who took the reins in managing these institutions played a complex role both within and beyond them. While they were expected to oversee the workings of the institutions, they were also students of intellectual disability in these new laboratories. They were experts on the conditions and individuals housed within the institution's walls, and they represented the public and political face of intellectual disability in trying to raise funds to support this new class of individuals. In speaking about Pinel[27] and Tuke, the French and British reformists who were part of the humanitarian[28] crusade that gave birth to the asylum in its modern incarnation, Foucault says of this new medical personage, *homo medicus,* "it would authorize not only new contacts between doctor and patient, but a new relation between insanity and medical thought. . . . Hitherto we find in the asylums only the same structures of confinement, but displaced and deformed. . . . With the new status of the medical personage, the deepest meaning of confinement is abolished: mental disease, with the meanings we now give it, is made possible."[29] Similarly, these new American "schools" were intended to remedy the harsh and inhumane confinement of idiots in almshouses and jails. Thus the superintendents were responsible for the salvation of these individuals, as well as their care and education, for which they were uniquely qualified and through which they too could give new meaning to idiocy.

This new class of experts came together in 1876 to form the Association of Medical Officers of American Institutions of Idiotic and Feeble-minded Persons, the first professional organization devoted to the study and treatment of feeblemindedness. They named Seguin their first president, and in its constitution explained that among its objectives "shall be the discussion of all questions relating to the causes, conditions, and statistics of idiocy, and to the management, training and education of idiots and feebleminded persons; it will also lend its influence to the establishment and fostering of institutions for this purpose."[30]

This professional statement reflects the fact that these were conceived as "total institutions" in Erving Goffman's sense: all aspects of life are conducted in the same place and in the company of a large batch of others, with tight daily schedules and enforced activities that are brought together into a single rational plan purportedly designed to fulfill the official aims of the institution.[31] The power at work in such institutions can be understood as a form of what Foucault has called disciplinary power, "a type of power, a modality for its exercise, comprising a whole set of instruments, techniques, procedures, levels of application, targets."[32] We see the development of this kind of power in eighteenth- and nineteenth-century schools, hospitals, factories, military schools, and ultimately the modern prison. Foucault explains that this form of power can be found in specialized institutions (e.g., penitentiaries) as well as institutions that use it toward a particular end (e.g., schools and hospitals). The institutions for the feebleminded monitored, studied, documented, taught, punished, and trained their inmates in hopes of making them into useful human beings.[33] The institutions that housed all forms of feeblemindedness were "omni-disciplinary," like the modern prison that Foucault describes. "Prison must be an exhaustive disciplinary apparatus: it must assume responsibility for all aspects of the individual, his physical training, his aptitude to work, his everyday conduct, his moral attitude, his state of mind."[34] Depending on the level of aptitude, the residents (or "inmates" as they came to be called as the view of the institution shifted from school to custodial facility) engaged in many kinds of work and tasks intended to be both instructive and therapeutic.[35] Yet the institution, as a site that produced knowledge about intellectual disability and had staff engaged in the care, education, transformation, and custody of its inmates, became a self-perpetuating machine. As we shall see, the institutions cannot be understood independent of their internal exigencies and the process by which the legitimacy of the superintendents was continually reinforced.[36]

The institution performed multiple functions: pedagogical, medical, therapeutic, custodial, and professional; it became the organizing principle amid an array of definitions, theories, categories, and proposed treatments. Many historians have rightly noted that the history of intellectual disability far exceeds the boundaries of the institution, however, and there is good reason to move beyond "expert discourse" and explore other dimensions of this rich history.[37] Moreover, there is the risk that exclusively focusing on this discourse "from above" will present a distorted picture of the history of intellectual disability.[38] Thus I want to underscore the fact that what follows in no way offers an exhaustive account of the meaning and reality of intellectual disability during this time period. Rather, I hope to bring to the foreground certain underlying tensions that are concomitant with the birth of this new space in which intellectual disability emerged as a new object of knowledge, in part so that we can better understand how they are still at play in other forms of expert discourse today.

"Man-Child" and "Household Pets": Quantitative and Qualitative Difference

Georges Canguilhem, in *The Normal and the Pathological,* describes a historical shift from a qualitative to a quantitative conception of disease. He states that, prior to the nineteenth century, disease was understood as ontological (a separate entity that we hope to cure) or dynamic (disease is a disruption of the general equilibrium of human beings); both accounts presented normal and pathological states as heterogeneous. However, in the nineteenth century, disease is understood in quantitative rather than qualitative terms: "Pathological phenomena found in living organisms are nothing more than quantitative variations, lesser or greater according to corresponding physiological phenomena."[39] The influence of this new conception of disease is echoed in the way idiocy was defined in the nineteenth century, though it marked an important departure from the very concept of disease.

This is evident in the work of Edouard Seguin, arguably one of the most influential figures in this new focus on idiocy and the desire to build institutions to house and teach those affected by it. Seguin, a student of famous French alienist Esquirol (who believed that idiocy is incurable), had begun to work with a group of idiots in Bicêtre and developed a theory of idiocy rooted in the belief that they could be educated. His book *Idiocy, and Its Treatment by the Physiological Method* is a testimony to the rise of physiology and the focus on function, rather than anatomical structure.[40] Seguin became convinced that idiocy was not incurable, as many before him had asserted; rather, "most idiots and children proximate to them, may be relieved in a more or less complete measure of their disabilities by the physiological method of education."[41] In 1850 he immigrated to the United States, where he worked with various

American institutions, and by 1876 had become the first president of the Association of Medical Officers of American Institutions of Idiotic and Feeble-minded Persons.

Seguin's belief in the curability, or at least improvability of "most idiots," is grounded in a conception of idiocy as a quantitative, not qualitative difference: it is a question of degree or intensity, not *kind*. Foucault characterizes this quantitative portrait of idiocy in terms of *development*, a key concept that allows idiocy to be distinguished from madness and from the category of disease more generally. In comparing Seguin's view with his mentor's, Foucault states that Esquirol's definition of idiocy points to a *lack* of development, a constitutional condition in which intellectual functions have never developed.[42] In Seguin's work, "the idiot and the mentally retarded are not patients: they cannot be said to lack stages; they have either not reached a stage or they have reached it too slowly."[43]

Seguin and the American superintendents who shared his view considered idiots to be human beings like the rest of us but at a lower level of development (be it physical, intellectual, or moral). "He is one of us in mankind, but shut up in an imperfect envelope."[44] This belief was echoed by many of the superintendents of the American institutions and provided justification for the institution as an educational facility. Dr. Hervey Wilbur, superintendent of the New York Asylum for Idiots, said in 1852, "At the basis of all our efforts lies the principle that the human attributes of intelligence, sensitivity, and will are not absolutely wanting in an idiot, but dormant and undeveloped."[45]

The belief that idiocy is simply a question of "less or more" with respect to various human attributes is, in part, what has allowed for the infantilization of this condition. Seguin was greatly influenced by Rousseau, and it is not coincidental that his definition of idiocy closely resembles the description of infancy in *Emile*. Seguin states, "The idiot moves, feels, understands, wills, but imperfectly; does nothing, thinks of nothing, cares for nothing (extreme cases); . . . isolated, without associations; a soul shut up in imperfect organs, an innocent."[46] Of our human infancy, Rousseau says, "We are born capable of learning but able to do nothing, knowing nothing. The soul, enchained in imperfect and half-formed organs, does not even have the sentiment of its own existence. The movements and the cries of the child who has just been born are purely mechanical effects, devoid of knowledge and of will."[47] Idiocy is akin to infancy, insofar as it is the lowest point of development of our human potential; in fact, Rousseau invites the reader to imagine this condition by introducing the idea of the "man-child": "Let us suppose that a child had at his birth the stature and the strength of a grown man. . . . This man-child would be a perfect imbecile, an automaton, an immobile and almost insensible statue."[48]

The parallels between Seguin's description of idiocy and Rousseau's portrait of infancy are striking. Though the language of infantilization did not begin with Rousseau, his expression "man-child" was later used by some superintendents of the American institutions, who referred to their inmates as "man-baby," "woman-baby," and "child-baby."[49] For example, the likening of the feebleminded to children can be seen in Samuel Gridley Howe's argument for adopting the language of feeblemindedness over idiocy so that these individuals would be viewed as differing from normal persons only in degree and thus worthy of protection and care: "Evil may arise from the misuse of the term Idiot, as the name of a class, if it causes them to be considered as a distinct order of persons, and different from other men in being utterly devoid of mind, for it will be considered useless to try to teach those who have no mind at all; but if they are considered as differing from others not in kind, but in degree only,—as merely having feeble mind, then their very feebleness, like that of little children, will commend them to our hearts."[50] What we see here is a definition of idiocy according to a temporal scale or chronology, and thus the "idiot" becomes interpreted against the backdrop of childhood more generally. Foucault writes, "The idiot is a certain degree of childhood, or again . . . childhood is a certain way of passing more or less quickly through degrees of idiocy, debility, or mental retardation. . . . The idiot belongs to childhood, as previously he belonged to illness."[51] Despite the negative effects of infantilization, this portrait acknowledges the place of idiots on the human continuum—human beings who remain at an early stage of development.[52]

From the early descriptions of idiocy in the mid-nineteenth century to contemporary definitions, intellectual disability has always been based on the notion of quantitative difference. Internally, it has always been a graded, hierarchical category. And with respect to the mentally "normal," it has been understood as part of a general hierarchy of ability (whether it is defined in physical, intellectual, or moral terms) on which all human beings are placed. This is reflected in Wilbur's explanation that idiocy, regardless of cause, must be understood as a stage of mental development: "What is called idiocy is a mental state. This is true no matter what our idea may be of the nature of the mind. It is true, whatever may be the physiological or pathological conditions associated with it. Thus, when we speak of idiocy or imbecility, or fatuity or feeblemindedness, we refer to grades and shades of mental states below the normal standard of human intelligence."[53] It is worth noting that this quantitative view was embodied in the eventual use of mental tests to classify levels of feeblemindedness as various degrees of intelligence, a method that continues to define mental retardation today.[54]

Besides this quantitative picture, however, we find the depiction of idiots as qualitatively different, a separate kind. They are viewed as animal-like, subhuman, or of a different race altogether. Generally, the most severe cases of idiocy were used to illustrate these qualitative differences. They were often described as human only in form, empty shells of humanity. Like those affected by madness, they borrowed their face from the face of the beast.[55] We see this other face of idiocy in Howe's work, for example. In exclaiming his dismay at the discovery of idiocy in his homeland, Howe wrote, "But alas! . . . [one] finds, even in our fair commonwealth, breathing masses of flesh, fashioned in the shape of men, but shorn of all other human attributes. . . . Idiots of the lowest class are mere organisms, masses of flesh and bone in human shape."[56] In a description of one case, he says, "He is, in form and outline, like a human being but in nothing else."[57] However, even the outward shape or form could be inhuman, and betray signs of animality. Howe speaks of the "peculiar look so common with idiots, and which may be better expressed by the word *monkeyish* than any other."[58] In some extreme cases, the individual is below the animal kingdom: "Very few cases (we were inclined to think none could) can be found in which a being in human shape is so much below even insects, and so little above a sensitive plant."[59] This subanimal nature was invoked in the appeals to the Pennsylvania government to open a school for idiots: "Even idiots can be raised, from a condition lower than that of brutes, to the likeness of men."[60]

These references to the animal nature of the feebleminded persisted through the turn of the century. Years later, in his famous hereditary study of feeblemindedness, *The Kallikak Family*, H. H. Goddard said of Deborah Kallikak's mother, "Her philosophy of life is the philosophy of the animal. There is no complaining, no irritation at the inequalities of fate. Sickness, pain, childbirth, death—she accepts them all with the same equanimity as she accepts the opportunity of putting a new dress and a gay ribbon on herself."[61]

Descriptions of idiocy as a distinct kind also relied on racial stereotypes and perceptions of inferiority. The relationship between race and intellectual disability is far too complex to do it justice here, but it is worth noting a few features of the ways in which this history is inevitably racialized.[62] From an institutional standpoint, the majority of state and private institutions served the feebleminded white only. Though many states (particularly in the South) campaigned for funds to build separate facilities for African Americans, few were opened.[63] The institutional form of idiocy I am discussing, then, was primarily white, while most feebleminded African Americans were housed in insane asylums for blacks or received no provision at all.[64]

However, from a conceptual standpoint, allusions to racial characteristics were being made as early as Seguin. He discredited phrenology as the sole means to diagnose idiocy, since many idiots had no cranial abnormalities, while suggesting that "any deviation from the Caucasian type among our children, in respect to [cranial] harmony of [cranial] proportions, must be looked upon, *a priori,* as representing some anomaly in their faculties."[65] A more explicit marriage of race and mental deficiency was Down's classification of a subspecies of idiocy that he named "Mongolian idiocy." Chris Borthwick, in his article "Racism, IQ, and Down's Syndrome," discusses the complex relationship between race and intellectual inferiority: "The analogy between 'Mongolian idiots' and Mongolians was, of course, insulting to Mongolians, and contributed to their dismissive treatment by Westerners in the colonial era. Analogies, however, point in two directions. If it was insulting to compare Mongolians to people with impaired functioning, it was also insulting to compare people with a disability to the Victorian stereotype of an uncreative, limited, passive race that had ceased its development before the British."[66] Allusions to inferior races permeate the discourse about feeblemindedness, though these references bear the mark of a broader debate that is another example of the qualitative/quantitative pair. As David Wright explains, nineteenth-century anthropological discourse about "races" betrays a similar question of whether these inferior races were different in kind or were simply lower on the scale of human development. Ironically, Down himself was on the more liberal side of this debate, as he favored the "unity of the human species" view, rather than the theory of "different types of man."[67]

Qualitative and quantitative portrayals of idiocy were central to the definition and description of feeblemindedness beginning in the mid-nineteenth century. Though these interpretations coexisted, they reflect two opposing views of the nature of intellectual disability. According to the quantitative picture, conditions like idiocy, imbecility, and feeblemindedness were defined according to a hierarchical ordering of certain human abilities. In taking this approach, Seguin's work paints a more holistic picture, evaluating the trinity of mobility and sensation, perception and reasoning, and affections and will.[68] As the IQ test became popularized, definitions depended almost entirely on a numerical score that was thought to represent intelligence. Though the relevant characteristics changed depending on the theorist and the historical period, the underlying assumption was that idiots and the feebleminded still fell somewhere along the human continuum. At the same time, however, the image of idiocy and feeblemindedness as animalistic and subhuman was equally powerful, and it drew on many assumptions and theories regarding the inferiority of certain races and ethnicities during that time period. The conviction that idiots were qualitatively different from other humans shaped descriptions of bodies and character, as well as technical and "scientific" definitions.

Intellectual disability has been and continues to be understood both in terms of difference in degree and kind, and the early language of infancy, IQ scores, animality, and race helped solidify and perpetuate quantitative and qualitative understandings of idiocy and feeblemindedness. Foucault speaks of the quantitative picture in terms of a "double normativity" whereby, in a developmental view, there are simultaneously two norms: the *adult* functions as a norm insofar as the idiot's development is halted, and the adult "appear[s] as both the real and ideal end of development; and the *child* functions as a norm insofar as the idiot's slowed development is compared to the majority of children."[69] Beside this, I think, we find another kind of normativity, whereby a conception of the *human* functions as a norm against which the feebleminded are defined or described as a fundamentally, qualitatively different kind.[70] Perhaps Dr. Isaac Kerlin's description of two of his students at the Pennsylvania Training School best illustrates this tension: "Two children have attached themselves to all of us, on account of their infancy and beauty, and are justly entitled to the appellation of 'pets' in our household."[71]

Organic/Non-Organic Idiocy: A Variety of the Nature/Nurture Debate

Another tension at work in the classification of intellectual disability is between the organic and non-organic. The nature of idiocy and its causes were discussed in terms of organic deficiency and in terms of the individual's relationship with his/her environment—non-organic or functional explanations.[72] In one sense, this can be understood as a form of the nature/nurture debate, though both sides are consistently at work in the understanding of intellectual disability.

Idiocy was clearly an object of medical knowledge, and its organic nature was discussed by many doctors, from the eighteenth-century French alienists to the nineteenth- and twentieth-century superintendents of American institutions. Seguin defines idiocy as a "specific infirmity of the cranio-spinal axis, produced by deficiency of nutrition in utero and in neo-nati" and goes on to discuss it in terms of its organic and physiological pathology.[73] Howe followed suit, defining grades of idiocy according to the nervous and muscular systems, the power of locomotion and speech, and the affective and intellectual faculties.[74] Further connections were made between idiocy and epilepsy, cretinism, hydrocephaly, microcephaly, encephalitis, paralysis, and brain lesions. The various organic explanations are too numerous and complex to discuss here. Suffice it to say that the medical gaze upon intellectual disability as some kind of natural, anatomical, or physiological defect has been a standard approach to its classification.

Simultaneous with these organic definitions and descriptions of idiocy were classifications based on the individual's relation to his or her environment. Many superintendents designated levels of feeblemindedness in pedagogical and vocational terms. In 1869 the institution for idiots in Ohio recognized three distinct classes: totally helpless and needing constant care, incapable of mental training but capable of physical training, and capable of schooling.[75] Dr. Hervey Wilbur of the Syracuse asylum recommended that American institutions adopt the following categories: "unimproved/retrograding idiots; moderately improved/ good for institutional work; and permanently improved."[76] Here again individuals were classified according to their ability to perform within the institution, as opposed to a medical, organic classification. Even in the Rome Asylum for Unteachables, Charles Bernstein classified inmates according to their vocational potential: unable to do any work, capable of self-care only, assist others in some work, usefulness in industrial departments, and good workers. The fact that functional and biological classifications coexist within the institutional framework points to the dual nature of the institution as a place of observation and treatment. Idiocy was defined in organic terms by a medical gaze that observed physical, anatomical, and physiological characteristics. At the same time, the fact that institutions were considered to be both therapeutic and educational facilities allowed idiocy to be defined functionally, in terms of the ability to be trained and perform institutional work.[77]

This organic/non-organic distinction manifests itself in more complicated terms at the level of etiology. The debate about whether idiocy is caused by nature or nurture has figured in the understanding of intellectual disability in various complex ways. Though endogenous causes of idiocy were identified (including malnutrition and lesions or abnormalities of the brain), it was also thought to be caused and influenced by environmental factors. Seguin discusses at length the importance of proper care during infancy. Mothers had to vigilantly look for signs of idiocy; with proper maternal education the effects of idiocy could be mitigated.[78] The entire campaign to build institutions was predicated on the belief that *environment mattered* and could change the face of idiocy.[79] And though the rise of the institution displaced the family's responsibility in certain cases, the family remained crucial in this endeavor. Foucault's characterization of the parental imperative, which emerged simultaneously with the growth of institutions, highlights the fact that, as he puts it, the disciplinary mechanisms of the asylum were transferred into the family as well: "This is how disciplinary power lives off family sovereignty, requiring the family to play the role of the agency that decides between normal and abnormal, regular and irregular, asking the family to hand over its abnormal, irregular individuals."[80]

The most complex manifestation of the tension between organic and non-organic explanations has been in the hereditarian discourse surrounding idiocy and feeblemindedness, much of which seems to fall in that gray area between nature and nurture. Howe asserts a direct relationship between the "sins of parents" and their disabled children: "It may be assumed as certain, that in all cases where children are born deformed, or blind, or deaf, or idiotic, or so imperfectly and feebly organized that they cannot come to maturity under ordinary circumstances . . . in all such cases the fault lies with the progenitors."[81] Though the five causes of "pre-disposition to idiocy" that he gives—the low condition of the physical organization, intemperance, self-abuse, intermarriage among relatives, attempts to procure abortions—suggest some kind of causal relationship between the parent's behavior and the child, he is not explicit about the actual biological connection.[82] He concludes that "the moral to be drawn from the existence of the individual idiot is this—he, or his parents, have so far violated the natural laws, so far marred the beautiful organism of the body, that it is an unfit instrument for the manifestation of the powers of the soul."[83]

The discourse about heredity allows us to see the close connection between etiology and treatment. In Howe's view, the obvious solution to the problem of idiocy was to recognize the "simple, clear, and beautiful" laws of nature. If they were "strictly observed," within a few generations "all possibility of its recurrence" could be removed.[84] As the connection between parents or ancestors and defective children became more deeply entrenched in the language of biology, this vision of improvability vanished. The language of "tainted blood" and "defective germ plasm" gained popularity with the rise of the eugenics movement in the early twentieth century, and approaches to treatment changed accordingly.[85] As Nicole Hahn Rafter points out, it was the rhetoric of eugenics that allowed the superintendents of institutions for the feebleminded to gain professional legitimacy, since they had struggled to carve out a particular niche of specialized knowledge, particularly with respect to etiological theories regarding feeblemindedness.[86] As this rhetoric began to take hold and feeblemindedness became increasingly associated with other categories of social deviance, the hope of prevention through the education of parents and the possibility of idiots improving within the therapeutic world of the institution began to disappear, and solutions like sterilization appeared. The coexistence of organic and non-organic explanations of intellectual disability, then, has not only affected the classifications and definitions of this condition, but has directly shaped the practices aimed at curing, treating, preventing, or eradicating it.

Static and Dynamic Definitions

Intellectual disability, as a classification, has encompassed a variety of physical, cognitive, and behavioral conditions, ranging from mild to severe. As already noted, the nature and ordering of these conditions has been the subject of research and debate, and the varieties of feeblemindedness discussed by superintendents were described qualitatively and quantitatively, and in organic and non-organic terms. Amid the confusion surrounding the etiology and nature of the many conditions encompassed by feeblemindedness, one question has directly influenced institutional practice: Is feeblemindedness (in any or all of its forms) curable or at least improvable, or is it an unchangeable condition? In the following discussion I will use the term "static" to refer to conditions believed to be incurable or not improvable by external influences or treatment; "dynamic" conditions are changeable (curable or at least improvable) through medical intervention, physical and/or psychological therapy, training, or education. Thus we can ask how the *categories* of intellectual disability were constructed, relying on its dual image as a both static and dynamic condition. Feeblemindedness has always included curable and incurable categories, but these designations have not remained constant. Why were certain types considered curable at one time and incurable at another? An examination of the ways in which these two conceptions influenced the classification and treatment of feeblemindedness will help illuminate the complex relationship between etiology, definition, and treatment in the world of institutional discourse and practice.

Initially it seems that this pair (static/dynamic) might be separated in a number of ways. Static and dynamic conceptions of feeblemindedness might parallel the distinction between organic and non-organic causes, severe and mild cases, or they might also correspond to historical periods: an age of optimism that views intellectual disability as dynamic, followed by an age of pessimism that views it as static. I will argue, instead, that the static and dynamic views of feeblemindedness are not so easily separated; in fact, this seemingly opposi-tional pair functions simultaneously.

As far as etiology is concerned, one could draw a parallel between the no-tions of intellectual disability as organic/non-organic and static/dynamic. For example, the following connection could be made: If intellectual disability is understood in organic or biological terms, then presumably there are certain immutable limits placed on the possibility of altering the condition (a treatment might exist, but it would have to act upon the biological organism, insofar as the condition is organic; changing the environment alone would not alter it). If intellectual disability is seen as *only* a function of the individual's environ-ment, then a change in the environment would change the condition itself.[87] But this parallel between organic/static and non-organic/dynamic is too sim-plistic. As we shall see, the roles of biology and the environment in explaining feeblemindedness as static and dynamic are extremely complex in the world of the institution.

The static/dynamic pair might also be seen as corresponding to the opposite poles on the severe-mild continuum. In other words, it seems likely that the more severe a person's condition is, the less likely it is that it would be curable, or even improvable. This is clear when feeblemindedness is defined in terms of educability. The subcategories—educable, trainable, incurable—are arranged in order of increasing severity, the latter group being the most severely dis-abled by cognitive and physical conditions. Though this picture has persisted throughout its history, we will encounter instances where the mildest forms of feeblemindedness have been considered hopelessly incurable. The dual concep-tion of intellectual disability as static and dynamic has functioned at both ends of the mild/severe spectrum.

In the mid-nineteenth century institutions for idiots grew, in part because these individuals were considered educable. As noted above, Seguin departed from Esquirol's belief that "idiots are what they must remain for the rest of their lives" and attempted to improve their condition through education.[88] The following statement illustrates the distinction between cure and improvement that was to remain important throughout the history of intellectual disabil-ity: "While waiting for medicine to cure idiots, I have undertaken to see that they participate in the benefits of education."[89] Interestingly, Seguin does not preclude the possibility of a cure (which could only come from the medical world) while his pedagogical project was aimed more modestly at improvement. Samuel Gridley Howe shared Seguin's optimism in the possibility of educating the feebleminded, but he too acknowledged that improvability should not be confounded with a cure: "We cannot remove idiocy; and we must be careful not to hurt our cause by promising too much in the way of lessening its evils. Idiocy is terrible,—it is radical,—it is an incurable defect."

Seguin had devised a program by which idiots could be taught through the development of their sensory functions: "The senses, being in man, the doors through which the mind issues and enters, we have treated them in idiots. . . . Some idiots are more afflicted in their minds . . . and others in their motor and sensory functions, even to the point of paralysis or anesthesia, but in either form their treatment must proceed more from the training of the senses, in order to improve the mind, than from the education of the mind in view of developing the sensory aptitudes."[90] This sensory training was accompanied by moral training since, for Seguin, "that which most essentially constitutes idiocy is the absence of moral volition, superseded by a negative will." The object of moral training, then, was "changing the negative will into an affirmative one."[91] The success of his pedagogical approach served to justify the new residential institutions, and soon American reformists were reiterating Seguin's belief in the educability of "idiots." An appeal to the citizens of Philadelphia to establish a school for idiots in 1853 states "a fact which is destined to become more and more widely known as schools for idiots multiply . . . that they are proper subjects for Education. . . . It is the torpor of their mental powers that we have to contend with, *not absolute incapacity.*"[92] Here we see idiocy presented as a changeable condition—not an absolute fate.

As these institutions developed, most grades of idiocy were assumed to benefit from training in a structured environment. Of course, the "higher grades" were more likely to be the subjects of educational efforts, while the more severe cases were the objects of training.[93] Finally, it was thought no amount of effort could change the condition of some. Even the most optimistic reformists believed that idiocy was a static condition for those most severely affected. Though this era of institutional growth is often called the age of optimism, the hope in the educability of idiots was tempered by the existence of "chronic" cases, where no improvement or education seemed possible.

Despite the existence from the beginning of these chronic incurables, the determination of which forms of idiocy were improvable did not remain constant. The taxonomy, from severe to mild (or low-grade to high-grade), was idiot, imbecile, and feebleminded. In the early period examined above, an inverse relationship between severity and improvability was posited: the more severe one's condition, the less curable or improvable one was believed to be;

thus, the idiots were the hopeless cases, and the feebleminded were targets of treatment and education. However, in the early twentieth century this relationship changed. The highest grades (renamed "morons" by Goddard) were now thought to be impervious to amelioration or cure. In his book on the Kallikak family, Goddard asserts, "Fortunately for the cause of science, the Kallikak family . . . [is] not open to argument. They were feebleminded, and no amount of education or good environment can change a feebleminded individual into a normal one, any more than it can change a red-haired stock into a black-haired stock."[94] There were a number of reasons for this shift. First, the practice of mental testing detected a new population of the "high-grade feebleminded" living outside the institution. Second, the emphasis on heredity made this group appear particularly dangerous because they were free to reproduce and spread feeblemindedness. Finally, there was a perceived association between this group and pressing social ills, such as pauperism, crime, and sexual immorality. One solution to these problems was to segregate the "dangerous" individuals; thus, institutionalization was no longer justified for its pedagogical effects but to prevent the spread of feeblemindedness.[95] The mildest cases were now presented as the least curable and most in need of permanent segregation, not education. In fact, the lower grades of feeblemindedness were no longer a concern. Goddard wrote, "We begin to realize that the idiot is not our greatest problem. . . . It is the moron type that makes for us our greatest problem."[96] In the case of the "moron," a dynamic view of intellectual disability as improvable was supplanted by a conviction in the hereditary and static nature of this condition. The proposed treatments reflected this belief: permanent segregation and sterilization were promoted rather than the importance of education and training.[97]

The static and dynamic views of intellectual disability, then, do not directly map onto the mild/severe continuum. Both mild and severe forms of intellectual disability were presented as dynamic, justifying the existence of the institution as a pedagogical and therapeutic instrument. Yet the static character of intellectual disability has also been ascribed to both ends of the spectrum: there were always severe cases—the incurables—who merited custodial care. However, the mildest forms of feeblemindedness were also deemed incurable as the association with immorality and crime developed.

Just as there is no clear parallel between dynamic/static and mild/severe forms of intellectual disability, there is no decisive historical shift from a dynamic, optimistic view to a static, pessimistic view of feeblemindedness. The period of "optimism" in the mid-nineteenth century included many custodial cases that were believed to be ineducable, and the age of pessimism witnessed growth in the special education system, predicated on the idea that at least some forms of intellectual disability are improvable.

As Ferguson has pointed out, chronic cases were always present, even in the earliest schools for idiots. It is a mistake to assume that the optimistic educational spirit touched the lives of all persons who were institutionalized. For some, the shift from schools to custodial facilities never took place: "In relation to the most severely retarded segment of the population, the nineteenth century cannot be understood as a brief golden age of experiment and reform followed by a gradual slide into custodialism. . . . When one begins to focus on severe disability, the mid-century institutional 'experiments' can be seen as somewhat self-serving endorsements of the status quo by the founders of the so-called schools. The social policy toward those judged unteachable or incorrigible in the nineteenth century was uninterrupted in its custodial orientation."[98] Though the period of optimism focused on improvability, a static conception of intellectual disability remained, and "hopeless" cases were treated by custodial means.

Conversely, the subsequent period of pessimism, drawing on the belief that feeblemindedness is a hereditary, hopeless condition and characterized by a rise in custodialism, was also a historical period of educational development. In 1896 the American Association on Mental Deficiency reported on the first American day classes for mentally retarded children in Rhode Island.[99] In the years that followed, numerous classes would open for children who were "backward" or "mentally deficient" (the two categories in place by 1900), while the idiots and imbeciles remained in institutions. Elizabeth Farrel, a teacher in the New York school system, was responsible for promoting ungraded classes in the public schools, and was the co-founder and first president of the International Council for Exceptional Children (1922).[100] Because I am focusing on residential institutions for the feebleminded, I will not discuss the development of special educational programs in public schools.[101] However, the period of eugenic fervor and pessimism concerning the feebleminded was also a time of growth in special education, based on the belief that certain persons with feeblemindedness are educable. Once again, the static and dynamic views of intellectual disability are present at the same time.

Protective and Productive Institutions

I conclude this section with the most interesting incarnation of the static and dynamic conceptions of intellectual disability: the complex way in which the institutional world relied on and perpetuated a picture of feeblemindedness as both static and dynamic. Within the walls of the institutions—called schools, life schools, and asylums—the discourses of cure, training, and education were transformed into a set of techniques, and the majority of residents were subjected to some kind of therapeutic and reformative practice.

Consider the static forms of feeblemindedness that seemed to offer no hope of improvement or education. Such individuals seemingly would have no place in a school. However, their presence was explained and justified in a number of ways. First, it was argued that families could not handle the burden of a feeble-minded child, particularly financially. Walter Fernald wrote, "Home care of a low grade idiot consumes so much of the working capacity of the wage earner of the household that often the entire family becomes pauperized. Humanity and public policy demand that these families should be relieved of the burden of those helpless idiots."[102] There was also the concern that, if not placed in the proper environment, the idiot's condition could actually worsen: "If neglected, feeble-minded children deteriorate with fearful rapidity.... Were all such children subjected to patient and well-directed nurture through their earlier years, a large proportion of them would doubtless be saved from the abject and disgusting condition in which they are usually found. Such nurture, however, is not to be expected, even in the families of the wealthy.... Hence the necessity of *special* schools."[103] Even those severely affected could benefit from institutionalization, for neither rich nor poor parents were equipped with the time and knowledge to properly care for these children. It was crucial to prevent more children ("idiotic at birth") who, "because of the ignorance and neglect of their parents have become filthy, gluttonous, lazy, vicious, depraved, and are rapidly sinking into driveling idiocy."[104] Foucault explains the "colonization of idiocy by psychiatry"[105] in terms of the parents' ability to work: rather than serving the end goal of education, the process of institutionalization served "the aim of releasing parents from taking care of their children so as to put them on the labor market."[106]

The superintendents' explicit discourse on idiocy presented the institution as the best solution for incurables. However, there was also a self-serving motive for the custodialization of static cases. In his history of the low-grade population, Ferguson argues that the institutional population of incurables was necessary to explain the superintendents' failure to educate or improve many of their inmates and re-integrate them back into the community. Therefore, "nineteenth century reformers always ensured the continued existence of a residual population who could not be helped by their reforms."[107] The debate over whether these incurable cases should be housed in a separate custodial department of the larger institution or have their own facilities confirms this. While some super-intendents thought that the presence of unteachables "embarrasses the general management"[108] and argued for separate institutions, they were outnumbered by those who accepted the "cottage" or "colony" plan. In this new design, we find the concretization of the classificatory system in architectural form. Trent explains that with the colony plan, individuals were divided based upon their "ability to perform tasks"[109] that were necessary for the institution to function (e.g., farmwork, construction, sewing, and cooking). Eventually most institu-tions adopted this approach, and the architecture of the institutions mirrored the dual classification of custodial (static) and educable (dynamic) cases, so that the high-grade and low-grade cases were housed separately.[110]

For the most severe cases, then, the institution was considered necessary for their own sake and for the sake of their families, and it was also in the best interest of the superintendents to house them in custodial departments. Yet in addition to the lowest-grade idiot whose condition was thought to be im-mutable, there was another class of feebleminded individuals who were also portrayed as static, and were housed with the low-grades in the custodial de-partments: the moral imbeciles.[111] Beginning in the late nineteenth century, the high-grade form of feeblemindedness was interpreted as the least hopeful because, while possessing greater intellectual capacity than the lower grades of idiocy and imbecility, the moral imbecile was afflicted with a permanent moral defect. In his influential work on moral imbecility, Isaac Kerlin (responsible for introducing the term) underscores the static nature of this condition: "As there are persons in whom we discover a partial or entire absence of color perception, or of the musical perception, and others who are partially or entirely destitute of the power of numbers, of distance, of analysis, of logic, or of any other special faculty,—*nor can the absence be supplied by education,*—so we have individuals who, from some inherent fault in, or some radical defect of the receptive cen-ters, are destitute in part and sometimes wholly of the so-called moral sense, and no environment and no education will supply the deficiency."[112]

Institutions protected society from these dangerous individuals and pre-vented them from propagating. Just as he justified the existence of the insti-tution for the low-grade idiot, Fernald asserted its importance for this other group of incurables, who needed permanent care or they would become va-grants, drunkards, and thieves or, worse, reproduce their own kind.[113] This "brighter class of feebleminded" was institutionalized for the benefit of society as a whole, not for their individual improvement. These static cases justified the existence of the institution as a *protective* instrument in a number of ways. The incarceration of low-grade idiots protected them from the injustice of being housed with the poor and the insane, and from being neglected and harmed in an unsuitable family environment. The families of these burdensome cases of idiocy were protected from hardship and financial ruin. Finally, the superintendents were protected from being criticized for the existence of unteachable cases within their institutions. The incarceration of the moral imbecile, on the other hand, protected the rest of society from their immoral and criminal behavior and kept them from reproducing. As Rafter writes, "The moral imbecile formed a bridge, the crucial conceptual link between the feebleminded and the criminal. Essays on moral imbecility . . . became the main form of specialized knowledge produced by . . . superintendents in the late nineteenth century. And in these writings the superintendents identified yet another new client: society itself. Using eugenics, they would cure the nation of its evils and restore it to health."[114]

While the institution justified its existence on the basis of hopeless static custodial cases, the institution also relied on and perpetuated the notion of feeblemindedness as a dynamic condition. The assumption that feeblemindedness was changeable lay at the core of the campaign to build institutions for the feebleminded. The rhetoric of improvability and educability, and the belief in the importance of a proper environment pervaded the calls for new facilities. Institutional practices, which ranged from education and training to supervision and punishment, were predicated on the belief that the proper environment could *improve* feeblemindedness and, more importantly, make its victims *productive* individuals. Here we find the institution portrayed not as a custodial, protective facility but as a reformative and productive one.

By the late nineteenth century, despite faith in the educability of the feebleminded, which provided the impetus and justification for the new institutions, the notion of training, not education, dominated institutional practice.[115] There were educational programs for the high-grade inmates, and many in the school departments were instructed "in the ordinary branches of the common schools. As compared with the education of normal children, it is a difference of degree, and not of kind."[116] However, as Burton Blatt observes, "ironically, state institutions provided education only for those who didn't belong there—the mildly retarded."[117] Most individuals living in institutions were improved through rigorous training and supervision, the goal of which was *productivity*. Though some were taught to read and write, Fernald, the superintendent of the Massachusetts School, raised concerns regarding its failure to fulfill this role: "The most prominent feature of our educational training today is the attention paid to instruction in industrial occupations and manual labor."[118]

Education, then, became conflated with training. Though superintendents justified their methods in terms of their students' mental abilities (or lack thereof), the conviction that training was more appropriate than education must also be explained in terms of the institution's need for productive inmates. There was no hiding the economic advantage provided by the use of inmate labor. Fernald wrote, "the average running expenses of these institutions have been gradually and largely reduced by this utilization of the industrial abilities of the trained inmates."[119] Since so many of the institutions had farms, students began learning farming techniques, along with other forms of vocational training, at a very young age.[120] Even those who could not be taught particular skills, the low-grade cases, were trained in life skills (bathing, feeding, dressing and undressing, cleanliness, etc.). "As a result of the kindly but firm discipline, the patient habit-teaching, and the well-ordered institution routine, a large proportion of these children become much less troublesome and disgusting, so much so that the burden and expense of their care and support are materially and permanently lessened."[121] Though it was argued that both the mild and severe cases could benefit from training, the need to engage in this "habit training" for the sake of institutional efficiency was exposed as well. As Trent explains, by the early 1900s "habit training of young children was directed at institutional adaptation, not skills needed on the outside."[122]

Insofar as the institution relied on both static and dynamic depictions of feeblemindedness, a paradoxical relation between these two supposedly disparate kinds of feeblemindedness emerges, particularly when we look at the characterization of inmate labor. Outside of the institution, as the eugenic fervor regarding the "menace of the feebleminded" grew in the early decades of the twentieth century, feeblemindedness was considered incurable (no family environment is adequate), hopeless, and dangerous (high-grades are a danger to society, and low-grades are in danger from society): a static condition. Within the institutional walls, however, the same condition was seen as improvable.[123] From the lowest to highest forms of feeblemindedness, disciplinary techniques were employed to make inmates productive. Even the custodial departments relied on routines, punishments, and physical tasks to prevent idleness among inmates. Charles Bernstein, superintendent of the Rome Custodial Asylum for Unteachable Idiots (opened in 1894), wrote, "I am convinced that I can do more for a low grade feebleminded boy, who soils himself and is destructive, through one summer's work for such boy with a pile of earth to be moved with pick, shovel and barrow, and a good attendant direct him, than could any teacher working with him in the schoolroom for the same length of time. . . . One-half the happiness in life is in having our minds occupied and in knowing that we are doing useful work, and the feebleminded are no exception to this rule."[124] There is a double irony in calling inmate labor "useful." The low-grades were often given futile tasks to keep them busy, while the work performed by high-grades served the purposes of the institution. One wonders what the "other half of the happiness in life" is for the productive feebleminded in the institution.

These institutions and the expert discourse produced by their superintendents disseminated the view of feeblemindedness as both a helplessly static fate and an improvable, dynamic condition. And as Trent argues, the presence of both groups was indispensable to the institution's very survival: "Within a decade of the founding of the first schools . . . the education of idiots with all its promise to train productive workers was becoming a means of institutional perpetuation."[125] Yet the fate of the institutions and the superintendents' claim to expert authority would change radically in the wake of a new technique: the IQ test. And with it came another new species of feeblemindedness: the moron.

Visibility and Invisibility

The institutions for the feebleminded that emerged in the mid-nineteenth century were arguably the most significant means by which knowledge about intellectual disability was produced and organized. As we have seen, the superintendents' expert discourse produced numerous classificatory systems and philosophies of training, education, and management. It also perpetuated dual portraits of intellectual disability as both static and dynamic, qualitative and quantitative departures from a *norm,* and organic and environmental explanations of etiology. The eugenics movement that took hold in the early twentieth century, with its attendant theories of degeneracy, hereditarian explanations of deviance, and campaigns to eliminate undesirable and unfit populations (e.g., immigrants, criminals, paupers, and the feebleminded), changed the face of intellectual disability.[126] It was the introduction of Alfred Binet's IQ test in this milieu of heightened concern about mental and moral deficiency that allowed the newest face of feeblemindedness, the moron, to eclipse all others for a period of time.[127] And it was one man, psychologist H. H. Goddard, who was responsible for introducing both this new technique and a new kind of feeblemindedness to the United States. Drawing on Goddard's landmark 1912 study, *The Kallikak Family*, I will consider the impact of mental testing through the lens of another conceptual pair: the visibility and invisibility of intellectual disability.[128] Specifically, we can examine how the IQ test generated shifts at three levels: the social, the individual, and the etiological.

One way to read the history of intellectual disability would be to focus on the ways that it has been made both socially visible and invisible. The incarceration of idiots in institutions far from public view was, in part, an attempt to render feeblemindedness invisible to the rest of the population, though paradoxically it was the humanitarian campaign that exposed the horrific conditions in which they were living that brought them under the public's gaze. Within the walls of the institutions, they were subjected to the expert's normalizing gaze, which controlled and classified them and brought both their defects and their potential to light. With the development of the intelligence test, this gaze extended beyond institutions for the feebleminded to other social institutions and settings where feeblemindedness could be found. Tests administered in prisons, reformatories, the army, and schools concluded that feeblemindedness was a problem that affected many beyond the institutional walls. Intelligence tests heightened the visibility of feeblemindedness: countless prisoners, prostitutes, schoolchildren, paupers, and immigrants were identified as feebleminded.[129] The results of this testing fueled a campaign against the dangers of feeblemindedness by linking it to other social ills (criminality, sexual vice, alcoholism, pauperism), thus making it visible as a social problem.[130] Underlying this increased social visibility, however, was a more fundamental *invisibility* at the level of the feebleminded individual.

As we saw with the institution, certain *kinds* of individuals emerged hand in hand with new techniques of gathering knowledge about them. This is true of the intelligence test as well; it appeared simultaneously with a new type of feeblemindedness: the moron. Goddard pronounced morons the most dangerous class of mental defectives *because of their invisibility*. Unlike the idiots and imbeciles, who were easily identifiable and had a place within the institution, the moron was able to pass for normal: "These are people of good outward appearance, but of low intelligence, who pass through school without acquiring any efficiency, and then go out into the world and must inevitably fall into some such life as we have pictured."[131] This life was one of criminality and immorality. The moron provided a causal explanation for deviance. Thanks to the numerous tests administered to prisoners and prostitutes, the scores of their intelligence tests confirmed that feeblemindedness in the form of the moron (i.e., high-grade intellectual and moral deficiency) had a direct link with criminality: "So we have, as is claimed, partly from statistical studies and partly from careful observation, abundant evidence of the truth of our claim that criminality is often made out of feeblemindedness. . . . Lombroso's famous criminal types, in so far as they were types, may have been types of feeblemindedness on which criminality was grafted by the circumstances of their environment."[132] From this passage it is clear that, in one sense, feeblemindedness had become a more fundamental category: it was considered the *cause* of criminality.

The belief in the criminal and immoral nature of the moron reinforced the danger of this particular class, and the success of mental testing in rendering morons visible to the public prompted further steps to be taken in treating the problem (e.g., institutional segregation and sterilization as means of controlling the spread of feeblemindedness). Whereas earlier emphasis had been placed on lower grades of mental deficiency (idiots and imbeciles), attention was now focused on morons, particularly because of the possibility that they would reproduce: "[The idiot] is indeed loathsome; he is somewhat difficult to take care of; nevertheless, he lives his life and is done. He does not continue the race with a line of children like himself. Because of his low-grade condition, he never becomes a parent. It is the moron type that makes for us our greatest problem. And when we face the question: 'What is to be done with them . . . ?' We realize that we have a huge problem."[133] This new class of feeblemindedness could not have emerged and gained such prominence without the intelligence test, which was able to pick out individuals who would otherwise have gone undetected. Since the moron's invisibility was believed to have drastic consequences—particularly crime and the propagation of feeblemindedness—the existence of this class of individuals reinforced the necessity and success of these tests. Much like the delinquent and the penitentiary technique that Foucault described, the moron and the IQ test "are in a sense twin brothers. . . . They appeared together."[134] In defining the moron, or criminal imbecile, Goddard cemented the connection between criminality and feeblemindedness and was able to conclude that "the so-called criminal type is merely a type of feeblemindedness. . . . It is hereditary feeblemindedness not hereditary criminality that accounts for the conditions."[135]

Alfred Binet, the father of the IQ test, confirmed that the type and technique came hand in hand. In his criticism of earlier methods of assessment, he stressed that while lower forms of mental deficiency like idiocy and imbecility are more easily identified by physical signs and pedagogical defects, the moron is the most difficult to diagnose by virtue of the invisibility of symptoms, hence the importance of the psychological method (the intelligence tests) over all other approaches: "The physical descriptions of the idiot and the imbeciles that one finds in classic treatises are not always correct; and even if they were, they would not apply in the least to morons. But the morons constitute the majority. It is the morons that must be recognized in the schools where they are confounded with normals; it is they who offer the greatest obstacle to the work of education. The diagnosis of moronity is at the same time the most important and the most difficult of all."[136]

This statement points to another effect these tests had on the visibility of feeblemindedness: they prompted a shift from defining its nature in terms of visible symptoms and behavior, to representing an invisible capacity—intelligence—in the form of a numerical score. Recall the earlier descriptions of idiocy by Howe and Seguin, which relied heavily on anatomical and physiological signs of idiocy. Binet argued for a new classificatory scheme that would *directly* test that which distinguishes feeblemindedness from all other conditions: intellectual defect. He identified three methods of recognizing inferior states of intelligence: medical, pedagogical, and psychological. The medical method studies the anatomical, pathological, and physiological signs, and is indirect "because it conjectures [sic] the mental from the physical."[137] The pedagogical method tests the sum of acquired knowledge, but accumulated knowledge is different from intelligence. Only the psychological method, which "makes direct observations and measurements of the degree of intelligence," can give an accurate assessment of the individual's intellectual defect.[138] For Binet, judgment was the fundamental faculty of intelligence: "To judge well, to comprehend well, to reason well, these are the essential activities of intelligence."[139] Feeblemindedness was no longer understood in terms of Seguin's trinity, "man's . . . three prominent vital expressions: activity, intelligence and will."[140] It was reduced to one faculty—intelligence—which was the only thing this new technique measured.

The IQ test was so successful in the United States because it was seen as an effective and scientific way of picking out this new type of individual, and was thought to offer a solution to the limitations of medical and pedagogical methods. Goddard, in his report *Feebleminded Children Classified by the Binet Method,* echoed the limitations of purely medical classifications: "We should certainly emphasize here what is known to all of you, that the old terms of classification, while of interest to physicians, perhaps, are of no practical value to us, and in accordance with this classification it could be made very clear that for instance a microcephalic child might be a moron, an imbecile or an idiot;

a hydrocephalic the same, and so on thru the list. In other words, these words do not help us to know about what the child is capable of in the way of training and development."[141] The IQ test, according to Binet, Goddard, and many others who promoted it, provided a direct line to the defective intellect that was the defining feature of feeblemindedness. In contrast with the multitude of visible signs of mental deficiency that had failed to provide a clear picture of feeblemindedness, the IQ test was able to definitively fix the level of this elusive, invisible, yet indispensable feature of humanness: intelligence. In this sense, invisibility triumphed over visibility.

Finally, mental tests affected the visibility of feeblemindedness at the etiological level. Here we find a sharp departure from Binet's original intent by Goddard and other Americans, a break that allowed the tests to flourish and remain a dominant source of knowledge about feeblemindedness. Binet and Simon explained that the intelligence test measures the *actual state of intelligence:* "Our purpose is to be able to measure the intellectual capacity of a child who is brought to us in order to know whether he is normal or retarded. We should therefore, study his condition at the time and that only. We have nothing to do either with his past history or with his future; consequently we shall neglect his etiology . . . and we leave unanswered the question of whether this retardation is curable, or even improvable.[142] Walter Fernald's presidential address to the American Association for the Study of Feeblemindedness illustrated that these tests were put to the opposite use in America: "The theory and practice of mental testing and the discovery of the concept of mental age did more to *explain* feeblemindedness, to simplify its diagnosis, and to furnish accurate data for *training and education,* than did all the previous study and research from the time of Seguin [emphasis mine].[143] While Binet refused to use his tests to explain etiology or dictate treatment, the IQ tests in the United States became inextricably bound with hereditarian explanations of feeblemindedness and with methods of controlling it.[144]

Goddard wrote his book *The Kallikak Family* as evidence of the connection between intelligence and heredity: "If both parents are feeble-minded all the children will be feeble-minded."[145] In hereditarian rhetoric, the notion of invisibility arises once again. "Defective germ plasm" or "bad blood" was responsible for mental deficiency and was passed along from one generation to the next. Since this invisible substance could not be seen any more than intelligence could be, techniques were devised to bring it to light. Intelligence tests and family histories could confirm the presence of the invisible cause (bad blood) and the invisible defect (low intelligence).[146]

Given the belief in the hereditarian nature of feeblemindedness, a host of treatments and solutions were proposed. Sterilization, segregation, marriage restrictions, and immigration laws were all enforced to stop the spread of feeblemindedness. The two aspects of feeblemindedness that Binet meant to avoid in his intelligence tests—etiology and treatment—became the focal point of their use in the United States. The *actual mental state* of the individual seemed far less important than what caused this defect and what was going to be done about it.

In addition to revealing how the emergence of this new class of disability—the moron—affected the social, individual, and etiological visibility and invisibility of intellectual disability, one can also read Goddard's *The Kallikak Family* in the context of the other conceptual tensions I have explored in this chapter. While the IQ test clearly embodies a quantitative view of intellectual disability, defined according to graded departures from a set norm, Goddard's descriptions of the feebleminded half of the Kallikak family and his definition of this new class represented intellectual disability as qualitatively distinct from the normal. (Recall Goddard's description of Deborah Kallikak's mother: "Her philosophy of life is the philosophy of the animal.")[147] Hereditarian explanations pointed to something even more fundamental in the moron, something that would mark her apart as radically other: the taint of bad blood, of defective germ plasm.[148]

Thus the etiology of this high-grade form of feeblemindedness is explained by positing some organic defect. In Goddard's words, "The question is, 'How do we account for this kind of individual?' The answer, in a word 'Heredity'—bad stock."[149] And this endogenous explanation, combined with the fears and dangers surrounding high-grade feebleminded individuals who could easily pass and procreate, in turn gave credence to the view of the moron as a hopelessly static case. Although Goddard's book acknowledged the many tasks, skills, and talents that Deborah exhibited at Vineland, he assumed that no amount of training or education could rehabilitate or erase her moral defect: "To-day if this woman were to leave the Institution, she would at once become a prey to the designs of evil men or evil women and would lead a life that would be vicious, immoral, and criminal, though because of her mentality she herself would not be responsible. There is nothing she might not be led to, because she has no power of control, and all her instincts and appetites are in the direction that would lead to vice."[150]

Was there anything significant about the fact that Deborah, this new face of the moron, was a woman? Were there distinctly *gendered kinds* of feeblemindedness? This leads to broader questions concerning the relevance of gender difference to this history. What do we make of the fact that the attendants in the institutions and the field-workers who engaged in these family pedigree studies were primarily women? And how did early feminist rhetoric and calls for reform shape what was being said and done about feeblemindedness during this period? To answer these questions, let us retrace this historical ground from the perspective of the women, disabled and non-disabled alike, who, as active human subjects, shaped intellectual disability as an object of knowledge.

2

Gendered Objects, Gendered Subjects

We have to understand what one's oppression
"as a woman" means in each case.

—ELIZABETH SPELMAN

In critically revisiting his work on madness in *The History of Madness*, Foucault saw a need to dislodge the asylum from its central place in the history of madness: "We should show, rather, that what is essential is not the institution with its regularity, with its rules, but precisely the imbalances of power that I have tried to show both distort the asylum's regularity and, at the same time, make it function."[1] Aside from briefly describing the workings of disciplinary power in the institution, I excluded notions of power and oppression from the discussion in chapter 1. I accounted for intellectual disability as a classification created and perpetuated from above by superintendents, institutional discourse and practice, and mental tests.[2] I did not represent the perspective of active subjects who were classified and oppressed but discussed them as objects of knowledge. In this chapter I take Foucault's suggestion seriously and explore the complex power relations embedded in both the institutional world and the social fabric in which intellectual disability emerged as a distinct category.

Although many institutional histories have looked at the question of power in the asylum and in schools for the "feebleminded," a sustained analysis of the ways in which gender figured into this story of power has yet to be written.

At first glance, it seems that the discourses and practices regarding the intel-lectually disabled affected men and women equally. From the time "idiocy" became a focal point in the mid-nineteenth century, through the eugenic fer-vor surrounding the feebleminded leading up to World War I, both men and women were placed in the new schools and asylums for idiots, were given IQ tests and placed in special educational programs, and the various categories of feeblemindedness (idiots, imbeciles, morons, moral imbeciles) were applied to both. On closer examination, the role of women in the history of intellectual disability emerges as complex and important, and it provides an illuminating example of the kind of "relations of force . . . that permeate institutions" and impact the lives of both disabled and non-disabled women.[3]

The concerns and contributions of women with disabilities to feminist dis-course and academic scholarship more generally have become increasingly evi-dent.[4] The question of intellectual disability remains somewhat marginalized, however, even in the literature on feminism and disability. Similarly, histories of intellectual disability include discussions of differential treatment of men and women, but there are fewer explicit analyses of the role that gender has played in the history of intellectual disability.[5] In an effort to redress this dual invis-ibility, I enter into the fascinating world of intellectual disability as a gendered classification.[6]

This chapter is structured around five groups of women who have played a part historically in the world of intellectual disability: (1) "feebleminded women," (2) institutional caregivers, (3) mothers, (4) researchers, and (5) reformists.[7] As I discuss these five groups, some of the features of classification mentioned in the previous chapter will emerge (e.g., prototype effects, the relationship between etiology and definition, and techniques of identifying the "feebleminded"). In addition to the insights these five groups will provide into the mechanisms of this classification, the complex relationships between them demand an analysis of power and oppression.

Before I turn to the first group of women, I will briefly outline the theoretical basis for my discussion of power and oppression, which draws on the work of Michel Foucault and Iris Marion Young.

Social Groups and Modes of Power

In chapter 1, I examined one form of power—disciplinary power—as it relates to intellectual disability. Foucault explores multiple forms of power in his histories.[8] He does not believe that power can be defined independently of its exercise in a particular social context. Thus he defines *"the exercise of power* as a way in which certain actions may structure a field of other possible actions."[9] For Foucault, power is relational, and an analysis of power relations cannot be reduced to the acts and motives of a particular individual; in this respect, it is non-subjective.[10] Though power relations are inevitable and "rooted deep in the social nexus," they are not necessarily oppressive.[11] Domination is one form, for instance, but there are many ways in which "certain actions may structure the field of other possible actions" that are not harmful, and some give rise to forms of resistance.[12] Power relations are a fact of social existence, and "a society without power relations can only be an abstraction." Given the pervasiveness of these relations, what interests Foucault is their role in the process by which "human beings are made subjects."[13]

The theory of oppression that Young presents in *Justice and the Politics of Difference* has a number of things in common with Foucault's definition of power. I interpret her concept of oppression as one mode of power in the Foucauldian sense. Like Foucault's notion of power, Young defines oppression relationally and does not think there is one essential definition. Her pluralistic approach to defining "five faces of oppression" shares the Foucauldian conviction that power must be analyzed in its particular forms, which vary depending on the context.[14] Oppression, like power, is non-subjective. In an effort to depart from traditional notions of oppression as the "exercise of tyranny by a ruling group,"[15] Young argues that "oppression . . . refers to systemic constraints on groups that are not necessarily the result of the intentions of a tyrant."[16]

Though I maintain that the five faces of oppression are modes of power in Foucault's sense, they are not exhaustive of all possible power relations. Foucault emphasizes that power relations need not involve domination, while Young associates domination with oppression. In her introduction she writes, "Oppression and domination should be the primary terms for conceptualizing injustice."[17] Furthermore, Young's entire project is based on the belief that oppression is avoidable, and while Foucault would agree that specific modes of power can be altered or avoided, he maintains that there will always be some form of power relations at play.

Given this interpretation of oppression as one mode of power in Foucault's sense, I now turn to Young's five faces of oppression: exploitation, marginalization, and powerlessness (which all deal with the social division of labor), cultural imperialism, and violence. Young states that these forms of oppression should be understood as applying to social groups, not to atomistic, autonomous individuals. She defines a social group as "a collective of persons differentiated from at least one other group by cultural norms, practices, or way of life. Members of a group have a specific affinity with another because of their similar experience or way of life."[18] Young finds that this concept of groups allows for a more thorough and complex analysis of oppression. Rather than the traditional view of oppression as the actions and policies of a few "tyrannical individuals,"[19] her theory defines oppression as a relation between groups.[20] Her five faces of oppression provide the means by which to evaluate whether a particular social group is oppressed, and in what ways. For the purposes of my discussion, I will focus on the first four forms of oppression as they apply to the history of intellectual disability.[21]

Drawing on the Marxist notion of exploitation, Young states, "The central insight expressed in the concept of exploitation . . . is that this oppression occurs through a steady process of the transfer of the results of the labor of one social group to benefit another."[22] She points to the work of various feminists who have identified the many ways in which women have performed devalued "feminine jobs" for the benefit of those on whom they are dependent (usually men), thus transferring the results of the labor from one social group to another.[23] In the case of the feebleminded, it will become apparent that the use of inmate labor was a form of exploitation.

The next two forms of oppression played a role in the lives of both feebleminded and "able-minded" women. Marginalization, Young says, is "perhaps the most dangerous form of oppression. A whole category of people is expelled from useful participation in social life and thus potentially subjected to severe material deprivation and even extermination."[24] Young identifies a number of groups that have been marginalized because they cannot contribute to the labor force, including the elderly, the sick, and the disabled.[25] The present chapter reveals that the feebleminded were marginalized at many levels. Powerlessness, the third face of oppression, happens to groups that "lack authority and are those over whom power is exercised without their exercising it."[26] Though this form of oppression is clearly at work in the history of intellectual disability, I will argue that Young's definition is not entirely equipped to deal with the complex relationships that operated in the definitions and practices surrounding feeblemindedness.

The final face of oppression I analyze is cultural imperialism. Young says, "To experience cultural imperialism means to experience how the dominant meanings of society render the particular perspective of one's own group invisible at the same time as they stereotype one's group and mark it out as the Other."[27] As we shall see, most of the women I discuss suffered this form of oppression at some level. Researchers, reformists, and mothers were oppressed as a result of being women in a predominantly patriarchal society. The women labeled "feebleminded" experienced cultural imperialism at another level, by virtue of being both female and defined as feebleminded.

As I examine these instances of exploitation, marginalization, powerless-ness, and cultural imperialism, it will become clear that the dynamics of op-pression had a significant impact on the classification of intellectual disability. This new focus on power relations both within and without the institutional world adds an important dimension to this history. While the previous chap-ter focused primarily on the expert/object dichotomy and examined the ways various "experts" produced knowledge and devised practices to deal with their object of study and treatment, an analysis of the five roles women played in this story will begin to reveal the complex relationships between active human subjects embedded within social groups and structures.

Feebleminded Women: A Prototype Effect

Mental retardation never became a "female malady" in the way that hysteria and other mental illnesses have become associated with women and feminine characteristics.[28] However, in the first decades of last century, the feebleminded woman became representative of the nature and dangers of the category as a whole. As we shall see, this asymmetry was largely due to the intersection between conceptions of feeblemindedness and stereotypes of femininity. By virtue of her membership in two socially defined groups—women and the fee-bleminded—the "feebleminded woman" was singled out as a perversion of the former group and a symbol of the latter.

Beginning in the late nineteenth century, there emerged a distinctly gendered class of "mental defectives" who received the attention of doctors, superinten-dents, legislators, and philanthropists: the "feebleminded woman." Evidence of the preoccupation with this new group can be found in written documents concerning the nature of feeblemindedness,[29] the meetings of the American As-sociation for the Study of Feeblemindedness,[30] in the legislation that provided funds to research and build institutions for these women, and in the number of custodial facilities built explicitly for women.[31] What accounted for this new concern with feebleminded women?

The emergence of this female class would not have been possible without the new category of moral imbecility, which in its early forms was usually male. As Trent explains, "Before the [Civil] war, moral idiots were almost always male. . . . When superintendents wrote about this type of idiot, their illustrations were of 'boys' who had improved both intellectually and morally under the tutelage of the institution. A decade after the war the discovery of female moral imbeciles, whose moral imbecility included the ability to bear illegitimate children, added a new urgency to the type."[32] The "moral imbecile" was differentiated from the "idiot" and "imbecile" insofar as he was far more deficient in the moral faculties than the intellect, while the "idiot" and "imbecile" were simply *mentally* deficient (and quite likable morally). This category quickly became prominent because it was more dangerous than idiocy for two reasons. First, moral imbeciles were closely linked with crime, pauperism, and degeneracy, and were considered a menace to society. Isaac Kerlin's typology of moral imbeciles confirms this. He divided them into four classes: the alcohol inebriate, the tramp, the prostitute, and the habitual criminal.[33] There was the added danger that, because of their higher mental functioning, moral imbeciles could pass for normal and thus go undetected.

The emergence of female feeblemindedness as a distinct problem relied on the existing emphasis on the moral imbecile (later known as the moron).[34] The high-grade forms of feeblemindedness, particularly those associated with *moral* deficiency, became representative of the category as a whole. The female incarnation of this type of feeblemindedness became symbolic of this prototypical group and represented the dangers of feeblemindedness generally.

The belief that feeblemindedness was hereditary contributed greatly to the new focus on the feebleminded woman. If mental deficiency was transmissible from one generation to the next, then it was of utmost importance that the feebleminded not be allowed to procreate. Women, as the symbols of procreative power, were particularly dangerous: "The sooner you can make people understand that the most economical thing we can do is to shut up every one of these children, *especially the female,* the more economical it is going to be for every state in the union."[35] Much of the focus was on the tendency of these women to have illegitimate children. Walter Fernald, the superintendent for the Massachusetts School for the Feebleminded from 1887 to 1924, stated in 1893, "There is hardly a poorhouse in this land where there are not two or more feebleminded women with from one to four illegitimate children."[36] By 1912 he had made the link between feeblemindedness and immorality in women definitive: "Feebleminded women are almost invariably immoral and if at large usually become carriers of venereal disease or give birth to children who are as defective as themselves. The feebleminded woman who marries is twice as prolific as the normal woman."[37]

There are countless descriptions of the dangers of female feebleminded-ness. Yet what is striking about this concern is the way Victorian feminine stereotypes influenced the classification and treatment of these women. In his article "Denied the Power to Choose the Good: Sexuality and Mental Defect in American Medical Practice, 1850–1920," Peter Tyor argues that "nineteenth century sexual norms and gender roles encouraged physicians to treat devi-ant female sexual behavior as evidence of mental retardation which warranted stringent measures of social control."[38] He shows that women's admission ages and retention time were higher after the 1870s, a fact that reflects the percep-tion of women of childbearing age as the most dangerous. Stereotypical views of female vulnerability only added to the need to protect this class; in Fernald's words, "a feebleminded girl is exposed as no other girl in the world is exposed. She has not the sense enough to protect herself from the perils to which women are subjected."[39] As stated in the *Second Annual Report of the Trustees of the New York State Custodial Asylum for Feebleminded Women* (1887), "the purpose of the asylum was to take women 'who grade in mind from being erratic to idiotic, one-fifth of whom being mothers from no wedlock' and who because of mental defect were 'ungoverned and easily yielding to lust, denied the power to choose the good, and to see them sheltered from the vices of vicious men.'"[40] As these quotes suggest, the problem was not simply the moral deficit in the female moral imbecile; by virtue of her womanhood, she was even more vulnerable and in need of protection.

Though this group needed protection from society, society also needed protection from it. Consequently a steady campaign began to segregate these women in all-female institutions and to separate women from men in existing asylums. The first custodial facility for women was built in New York in 1878, and many followed.[41] In 1905, four state governors recommended increasing the facilities for feebleminded girls or women of childbearing age.[42]

Although countless feebleminded men played out their lives in institutions, it seems that gender was a decisive factor in retaining women, insofar as the stereotypes of women as passive and vulnerable put feebleminded women at even greater risk than men upon leaving the institution. A study (1920s) on pa-roled inmates at Letchworth Village,[43] for example, concluded that "males are far more successful in extra-institutional adaptation" than females due to the sexual vulnerability of feebleminded women: "At times of relaxed supervision the girl is the easy prey of unscrupulous persons and, pursued, falls a ready victim to sex delinquencies. The boy, belonging to the aggressive sex, because of his dull wit, cannot successfully compete with his more normal brethren in the game of procreation."[44] Here again we see the effect of sexual stereotypes: feebleminded women, insofar as they are passive, are at greater danger of "falling prey" to sexual vice. Feebleminded men, on the other hand, are deprived of their aggressive nature due to their deficiency and are thus less likely to procreate. If the procreative potential of women were removed, they would be perfectly fine candidates for parole, as the Letchworth study indicates:[45] "These girls who have gone out from our institution and have come back as failures would have been successes if they had been sterilized. . . . They are successes— they have good personalities, but from our standard and the standards of the social workers, they are failures. They cannot go out year after year and keep absolutely straight."[46] Tyor's data supports this reluctance to grant parole to women inmates. Women were admitted in greater numbers at childbearing age and were retained in the institutions for longer periods of time than their male counterparts.[47] Thus, not only were women incarcerated at childbearing age due to the dangers of procreation, but they were refused parole because of their feminine vulnerability and passivity.

As we have already seen, the moral imbecile (male and female) acquired a new name with Goddard's 1910 taxonomy: the moron. In many ways, the moron became a prototypical example of feeblemindedness because of his or her invisibility and thanks to the ability of IQ tests to identify so many cases of high-grade feeblemindedness. However, of this class, the *female* brand became the most representative. An example of this is found in Goddard's study of the Kallikak family. Though both male and female cases of feeblemindedness were identified, the focus on Deborah Kallikak, the feebleminded girl supposedly responsible for this "defective line," contributes to the asymmetrical nature of this category: its female form is infused with significant symbolic power.

The case of Deborah Kallikak became the paradigmatic example of the high-grade class of the feebleminded, and her descent from a long line of bad ancestors underscored the dangerous consequences of procreation by the feebleminded. I quote Goddard's description of Deborah at length because I think it exemplifies the prevailing view of the female moron:

> [Deborah] is a typical illustration of the mentality of a high-grade feeble-minded person, the moron, the delinquent, the kind of girl or woman that fills our reformatories. They are wayward, they get into all sorts of trouble and difficulties,

sexually and otherwise. . . . It is also the history of the same type of girl in the public school. Rather good-looking, bright in appearance, with many attractive ways, the teacher clings to hope, indeed insists that such a girl will come out all right. Our work with Deborah convinces us that such hopes are delusions. Here is a child who has been most carefully guarded. She has been persistently trained since she was eight years old, and yet nothing has been accomplished in the direction of higher intelligence or general education. Today if this young woman were to leave the Institution, she would at once become a prey to the designs of evil men or evil women and would lead a life that would be vicious, immoral, or criminal, though because of her mentality she herself would not be responsible. There is nothing that she might not be led into, because she has no power of control, and all her instincts and appetites are in the direction that would lead to vice.[48]

Here we see all the features of female feeblemindedness: her sexual immorality, her vulnerability, her dangerous presence outside of the institution, and the hopelessness of education and parole. Because of her mental and moral defect, she is incapable of avoiding the evils and vices that would inevitably cross her path. Deborah's eighty-one years in the Vineland State School attest to the belief that institutionalization was the best fate for these vulnerable women.

A number of factors played a role in the definition of the feebleminded woman: (1) the emergence of moral imbecility as a representative subcategory allowed for the focus on the immorality of women in particular; (2) the emphasis on heredity and procreation made the segregation and retention of women paramount to avoid the spread of feeblemindedness; (3) the prevailing sexual stereotypes of women as passive, vulnerable procreators; and (4) the efforts by non-feebleminded women to pick out their feebleminded counterparts, institutionalize them, and use them to advance their own political agendas. (I will discuss this fourth factor at length in the section on reformists.) In the creation of the feebleminded woman as prototypical, we see the consequences of being identified in two overlapping social groups that are oppressed.

The feebleminded constitute a social group if we adopt Young's definition. She distinguishes a social group from an "aggregate—any classification of persons according to some attribute," and argues that while the aggregate model views the individual as ontologically prior to the collective, social groups "constitute individuals" insofar as one's identity is derivative from them.[49] As I have shown, it would be difficult to reduce the intellectually disabled to one common attribute. The many definitions and explanations for idiocy and feeblemindedness reflect a complex social process by which this group was picked out, and this will become even more evident in what follows. Furthermore, their segregation within institutions, the direct effect their classification has had on the education and treatment they received, and the lack of agency and control they have had over their lives are all evidence that in a very real sense, their identities have been shaped by their membership in the group labeled the feebleminded. Young also states that each oppressed group does not necessarily have a corresponding oppressing social group.[50] This is certainly the case for the feebleminded. It is impossible to point to one individual, or even one discipline or institution, responsible for the definition and treatment of feebleminded-ness. However, Young does say that every oppressed group has a corresponding *privileged* group, which will become equally clear in the examination of the re-maining four groups of women. Given that the feebleminded represent a social group according to Young's definition, then, in what ways were feebleminded women oppressed?

Women labeled feebleminded suffered cultural imperialism at a number of levels. The dominant patriarchal stereotypes of (white, middle-class) women as passive, vulnerable, procreative vessels were applied to feebleminded women as well, and in fact justified their incarceration. At the same time, the great importance placed on mental ability and proper sexual conduct rendered them invisible, not just in suppressing their particular perspective but in the physi-cal sense. The institutionalization of feebleminded women marginalized them, making them completely socially invisible.

In addition to her prototypical status and her oppression as a member of two social groups, we also see in the feebleminded woman the instability of this classification. As Tyor rightly suggests, it was sexual misconduct (i.e., birth of an illegitimate child) that became the new sign of feeblemindedness; the feebleminded woman as a new recognizable type emerged simultaneously with a new diagnostic method. The boundaries that defined the nature of feeble-mindedness were highly permeable. In its female form, the definition and de-tection of feeblemindedness were inseparable from dominant moral codes and expectations.

Institutional Caregivers: The Paradox of Inmate Labor

From their birth in the 1840s, the earliest American educational institutions for idiots relied on female labor. Edouard Seguin was explicit about the impor-tance of women working in the institution as attendants, teachers, and matrons. In his description of the institution, he explained the duties of each female employee. The attendant must be a gentle, caring woman and, given that her nature cannot go beyond that, must defer to the male scientific authority when she runs into trouble:

> The attendant cannot be empowered to punish or coerce children, but to help and incite them only; hence the necessity of choosing for that function women very kind, gay, attractive, endowed with open faces, ringing voices, clear eyes, easy movements, and affectionate propensity towards children. These are their only real power; when it fails they have to refer to their presumed superiors in intelligence, and to borrow of them an authority which cannot be exercised but with a complete knowledge of the physiological anomalies of each case. Thus is spent the time of these good women, who attend to the idiots much in the same manner as the monks of Spain of yore, and the farmers of Ghel later, took care of the insane, with little science, but a great deal of charity.[51]

Seguin suggested that science was beyond a woman's reach, but her propensity to care, nurture, and provide charity made her a perfect candidate for attending to those in need. Similarly, women teachers were not allowed to teach physical activities; the role of the gymnast was filled by men: "The gymnast seems to need more than the teacher, the quality of judging the point at which each exercise must be carried by each child, to be physiological and safe."[52] Once again, women were thought unfit to make the more sophisticated decisions that rely on scientific knowledge of physiology, which lay at the core of Seguin's method.

According to Seguin, the woman who has the most power in the institution is the matron. She is responsible for overseeing the attendants and seeing that each child is cared for. She presides over festivities and examines children who get hurt. Yet despite this active role, she is not considered in charge of the institution. The superintendent (who throughout the nineteenth century was almost always a medical doctor) is the man who oversees the entire operation. Seguin states he "is or should be the head. He is supposed to be prepared by special studies to confront the important problem enclosed in the yet mysterious word idiocy."[53] Isaac Kerlin's *Manual of Elwyn* describes the importance of the matron acting in natural mothering role: "To be true Matrons they should be the centre and example of the ladyhood of the family, the constant friends and helpers of the Superintendents, and the generous and sympathetic foster-mothers of our dependent children."[54] Attendants, teachers, and matrons were expected to exhibit and act according to their "natural" feminine capabilities.

As we saw in chapter 1, the institutional world was the primary vehicle for studying and treating idiocy, and the superintendents were responsible for much of the knowledge generated about intellectual disability. This psychiatric power was built into the very structure of the institution, which was patterned explicitly on the middle-class patriarchal family: superintendent as commanding father, matron and attendants as the caregivers, and the inmates as children.[55] That these institutions, from their inception, exemplified accepted gender roles is hardly surprising. Yet there is another feature of the institution that makes this fact far more interesting: the use of inmate labor also conformed to these norms.

In his 1893 description of American institutions for the feebleminded, Walter Fernald explained the division of inmates into two departments: the high-grades were placed in educational facilities (which amounted to training them to work in the institution), while the low-grade idiots, juvenile insane, epileptics, and moral imbeciles were placed in the custodial department.[56] "The daily routine work of a large institution furnishes these trained adults with abundant opportunities for doing simple manual labor, which otherwise would have been done by paid employees."[57] It was both convenient and cheap for the institution to employ inmates to work for free. Though inmate labor was supposed to serve educational purposes, as Trent says, "it solved the two perennial problems faced by institutions: employee costs and employee retention."[58]

Trent goes on to point out that "all institutions relied almost exclusively on the care of custodial inmates by salaried attendants and higher-functioning inmates."[59] The caregiving, nurturing attendants (mostly female) were not the only women playing that role in the institution; the female inmates were responsible for caring for more severely feebleminded patients. While the men worked on the farm (many institutions were surrounded by farmland) and did manual labor, feebleminded women learned basket weaving, sewing, nursing, and, most importantly, they cared for the low-grade idiots and imbeciles. As Fernald explained, "Many of these adult females, naturally kind and gentle, have the instinctive feminine love for children, and are of great assistance in caring for the feeble and crippled children in the custodial department."[60]

As already noted, women were given the job of attendant because of their alleged innate feminine capacity to nurture. What is remarkable about feebleminded women caring for other inmates, as Fernald's statement illustrates, is that the very women who embodied these quintessential female traits were the same women who had given birth to illegitimate children, were considered the "paupers of paupers," and were thought to have perverted the sexual behavioral norms expected of women. Though the feebleminded woman needed to be segregated and protected by virtue of her deficient intellect and moral faculty, her caregiving nature remained intact.

Here we see static and dynamic conceptions of feeblemindedness operating simultaneously: high-grade feebleminded women were unteachable, static cases of moral and intellectual defect if left outside the institution (recall Kerlin's description of this moral defect as indelible), but malleable and ultimately useful workers within. I maintain that the tension between these two portrayals is more than a function of the belief in the therapeutic benefits of institutionalization. It was not simply that feebleminded women could lead worthwhile lives inside the protective facility. They were subjected to competing definitions of their very nature: on the one hand, they were inherently morally defective and the birth of an illegitimate child proved their feeblemindedness. On the other hand, they were seen as able to properly care for children—presumably in a morally acceptable fashion—which is why they were employed within the institution. Paradoxically, the same women who had perverted the virtues of feminine purity and motherhood in the outside world were called on to use them within the walls of the institution. One finds countless examples like the Sunset Sisters of the Indiana School, who cared for the idiots and imbeciles housed in Sunset Cottage: "Higher-functioning female inmates, were assigned the care of one or more of these low-grade inmates. Seven days a week, every day of the year, the Sisters fed, changed, bathed and attended to them."[61]

The mothering role played by these women was in part justified by the infantilization of the feebleminded, a constant feature of this classification. If all of the adults and children housed within the institution are thought of as children, then it is only natural that they need a mother to care for them. I think the following statement by the superintendent of the Indiana School captures this double vision of the childlike and feminine qualities of the feebleminded: "Most appealing of all the touching sights in an institution, is to see the tenderness and patience exercised by a big overgrown man-baby or woman-baby, towards a tiny child-baby when put in their care. The maternal instinct is almost always present, and is often as strong in the males as in the females; fortunately for them and for us it is much stronger than the sex instinct."[62]

Here we find a complex blend of definitions and stereotypes: the high-grade feebleminded woman (men too have this potential) is at once maternal, childlike, and asexual. The pathological sexual instincts which defined these women as "moral imbeciles" and sanctioned their admittance into the institution have disappeared, and we are left with the touching sign of a woman-baby caring for her child-baby. Thousands of incarcerated women who fulfilled this role were evidence of a goal accomplished, well articulated by the spokeswoman for the feebleminded of her sex, Josephine Lowell: "These unhappy beings need, first of all, *to be taught to be women;* they must be induced to love that which is good and pure, and to wish to resemble it; they must learn all household duties; they must learn to enjoy work [emphasis mine]."[63]

The use of feebleminded labor served a far more insidious purpose than teaching and training these women for rehabilitative purposes: the dramatic rise in the number of women institutionalized as feebleminded for violating sexual norms was also a convenient way of assembling a greater labor force.[64] The fact that the educational and reformative rhetoric surrounding high-grade cases was being abandoned at the same time that more of them were being trained to work within the institution indicates that a new kind of training was in place: one which served the purposes of the institution.[65] The rhetoric of educability and reform simultaneously created and fulfilled the need for institutional labor and ensured that the institution could remain a self-perpetuating mechanism.

Evidence of this can be found in the nursing programs developed in the institutions. Trent describes the one at the Rome Asylum in New York: "Bernstein [the superintendent] began a nursing class. By 1925, 38 female inmates had enrolled, 21 completed coursework. . . . The graduates of these nursing programs found employment at their own institution, became nurses and nurses' aides at other county or state institutions."[66] The dangers of procreation and immorality, and the fact that moral imbecility was incurable, ensured that feebleminded women would not be released from the institution; yet they were clearly moral and educable enough to be taught to be employed *within* the institution, as nurses, mothers, and caregivers, which, as Trent has pointed out, fulfilled both economic and practical demands of the institution. The female moral imbecile came to the forefront precisely at that time when the custodial institutions needed her most.

Feebleminded women, like the Sunset Sisters and the Rome Asylum attendants, were caught in a complex web of stereotypes, rhetoric, and institutional needs. Female inmates were viewed simultaneously as caregivers fulfilling their "natural maternal instincts" and as intellectually and morally deficient children. The rhetoric of heredity and menace ensured that they would play the role of "woman-baby" in the institution for the rest of their lives. As the ineducable and dangerous moron became prototypical, greater numbers of men and women were being trained to become a permanent labor force in the institution.[67]

In addition to interpreting the use of inmate labor from the perspective of institutional exigency, we can also analyze it in terms of its oppressive nature. The first three faces of oppression Young defines deal with the social division of labor, and all are at work within the institution. Feebleminded women as a group were exploited, marginalized, and powerless.

The feebleminded woman was exploited insofar as the benefits of her institutional labor were transferred to others. The low-grade inmates clearly relied on her care, but it was the institution that presided over her like a great paternal figure that ultimately benefited. Her labor served the needs of the very structure that limited her freedom. Thus, in addition to exploiting the feebleminded woman, the institution contributed to her marginalization.

The feebleminded as a class (men and women) were clearly marginalized. Their institutionalization was a sign of their lack of productivity and inability to contribute to or enhance society. As a result, they were subjected to material deprivation, which "blocks the opportunity to exercise capacities in socially defined and recognized ways."[68] However, *within* the institution, *because of their marginalization,* they were able to be exploited.[69] The institution provided for basic needs precisely so that the feebleminded *could be trained and expected to* "exercise capacities in socially defined and recognized ways." There are multiple layers of oppression at work here, and we can see the interrelation between marginalization and exploitation in the dynamics of institutional and extra-institutional definitions of feeblemindedness.

Young defines the powerless as "those over whom power is exercised without their exercising it; the powerless are situated so they must take orders and rarely have the right to give them."[70] Perhaps because Young discusses powerlessness primarily in terms of the power relations between professionals and non-professionals, her notion of powerlessness does not accurately describe the power relations within the institution.[71] To avoid confusion, I will discuss Young's concept of powerlessness in terms of authority (the ability to give orders, make rules and decisions, occupy a respected professional role) and what I call practical power: performing labor that does not confer authority (in the above sense) but allows one to directly affect the lives of others. I find this distinction helpful in analyzing institutional power relations that are not captured by Young's definition of powerlessness.

Both feebleminded and non-feebleminded female caregivers lacked authority with respect to the dominant male superintendents, and both were called on to perform "feminine labor." Nevertheless, there was an important difference in the oppression of feebleminded women as opposed to their able-minded counterparts. The paid female attendant had authority over the feebleminded "woman-baby" who cared for the more severely disabled. Feebleminded attendants were in a position of practical power, however, with respect to the low-grades in their care. As Trent says, "the attendant, not the educator or the physician, was, in fact if not in rhetoric, the most crucial actor in the lives of inmates after 1890."[72] Though the many feebleminded women who occupied this role may not have possessed the authority granted to able-minded attendants and superintendents, it would be an oversimplification to say that they were completely powerless.

The use of inmate labor puts into relief the multiple forms of oppression at work in the institution: exploitation, marginalization, cultural imperialism, and various degrees of powerlessness with respect to authority and practical power. More generally, these power relations point to the instability of the classification of feeblemindedness. Depending on her place within and without the institution, the very *nature* and *status* of the feebleminded woman changed.

Women as Mothers: The Role of Etiology

Women played a role as both inmates and employees of institutions for the feebleminded; they were painted as both dangers and saviors because of their femininity. Now I will move out of the context of the institution and consider the problem of etiology once again. One prominent etiologic explanation focused specifically on women: mothers as a group played an important part in explaining the cause of feeblemindedness.

We have already encountered the issue of motherhood in the context of intellectual disability. Giving birth to an illegitimate child was considered a sign of feeblemindedness and became integral to the classification and institutionalization of the feebleminded woman. The assumption that women have a natural capacity to nurture and fulfill their mothering instincts affected the division of labor in the institutions and justified the maternal roles of both paid attendants and high-grade female inmates. Yet there is also a way in which both feebleminded and able-minded women *as mothers* were portrayed as responsible for feeblemindedness. Pedigree studies identified both men and women as the causes of degeneracy.[73] Alcoholics, epileptics, sexually immoral men and women alike could pass on the bad blood, the "tainted germ plasm" that would perpetuate and worsen deficiencies in the family. Figures like Deborah Kallikak reinforced the notion that feeblemindedness is hereditary, but was there anything significant about women spreading this curse? Were mothers and fathers equally at fault for their feebleminded children? If we examine this history, it becomes clear that there was a preoccupation with mothers in particular, and the image of the "bad mother" played an important part in explaining feeblemindedness.[74]

In the context of etiology, a bad mother was one who in some way *caused* her child to be feebleminded. The paradigmatic case was the Kallikak family, where a good man fathered two families—one with the feebleminded girl and the other with a "normal" woman. Marouf Hasain, in his book *Eugenic Rhetoric in Anglo-American Thought,* links this dual representation of motherhood to the rhetoric of eugenics: "The characterization of American women in hardline eugenics stories often involved a rhetorical division between those moral women who had good habits and healthy germ plasm and the unhealthy 'shiftless' women who polluted America's genetic pool. Normal women married, had the requisite number of children to perpetuate the race, and raised their children eugenically. Unhealthy or abnormal women were biologically 'feebleminded' or otherwise inferior."[75]

This good mother/bad mother dichotomy can be analyzed at two levels. First, I will explain why the feebleminded woman came to symbolize the bad mother with respect to the spread of feeblemindedness. Then I will examine how normal women could be considered bad mothers insofar as they too could cause feeblemindedness.

The concept of a good feebleminded mother did not exist in the early decades of the twentieth century. According to the hereditarian view of feeblemindedness, feebleminded women were likely to spread their tainted germ plasm on to their offspring. In the words of Walter Fernald, "[high-grade female imbeciles] are certain to become sexual offenders and to spread venereal disease or to give birth to degenerate children. Their numerous progeny usually become public charges or diseased or neglected children, imbeciles, epileptics, juvenile delinquents, or paupers or criminals."[76] Insofar as feebleminded women were seen as directly responsible for producing degenerate children, any woman who was feebleminded and chose to procreate represented a bad mother. Feebleminded mothers were also symbols of promiscuity and careless procreation, since giving birth to an illegitimate child was considered *proof* of feeblemindedness. As discussed earlier, this justified the incarceration of many of these women who, ironically, were then put to work as surrogate mothers caring for low-grade inmates within the institutions.

Thus the feebleminded woman was the quintessential bad mother in two respects: she symbolized careless and immoral procreation and represented the danger of spreading tainted germ plasm to one's offspring. Yet this image of the bad mother, embodied by the feebleminded woman, could be applied to able-minded women as well.

The image of the feebleminded mother as an immoral, careless procreator was countered by the myth of the good, able-minded mother, whose vigilance prevented her from having a feebleminded child. Though there was concern with feebleminded men reproducing, the fact that women carried children and gave birth to them was not unimportant. Many doctors argued that the state of the mother during intercourse "has much power in the formation of the foetus, both in modifying its physical constitution and in determining the character and temperament of its mind."[77] Able-minded women, *as mothers,* were considered crucial to the prevention of feeblemindedness.[78]

Seguin identified a number of important ways of preventing idiocy: keeping the woman in good mental and physical health during pregnancy, teaching women the signs of idiocy in their newborns so they might get immediate attention, and ensuring that the mother gives enough attention and love to the child:

> How much more sensible it would be for young couples to try to live according to hygienic rules, to keep the pregnant woman in comfortable conditions . . . sooner than to act as if relying upon the wisdom of the embryo to feed himself out of no food and to keep himself unmoved amidst the emotions of his mother. . . . [Of the signs of idiocy] Who could watch over the tardy coming of these functions better than a mother, if she were timely advised by a competent physician? The skill of the latter is of no avail without her vigilance, and her zeal may be very blind, even mischievous indeed without his advice; stuttering, squinting and all sorts of bodily defects, besides the perpetuation of the worst symptoms of early idiocy, are too often due to the want of this concerted action of love and knowledge.[79]

The belief that vigilant mothers, *under the guidance of a male physician,* could prevent idiocy or at least mitigate its effects is evidence of a tension between two competing myths about mothers: that "only the experts know how to raise children" and that "women are born nurturers."[80] Seguin's rhetorical question captures this dual picture of a woman's "natural" capacity to mother, and her dependence on the epistemological authority of the doctor: "Who could watch over the tardy coming of these functions better than a mother, if she were timely advised by a competent physician?" This embodies the transfer of disciplinary power into the family that Foucault exposes: "Just as the family model is transferred into disciplinary systems, disciplinary techniques are transplanted into the family. . . . I think we can say that, on the basis of disciplinary systems, family sovereignty will be placed under the following obligation: 'You must find for us the mad, feeble-minded, difficult, and perverse, you must find them yourself, through the exercise of disciplinary kinds of control within family sovereignty.'"[81]

This vigilance could take many forms, and there were concerns among male "experts" that women pursuing higher education and other traditionally male goals were endangering their children.[82] Seguin noted that the stress of emancipation had made women more vulnerable to the dangers of pregnancy, and his cautionary words made quite a stir. At the 1887 annual meeting of the Association of Medical Officers of American Institutions of Idiotic and Feeble-minded Persons, a prominent Philadelphia lawyer included the following reference to Seguin in his paper "A Medico-Legal Study of Idiocy":

> It is rather depressing to those of us who may favor the extension on what is called "The Sphere of Women" to be told that a modern factor of idiocy has arisen through the influence of gynagogues. This delightful term . . . is supposed to represent the class of agitators of women's rights. Concerning the result of their labors, Dr. Seguin says, "We overburden women, they overburden themselves, and choose or accept burdens unfit for them. . . . As soon as women assumed the anxieties pertaining to both sexes they gave birth to children whose like had hardly been met with thirty years ago—insane before their brain could have been deranged by their own exertions—insane, likely, by a reflex action of the nervous exhaustion of their mother. Children gotten under such moral and other pressures cannot truly be said to be born from the union, but rather from the division of their parents; conceived in antagonism, they can only be excessive in their tendencies or monsters in their organization."[83]

The stress resulting from pursuing goals thought to be unfit for women's sex and constitution was viewed as a cause of idiocy and insanity, monstrosity and excess.

Thus a cult of proper motherhood developed. Mothers were expected to be vigilant at every stage in order to prevent feeblemindedness in their offspring: in proper procreative habits, low stress and appropriate care during pregnancy, and attentiveness to signs of idiocy in the newborn. Gordon describes the double standard operant at the time: "The very attitudes that were attacked in women— social ambition, desire for wealth—were applauded in men. . . . In order to preserve the 'race' nature had ordained not only a division of labor but an ultimate division of values as well, that required of women *absolute selflessness*."[84]

This demand for vigilance extended to potential mothers as well. Many popular women's journals (*Good Housekeeping, Cosmopolitan, Ladies Home Journal*) reminded able-minded women of the hereditarian nature of feeblemindedness and urged women to investigate the possibility of "defective stock" in their own family background and in their prospective mates.[85] Hasain explains: "Those stories told in women's journals often integrated a variety of eugenical interpretations. . . . On the one hand women were warned that if 'two neurotic taints' were brought together, this would be like 'fire and tinder' in that 'your offspring will be neuropathic—feebleminded or epileptic, or sexually perverted or destined to become insane.' [*Cosmopolitan*, 1913] Yet at the same time they were asked to educate themselves and their children on the ways that even those without training could follow the rules of heredity. The really good parent was supposed to be a cautious person who checked his or her prospective mate's ancestry and background."[86] These magazines advised women how to avoid feebleminded children and reminded them of the danger posed by the feebleminded woman. One article in *American Magazine* in 1913 warned its readers that "the village girls who had illegitimate children might be medically, pedagogically, psychologically or sociologically 'feebleminded.'"[87] Though *all* women, from cities or villages, upper or lower class, were at risk, be it from their tainted ancestry, the poor choice of an afflicted mate, or the unfortunate consequences of their drive for emancipation, the feebleminded woman still symbolized the prototypical threat.

Janice Brockely points to another dimension in which this discourse was gendered: disabled offspring and their dependency were depicted differently for male and female children. "A permanently dependent idiot son was an anomaly of note in American popular culture, while a permanently dependent daughter was simply routine."[88]

The female potential to mother played a significant role in the etiologic arguments surrounding feeblemindedness. As we have seen, both feebleminded and able-minded women could be the cause of feeblemindedness. For the latter, being a good mother (i.e., preventing feeblemindedness) meant constant vigilance. Pregnant women were responsible for ensuring a healthy environment, physically and mentally, for the baby in the womb. Mothers of newborns were taught to watch for signs of idiocy, and were urged to give the proper love and attention to avoid adverse consequences.[89] The backlash against the women's movement advocated the selfless duty of women to bear and raise children, and so-called liberated women were warned that they could bring about the birth of a feebleminded baby.[90] Finally, the utmost care was required in selecting a mate and investigating his personal ancestry, given the hereditary nature of feeblemindedness.

Women labeled feebleminded had no hope of being a good mother but could, however, play a role in preventing the spread of feeblemindedness: they symbolized the prototypical bad mother against which able-minded women could measure themselves. Deborah and the entire defective line of Kallikaks represented the hereditary nature of feeblemindedness, while the institutionalization of countless feebleminded women who gave birth to illegitimate children served as a constant reminder of the dangers of transgression.

These two images of motherhood directly affected the classification of intellectual disability at the etiologic level. They were so powerful that thinking about the causes and prevention of feeblemindedness without taking the mother into consideration was impossible. With respect to the two social groups we have been examining (women and the feebleminded), it seems that at the level of etiology, the entire social group of women—feebleminded or not—was indispensable to an understanding of feeblemindedness, and was implicated in its perpetuation. Fernald's choice of words seems only too appropriate: "It has been truly said that feeblemindedness is the mother of crime, pauperism and degeneracy."[91]

Female Researchers: Pedigree Studies as "Woman's Work"

As we saw, there was little consensus as to the best method to identify feeblemindedness. However, with different techniques of detection, new types of feeblemindedness emerged. As mentioned earlier, one technique that became popular along with IQ tests in the first decades of this century was the pedigree study. Family histories were traced in order to confirm the feeblemindedness of a particular individual and to study the hereditarian nature of feeblemindedness.

Numerous pedigree studies were done on "defective families" from the late nineteenth century into the 1920s. Both Goddard's Vineland Training School and the Eugenics Records Office (founded by Charles Davenport in 1910 and funded by Mrs. Harriman, a wealthy philanthropist who gave money to help prevent feeblemindedness) offered training programs for field-workers. As Nicole Hahn Rafter points out in her collection and analysis of pedigree studies titled *White Trash: The Eugenic Family Studies, 1877–1919,* most of the researchers trained were women. In fact, thousands of women were employed in this new means of gathering knowledge about feeblemindedness.[92]

Elizabeth Kite is an important figure in this history. She was Goddard's main field-worker and was responsible for the stories about Deborah Kallikak and her feebleminded ancestry that underscored the sense of women's culpability in the spread of mental deficiency.[93] In addition to the Kallikak study (which, according to Rafter, was the first family study "to realize the potential of the bad-mother theme"), Kite published another study called *The Pineys* (1913) in which she investigated mentally deficient families in the New Jersey Pine Barrens.[94] This study directly resulted in the construction of an institution for the mentally deficient in that area of New Jersey, and contributed to the growing body of work which offered "proof" of the heritability of feeblemindedness. In addition to her role as a researcher, she was also responsible for translating two influential books into English: *Development of Intelligence in Children* and *The Intelligence of the Feebleminded* by Binet and Simon.

Women researchers such as Elizabeth Kite played a significant role in the identification of feebleminded men and women. By virtue of their social status and their position as field-workers, these women were allowed entrance into the world of feeblemindedness and were able to make tangible contributions to both conceptual and institutional developments. However, the fact that the role of the researcher was occupied by women is not incidental. As with the institutions, the division of labor in this new method of generating knowledge about feeblemindedness ran along gender lines.

Rafter points out that fieldwork offered women an opportunity to participate in the science of eugenics in ways suited to their femininity: "Eugenic field investigation was women's work in several senses. First, it involved intuition and an eye for detail, abilities with which women were thought to be particularly well endowed. . . . Second, women (perhaps because less intimidating) were better able to elicit personal information from strangers. . . . Third, in serving as assistants to men such as Goddard and Davenport, field workers elaborated the traditional division of labor."[95] This "women's work" can be analyzed on a number of levels. First, the definition of this role clearly relied on dominant stereotypes of women as intuitive, personable, and subservient. Second, these women lacked the authority possessed by their male superiors (usually doctors and superintendents). However, these factors also served to empower female researchers. Though their position was defined according to stereotypes of femininity, they were also considered to possess abilities that men lacked: "Because of their supposed emotional and intuitive powers, eugenicists believed that women were more adept than men at quantifying the numbers of the feebleminded. After a few weeks' training, field workers were thought to be able to tell at a glance whether someone had pure or tainted germplasm."[96] Here is a case where gender stereotypes directly influenced *how* feeblemindedness was diagnosed. In a sense, women provided a solution to the problem of etiologic invisibility: they supposedly had the ability to trace lines of "defective stock" and identify the quality of a person's germ plasm.

These women occupied an epistemic position similar to the vigilant mothers who watched closely for signs of feeblemindedness in their children. For both groups, their alleged ability to recognize these signs was attributed to their feminine intuitiveness, whether it was put to use in the nursery or the interview. However, this authority was mediated by the guidance of a male expert. Both fieldwork and motherhood, as forms of "woman's work," were defined in contrast to the more authoritative positions occupied by men.

Though they did not have the socially recognized authority of the male superintendents, female researchers had significant epistemic authority insofar as they were given the task of identifying cases of feeblemindedness and tracing histories. They also had significant practical power with respect to the feebleminded persons they picked out.[97] As Elizabeth Kite's story illustrates, these studies often had a direct effect on which feebleminded persons would be placed in institutions. In this sense, women researchers perpetuated the marginalization of the feebleminded by identifying them and justifying their incarceration. Moreover, it enhanced the organic and biological interpretation of feeblemindedness: "By closely linking moral and mental deficiencies, Kite's data and Goddard's interpretations suggested new biological explanations for a broad range of social problems that afflicted American society in the early twentieth century."[98] Feebleminded women were objects of study, often by fellow women whose feminine qualities and able minds offered these researchers the opportunity to have a direct effect on their feebleminded counterparts.[99]

Female Reformists: Lady Bountiful and the "Dawn of Womanhood"

The final group of women, the reformists, also had a hand in developing and perpetuating the category of feeblemindedness. In this section I will discuss two kinds of reformists: female philanthropists who had a direct effect on the lives of feebleminded women, and feminists who exploited the image of the feebleminded woman to advance their own political reforms.[100] I categorize these two types of women as reformists because they shared three things with respect to the history of intellectual disability. First, unlike field-workers and the (able-minded) women working in the institutions, these women did not work under male supervision; therefore, the power dynamics were different. Second, reformists were responsible (in different ways) for promoting negative portraits of feebleminded *women* specifically. This leads to the third point: while at the level of etiology, *all* women were defined by male authorities as capable of spreading feeblemindedness, the reformists separated *themselves* from feebleminded women. They divided the categories of womanhood and motherhood into "us" and "them." As we shall see, the feebleminded as a class provided a social cause for philanthropists and fodder for the arguments of the newly emergent feminist movement.

To illustrate the complex power dynamics at work in the role of women reformists, I will focus on Josephine Shaw Lowell and Margaret Sanger.[101] These two women are important to the history of intellectual disability for many reasons, chief among them the fact that in their campaigns to build institutions specifically for feebleminded women and to empower women to take control over their reproductive practices, respectively, Lowell and Sanger had both a direct and indirect impact on the lives of feebleminded women. But their professional lives and aspirations also raise broader questions for both the feminist and eugenics movements. The historical and biographical scholarship on their lives points to this fact. In both cases, scholars tend to either downplay their associations with eugenics in an effort to herald them as feminist heroines, or vilify them for embodying the eugenic spirit of the day and profoundly distorting the goals of feminism.[102] But there is an even more intriguing dimension to both women's lives that further complicates a straightforward reading and critique of them in these terms. In adopting a form of cultural imperialism, whereby they set up an us/them dichotomy between themselves and the problem of the feebleminded woman they hoped to address, they distanced themselves from a perceived other with whom they may have shared much more than their womanhood. Alexander Sanger writes that his grandmother "came from one of the classes that Protestant eugenicists looked down upon and discriminated against—Irish Catholics. She was also poor and female. She had married a Jew. She had a criminal record from her days as a labor organizer. She had inherited diseases. No eugenicist would call her 'fit.'"[103] Similarly Rafter explains that "Lowell herself was something of a deviant. Like the feebleminded woman whom she sought to bring under control, Lowell was a single mother."[104] Questions about what allowed these potentially "deviant" women to gain professional power and adopt a place of authority in relation to both their male counterparts and the group of feebleminded women that caught their attention will have to wait for another time. However, these questions loom as large on the historical horizon as they do in considerations of the contemporary roles that women play today in relation to disability, feminism, and the prospect of a new eugenics.[105]

Josephine Shaw Lowell

Josephine Shaw Lowell was born in 1843 to a good family, married Colonel Charles Russell Lowell at the age of twenty, and was widowed in less than a year. After the death of her husband, she began to develop what would be a forty-year career of public service.[106] She practiced a brand of "scientific charity," a movement that was "predicated on the belief that the principles of science could be applied to solve social problems."[107] In 1876 she was the first woman to be appointed as a commissioner to the New York State Board of Charities, and her thirteen-year membership was a fruitful one.[108] She campaigned for the construction of a Reformatory for Women (patterned on the reformatory that opened in Elmira, Massachusetts, in 1887), arguing that women were the cause of many of society's present ills: "One of the most important and most dangerous causes of the increase of crime, pauperism and insanity is unrestrained liberty allowed to vagrant and degraded women. . . . In order to grapple with this gigantic evil and to stop the increase of pauperism, crime and insanity in this community, a reformatory for women, under the management of women . . . is required."[109] She explained her two separate objectives: reforming these women, and if that was impossible, cutting off all hereditary lines that would transmit pauperism, crime, and insanity.[110] She lived to see three state reformatories for women open in Hudson, Albion, and Bedford, New York.[111]

Lowell clearly subscribed to the views of her time concerning the hereditary nature of degeneracy.[112] What sets her apart was her particular concern for women, many of whom were confined in almshouses where they fell prey to "lustful men."[113] Women who were feebleminded (identified by having given birth to an illegitimate child) required special attention. They needed to be "taught to be women," and this was only possible in an environment isolated from the vices and temptations of men.[114] Thus, after she appealed to the State Board of Charities, the Board of Trustees of the Syracuse institution agreed to open an experimental facility in Newark for feebleminded women between the ages of sixteen and forty-five (of childbearing age), and the state legislature gave $18,000 for its construction. The State Custodial Asylum for Feeble-Minded Women at Newark opened as an experimental facility in September 1878. In response to Lowell's call for "the establishment of further and definite provision for the custodial care and sequestration of idiotic and feeble-minded girls and women, for their protection and the protection of the State," the institution became a permanent custodial facility in 1885.[115] By October 1910 the asylum had 792 inmates, classified according to degree of intelligence.[116]

Superintendents believed that the institution was decreasing the number of vagrant feebleminded women on the streets, and thereby containing the spread of feeblemindedness. As J. C. Carson, the president of the Association of Medical Officers, reported at its annual meeting (1889): "There are at the present time over 200 of these feeble minded girls and women provided for in this institution. . . . There is no doubt that the propagation of idiocy, which was formerly carried on through the medium of weak-minded girls among the homes and poorhouses of our State, will henceforth be materially lessened."[117] Lowell employed similar rhetoric to make her case, arguments based on what Rafter has identified as two-sided tactics: "She simultaneously argued that helpless women must be protected against wickedness (her appeal to rectitude) and that society must protect itself against such wicked women (her appeal to rationality.) This double-pronged appeal enabled Lowell's audience to rationalize eugenic institutionalization as an act of kindness, and it led directly to Lowell's conclusion that an asylum was necessary."[118] The influence of Josephine Lowell's campaign was felt beyond the walls of the institution that would have borne her name had she not refused. By the end of the 1880s, institutions in Pennsylvania, Ohio, and Illinois built separate cottages for women of childbearing age.[119] The intensified threat of feebleminded women was clearly reflected in the institutional structure: women were now believed to need separate quarters or their own facilities.

Lowell's accomplishments in singling out the "weaker" members of her sex and campaigning for their segregation are indicative of the authority and practical power some women had in the sphere of social reform. The tributes Lowell received after her death give a sense of the vast influence she had in the philanthropic world.[120] In addition to her work on behalf of feebleminded and vagrant women, she founded the Charity Organization Society, which coordinated the charitable work done by the myriad of smaller organizations and reform efforts. Her success, however, also reveals her role in the oppression of the feebleminded.

Anne Firor Scott writes, "American women were as much a part of the larger culture as men were, and while their outsider status may have made them sensitive to some human needs, they shared the unexamined assumptions of their own time about race, class, ethnicity."[121] To this list we must add mental ability and morality, since Lowell's concern for feebleminded and criminal women certainly echoed the dominant male discourse about feeblemindedness: that it was heritable, dangerous, and in desperate need of containment. Insofar as female philanthropists like Lowell subscribed to the dominant assumptions about the nature and dangers of feeblemindedness, feebleminded women suffered cultural imperialism at the hands of able-minded men and women.

Lowell also contributed to the social marginalization of feebleminded women by constructing institutions to house them. Furthermore, her statement that "women have proven themselves entirely adequate to the control and management of women" reflects the benefit these institutions could have for able-minded women: like fieldwork, they provided women with a new form of labor and authority (not only as attendants and teachers but as superintendents and physicians).[122] This statement also suggests that Lowell divided the general category of woman into two separate groups of women—able-minded and feebleminded. She emphasized that the latter aberrant breed of women, though in need of assistance and care now, must ultimately be eradicated.[123] "For self-protection, the state should care for these human beings who, having been born, must be supported to the end; but every motive of humanity, justice and self-interest should lead to the extinction of the line as soon as possible."[124] Here we see the brand of philanthropy Lowell practiced; her concern for her fellow women (and there is little evidence that she would have thought of them in this way) only extended to the current generation. Underlying Lowell's demand for the construction of institutions for feebleminded and delinquent women was the assumption that their segregation would prevent the propagation of their defective lines. The boundaries demarcating the feebleminded as a social group served to exclude feebleminded women from membership in the group of women to which Lowell belonged. These defective members of her sex were in a class separate from her own.

Margaret Sanger

This division between feebleminded and non-feebleminded women was present in the feminist movement as well. Many feminists around the turn of the century used the rhetoric of eugenics to bolster their causes.[125] However, with respect to able-minded women perpetuating feeblemindedness, their arguments departed from the good/bad mother myth advanced by male experts. Rather than focusing on responsible and vigilant procreation/pregnancy/infant care as a means to avoid a feebleminded child, these female reformists argued that "voluntary motherhood" was essential to preventing feeblemindedness. The call for women to control their sexuality and reproduction (particularly through contraception) relied on arguments concerning the deleterious effects of able-minded women having unwanted children. Many feminists played on the fear of feeblemindedness and "raised traditional eugenic bogies: that unwanted children would be likely to be inferior; that children also had a right not to be born if they would be weak or deprived or defective."[126] In fact, Gordon says that it would be nearly impossible to find discussions of voluntary motherhood between 1890 and 1910 that didn't claim that unwanted children were likely to be morally and/or physically defective.[127]

Margaret Sanger, a leader of the birth control movement in America and founder of Planned Parenthood, is a complex and important figure in this history. Historians and feminists have interpreted her legacy in a variety of ways, and she has been viewed as both a liberator and an oppressor of women.[128] Though her association with eugenics has been debated, her writings attest to her belief in the hereditary nature of feeblemindedness, as well as a strong conviction that feebleminded women should not be allowed to reproduce.[129] In her book *Women and the New Race*, Sanger repeatedly invoked the dangers of feeblemindedness in her call for the emancipation of motherhood. She referred to the number of feebleminded who were not in institutions, "being free to propagate their kind," and claimed that the feebleminded "are notoriously prolific in reproduction."[130] With examples of women pleading for help in avoiding defective children, Sanger claimed that "by all means there should be no children when either mother or father suffers from such diseases as tuberculosis, gonorrhea, epilepsy, insanity, drunkenness and mental disorders."[131]

Sanger, like many eugenicists, saw the problem through the lenses of poverty, race, degeneracy, and immigration: "Anybody in this vast country is at perfect liberty to become a father or a mother! You may be diseased, you may be a mental defective, a moron, a pauper, a habitual criminal; you may be insane, irresponsible, with no knowledge of the laws of health, hygiene, or common decency; yet you may bring not merely one child into these United States. You are encouraged to bring a dozen. . . . it is high time to recognize that if it is not right to import into our country individuals from whom we must later protect ourselves, it is even more imperative to protect ourselves and to protect

American society today and tomorrow from the procreation of such individuals within our gates."[132]

Similar to the underlying justification for institutions as providing a protective function, Sanger's movement toward reproductive freedom and control is grounded in the same discourse of protection. The solution, she believes, lies in the freedom of motherhood: "We must set motherhood free. . . . Motherhood works in wondrous ways. It refuses to bring forth weaklings, refuses to bring forth slaves. . . . It withholds the unfit, brings forth the fit. . . . Instinctively it avoids all those things which multiply racial handicaps."[133] As we can gather from her statements, however, those who are feebleminded or defective in any sense should not be included in the category of motherhood. Thus we find a dichotomy in motherhood as well as in womanhood, between the good, free woman working to improve the race, and the feebleminded, deficient woman for whom motherhood must be avoided. Whereas the male discourse about etiology targeted women *as a group*, here we see able-minded women separating themselves from feebleminded women once again (recall Lowell). When Sanger proclaims that "we must set motherhood free," she is calling on those other women who continue to burden society to relinquish motherhood. In describing Sanger's brand of feminism, Frank says that she "had a eugenically vitiated view of woman's liberation, which did not mean the freedom for every woman to decide, without coercion, the number of children she desired to have; rather, it meant sexual freedom for the 'fit.'"[134] That the emancipation of motherhood and womanhood required the bondage of the feebleminded and the inferior is obvious in the concluding words of her book: "This is the dawn. Womanhood shakes off its bondage. It asserts its right to be free. Like begets like. We gather perfect fruit from perfect trees. The race is but an amplification of its mother body, the multiplication of flesh habitations—beautiful and perfected for souls akin to the mother soul. . . . When the last fetter falls the evils that have resulted from the suppression of woman's will to freedom will pass. Child slavery, prostitution, feeblemindedness, physical deterioration, hunger, oppression and war will disappear from the earth."[135] This utopian vision is predicated on the belief that imperfect trees would not bring forth fruit. Thus defective women could only hope to witness the dawn of womanhood and the emancipation of motherhood—neither of which included them—from behind the bars of the institution.

The power relations with respect to female reformists are complex. The relationship between this group of privileged women and feebleminded women illuminates the multiple layers at which oppression operated. By calling attention to their feebleminded counterparts, women like Lowell and Sanger had a direct hand in the concrete marginalization of feebleminded women. Lowell was responsible for the first custodial facility for feebleminded women, as well as the increasing segregation of institutions according to sex. Sanger too overtly supported segregation, and her promotion of reproductive control was made concrete in the practice of sterilization in the early decades of the twentieth century, a practice that she wholeheartedly supported. Franks points out the disturbingly close association between American eugenics and the Nazis' infamous 1933 sterilization law when she quotes Sanger's 1932 recommendation for "a stern and rigid policy of sterilization and segregation to that grade of population whose progeny is already tainted, or whose inheritance is such that objectionable traits may be transmitted to offspring . . . [and] to give certain dysgenic groups in our population their choice of segregation or sterilization."[136]

Reformists like Margaret Sanger directly and indirectly affected the lives of feebleminded women: they exploited this group for the advancement of their political agendas and for the benefit of able-minded women. They were responsible for concrete practices that both marginalized and did outright violence to these women, and they perpetuated a form of cultural imperialism in marking out this group as other and setting feebleminded women apart from themselves with respect to both womanhood and motherhood.[137]

Conclusion

There are many ways to interpret the relationship between gender and intellectual disability. Beyond simply pointing to how the definitions and corresponding practices associated with this category were impacted by gender, however, we see that an analysis of the gendered dimensions of this history reveals a kaleidoscope of issues much more colorful than the simple relationship between an object of knowledge and its knowers.

What we see is that the history and nature of this classification cannot be abstracted from the complex matrix of power relations out of which it emerged. In defending the importance of gender as an analytical concept (against the postmodern call to dismantle the notion entirely), Iris Marion Young explains the multiplicity of power relations that a *gendered* analysis of social structures can uncover:

> When describing social structures as gendered it is neither necessary to make generalizations about men and women nor is it necessary to reduce varying gen-

der structures to a common principle. . . . Structures of a gendered hierarchy of power differentiate men from one another according to social roles and dispositions, and do not simply differentiate men and women. The most important thing about the analysis is to understand how the rules, relations and their material consequences produce privileges for some people that underlie an interest in their maintenance, at the same time that they limit options of others, cause relative deprivations in their lives, or render them vulnerable to domination and exploitation.[138]

The analysis of the various roles women played in terms of Young's faces of oppression has revealed that social group membership can have profound consequences. As (white) women, both feebleminded and able-minded mothers were viewed as responsible for causing feeblemindedness; the roles assigned to women in the institutions relied on dominant stereotypes about femininity; and women were assigned to fieldwork because it was perceived as best suited to their feminine nature. However, the oppression of feebleminded women was different by virtue of their membership in both social groups, and they suffered distinct forms of marginalization, cultural imperialism, powerlessness, and exploitation. The force of Elizabeth Spelman's question in her book *Inessential Woman* is felt with particular poignancy and urgency when we consider these complex power relations: "Does the existence of those who can be defined as complete persons demand the existence of others who cannot be granted personhood?"[139] Spelman's question may be rephrased as, Does the existence of those who can be defined as complete women and mothers demand the existence of others who cannot be granted womanhood and motherhood?

3

Analytic Interlude

The foregoing window into the history of intellectual disability is by no means exhaustive but reveals certain tensions and dynamics that are important to consider when turning our attention to contemporary questions regarding intellectual disability. Though the emerging discourse of social construction in the past few decades has been conceptually, legally, and politically significant in changing the ways that disability is understood (primarily thanks to the disability rights movement and the work of disability theorists), there may be reasons to resist a facile application of the phrase "socially constructed" to intellectual disability in light of this tremendously rich and nuanced story that tells the evolution of mental retardation as a classification. Eva Kittay writes about her daughter, "The cognitive impairments of the severely and profoundly retarded are not merely contingently disabling. Unlike many disabilities, [Sesha's] are not simply social constructions. Someone such as my daughter could not survive, much less thrive, without constant vigilant attention. . . . We might say, however, that in the case of developmental disabilities, especially severe ones, though the disability itself is not socially constructed, the view that mental retardation is a 'problem' rather than a possible outcome of human physiology *is*."[1] What follows is a conceptual framework for theorizing intellectual disability. I offer a series of analytic tools intended to recast and amplify the discourse of social constructionism and shed light on precisely *how* and *why* intellectual disability is constructed as a problem.

The Status of Intellectual Disability:
Beyond Social Constructionism?

One of the problems highlighted in Ian Hacking's book *The Social Construction of What?* is the supposed tension or dichotomy that emerges in discussions about social construction: there seems to be a false binary drawn between the "real" and the "socially constructed."[2] If we consider this in the context of intellectual disability, the problem becomes immediately clear. At one level, the answer to a question like, Is mental retardation real? is obvious.[3] There are real people who have been labeled as "mentally retarded" and have been directly affected by that label. There are individuals who have various intellectual limitations, some a result of endogenous biological or genetic causes, others caused by external factors (e.g., poverty, deprivation, prenatal or postnatal trauma), and some for which there is no identifiable cause. There are persons who face social barriers, institutionalization, and violence because of their limitations, and/or because they are labeled "mentally retarded." I do not wish to dispute any of these claims. However, is mental retardation a "natural kind"? Does mental retardation pick out some real deficit or feature of human existence independent of the social, historical, and political context? Must one choose between pure constructs and real entities? And what is the difference between saying "*mental retardation* is socially constructed," "mental retardation *as a problem* is socially constructed," and "*mentally retarded individuals* are socially constructed"? We have entered into murky waters here and need some conceptual clarity.

First, the phrase "social construction" has various meanings when used in the context of disability.[4] "Construct" is a verb referring to a process, and "construction" is a noun—the product, or construct.[5] Some theorists are concerned with the process by which disability has been shaped. Michael Oliver, in *The Politics of Disablement,* undertakes the project of showing that "disability as a category can only be understood within a framework which suggests that it is culturally produced and socially structured."[6] His book explores the ways in which the social restrictions and oppressive practices of a capitalistic society produce disability. Susan Wendell also talks about the *process* by which disability is created: "I call the interaction of the biological and the social to create (or prevent) disability 'the social construction of disability.'"[7] She goes on to point out numerous social and cultural factors that construct disability: resource distributions, medical care and practices, the pace of life, expectations of performance, notions of a paradigm citizen, lack of realistic cultural representations of disabled individuals, stereotyping.[8] Though much of the literature on disability is restricted to physical disabilities, some have suggested that mental retardation is the result of a process of social construction. James Trent's book is titled *Inventing the Feeble Mind,* suggesting a process by which the feeble mind was produced. Throughout his history of mental retardation, Trent refers to the "cognitive and social construction" of mental retardation. For instance, he discusses the construction of sterilization, names one section of a chapter "Constructing Retarded Children," and defines nineteenth-century idiocy as a social and cognitive construct.

As early as the 1970s, theorists were talking about the social dimensions of labeling people as "mentally retarded." Jane Mercer, in *Labeling the Mentally Retarded,* distinguishes between the clinical and social systems approaches to mental retardation. The former falls under the medical/statistical model that views mental retardation as an individual pathological characteristic that transcends sociocultural groups, while the latter (her position) argues that mental retardation is "an achieved status in a social system and the role played by the person holding that status."[9] Again, we are told of a process by which disability (in this case mental retardation) is constructed. More recently, theorists from numerous disciplines have put forth theories regarding the processes through which intellectual disabilities are produced.[10]

Closely related to the notion of social construction as a process is the view that the social construction of disability involves a kind of interpretation. Harlan Lane, in "The Social Construction of Deafness," refers to two "constructions of deafness" that are dominant and compete for shaping deaf people's destinies: deafness as a category of disability, and deaf as designating a member of a linguistic minority.[11] In this article, "social construction" seems to refer to competing interpretations of deafness, not to any object or process. I think this is the way in which Adrienne Asch and Michelle Fine, in their article "Shared Dreams," use the term "social construction" to claim that experiences are socially constructed: "In the past twenty years both the study and politics of disability have undergone transformation. Activists and scholars have insisted that the *disability* (the *biological* condition) be conceptually disentangled from the *handicap* (the *social* ramifications) of the condition. . . . Scholars and activists within feminism and disability rights have demonstrated that the experiences of being female or of having a disability are socially constructed; that the biological cannot be understood outside of those contexts and relationships that shape and give meaning to femaleness and to disability."[12] This seems to suggest an interpretive step: a biological condition is given meaning by an ableist society, and the experience of it becomes disabling based on this interpretation. In a similar vein, Ron Amundson explores the ways in which disability is constructed based on the reification of "normal" and "abnormal function." The assumption that these categories are real, objective categories found in nature leads to the definition of certain impairments as objectively "abnormal" states.[13] Thus social construction with regard to disability can refer to the *process* of construction and the *interpretation* of a particular condition.

The term "social construction" also refers to the construct itself. Disability *as a category* can be considered a social construct,[14] as can disabled individuals and their bodies: "The disabled individual is an ideological construction related to the core ideology of individualism."[15] Wendell describes the construction of the disabled body by the medical authorities; Trent describes the invention of the feeble mind; Mark Rapley argues that the very concept of intellectual disability is a social construct. All of these point to the end product, an object or construct. (Notice that this construct can be an entity, like the feeble mind or the disabled body, or a concept—the construction of the concept of disability.)

Focusing on the product of the construction—the actual object that is constructed—Hacking makes a series of distinctions that are helpful in teasing out the multiple meanings of the phrase "social construction" in the context of mental retardation.[16] He identifies three broad categories of things that can be socially constructed: objects (things in the world), ideas (conceptions, concepts, beliefs, attitudes, theories), and elevator words (higher-level concepts like truth, reality, and knowledge). Considered in the context of mental retardation, a number of possible candidates emerge: *mentally retarded persons* themselves are social constructs (e.g., the feebleminded woman, the moron); *categories* like mental retardation or autism; *concepts* like IQ, intelligence, normalcy, or personhood; and *theories* (e.g., the belief in the superiority of the "mentally accelerated"[17] or the position that to be a person one must be rational). For the purposes of this brief glimpse into the world of social construction, let us take the broad *category* of "mental retardation" and consider it in relation to the claims that, according to Hacking, characterize the social constructionist position: "Social constructionist work is critical of the status quo. Social constructionists about X tend to hold that: (1) X need not have existed, or need not be at all as it is. X or X as it is at present, is not determined by the nature of things; it is not inevitable."[18] This claim captures the position of many advocates and theorists: the concept of mental retardation as it exists today need not have developed as it is, and is not inevitable. While one could say that persons with cognitive limitations have existed throughout history, the definition of mental retardation need not have developed in the way that it has.[19]

Hacking explains that some social constructionists go further and make one or both of the following claims: (2) X is quite bad as it is; and (3) We would be much better off if X were done away with, or at least radically transformed.[20] So what does it mean to say mental retardation as a category is quite bad? Many have argued that the definition of mental retardation (or intellectual disability more broadly) is highly objectionable for a variety of reasons, based both on the problematic nature of the category itself and on the deleterious effects of being thus classified. For example, Dan Goodley and Rapley argue that "the current modernist notion of intellectual disability as a given form of being in the world is unsustainable."[21] Others have challenged the notion of impairment as something that is fixed. Drawing parallels between the process by which both impairment and sex are naturalized and thus become viewed as ontologically given, Shelley Tremain argues that neither "sex" nor "impairment" should be viewed as prediscursively given; rather, both are performative and posited as "natural" by virtue of the systems of power that come to represent them as such. Thus, she argues, "inasmuch as the 'impairments' alleged to underlie disability are actually constituted in order to sustain, and even augment, current social arrangements, they must no longer be theorized as essential, biological characteristics of a 'real' body upon which recognizably disabling conditions are imposed."[22] If this is the case, then, the central distinction underlying the social model collapses, and the task for disability theorists is to reconsider the ways in which "impairment" itself is constructed through social, political, and conceptual practices. This would support the sentiment that the label "mental retardation" should be done away with altogether.

Yet this is a complex issue in the context of advocacy, rights, and legal protection. It is possible (and may be desirable) to level a critique of existing ideas or assumptions about intellectual disability, while at the same time maintaining that the category itself should not be completely discarded. For example, Eva Feder Kittay argues for a reconceptualization of the dependence associated with intellectual disability, but at the same time recognizes the need (politically, economically, and socially) for the category to exist in order for persons with severe intellectual disabilities to receive the care and support they require: "While dependence is often socially constructed—*all* dependence is not ... Neither 'labeling' nor environmental impediments create [Sesha's] dependence—although environment modifications are *crucial* for her to have a decent life."[23]

In *Ethical and Philosophical Problems of Mental Handicap,* Peter Byrne is explicitly critical of what he sees as a postmodern turn that views intellectual disability as pure social construction and expresses concern about its political implications: "If we abandon the label and the caring institutions which properly go with it, we will have cut off a significant minority of human beings from aid and help which they need."[24] These claims highlight one feature of mental retardation that makes generalizations about it difficult: it is internally heterogeneous (within the category there are multiple subcategories). In this case, the distinction between mild and severe mental retardation might make all the difference in arguing whether or not to dispense with the category, even if one recognizes its historically contingent nature. For example, self-advocacy movements like People First are challenging the veracity of their own status as mentally retarded, claiming that they were wrongly institutionalized and rejecting mental retardation as a viable, appropriate label. This echoes earlier historical examples whereby individuals became disabled by virtue of their lives in institutions, and where certain social mores and fears were intimately intertwined with definitions of feeblemindedness. However, it is not clear that this position adequately captures the concerns of Kittay and Byrne with respect to profoundly disabled individuals and the multiple forms of support that depend on a certain classification.

Amid the differences in interpretation and the various objects of social construction, however, Hacking explains that all proclaimed social constructionists share the following precondition: "In the present state of affairs, x is taken for granted; x appears to be inevitable."[25] It is against the perceived inevitability of mental retardation, not as a condition but *as a classification,* that many historians of mental retardation, disability theorists, and philosophers like me are arguing. Yet as we shall see in part 2, it is precisely this notion of contingency that has been traditionally left out of philosophical discussions of intellectual disability; rather, this category has been taken for granted as an inevitable and self-evident natural kind. That said, I do not necessarily think that the language of social construction is precise or capacious enough to be satisfying. I share Hacking's ambivalence about tidy resolutions: "Not only am I ambivalent, or worse, about social construction; I am also ambivalent about the use of rigid designation in connection with disease and disorder."[26] Thus, in a joint effort to recast social constructionist discourse and to challenge a certain kind of philosophizing about intellectual disability, I propose that intellectual disability can be analyzed in terms of the following concepts: heterogeneity, instability, prototype effects, and power relations. This framework emerges from the preceding historical analyses and will be useful in critically examining contemporary philosophical faces of intellectual disability. Ultimately, I think the case of mental retardation shows that when the false dichotomy between "natural kind" and "socially constructed kind" is rejected, a new array of philosophical questions emerge.[27]

A New Conceptual Framework

Heterogeneity

Mental retardation is a heterogeneous classification, both internally and externally. Internally, it is divided into subgroups, meaning that there is not just *one kind* of mental retardation. These subdivisions take two forms: they are ordered hierarchically (I imagine this as a vertical ordering) and horizontally—with discrete kinds existing side by side. There are a number of examples of vertical hierarchies: subcategories of mental retardation have been defined according to severity, degree of intelligence, and the ability to perform certain functions (e.g., educable, trainable). All of these descriptions organize forms of mental retardation on an ascending scale, where each type possesses less or more of a particular feature.

The subgroups of mental retardation have also been ordered horizontally as qualitatively different kinds. For example, the "moral imbecile" and the "idiot" were two varieties of feeblemindedness, one with a moral defect, the other suffering from an intellectual defect.[28] Forms of mental retardation were also grouped etiologically (e.g., congenital or non-congenital, endogenous or exogenous). Finally, the feebleminded were often classified according to anatomical or physiological phenomena (e.g., Down's Mongolian idiocy or epileptic idiocy).

Both horizontal and vertical subclassifications of mental retardation were operant in the historical period we have examined, and they signify an *internal* heterogeneity because they were not mutually exclusive ways of describing and defining. Rather, they coexisted within the broader category as two possible ways of organizing the variety of kinds and degrees of what was then called idiocy or feeblemindedness.

This classification is also externally heterogeneous: mental retardation has been defined in different ways by many different individuals and is an object of knowledge for multiple disciplines.[29] One of the most persistent features of this classification is the lack of consensus about the nature of mental retardation and the continual criticism of existing definitions. Seguin acknowledged this variety but saw no need to address other definitions in his own work: "Its definitions have been so numerous, they are so different from one another, and they have so little bearing on the treatment, that their omission cannot be much felt in a practical treatise."[30] In an article in the *American Journal of Education*, Dr. Brockett, a well-known writer who supported the new schools for idiots, wrote, "Of the many definitions which writers on the subject have essayed, no one appears entirely free from objection."[31] Even sixty years later, Alfred Binet and Theodore Simon addressed the lack of a proper method of classification in *The Development of Intelligence in Children*. Of the three kinds of error in diagnosing inferior intellectual states—ignorance, variable meaning of terms, and method—they conclude that the last is the most damaging: "In looking closely one can see that the confusion comes principally from a fault in the method of examination. When an alienist finds himself in the presence of a child of inferior intelligence, he . . . contents himself with taking a subjective impression, an impression as a whole, of his subject, and of making his diagnosis by instinct."[32] It is ironic that Binet's solution to the assessment of intellectual inferiority, in its mutated American form, has generated more criticism than perhaps any other classificatory system of mental deficiency.[33] Nevertheless, the IQ score is still a part of the definition of mental retardation, and the category remains a contested one.[34]

Amid competing definitions and methods of diagnosis, some superintendents recognized the limitations of their own classifications and admitted that the categories they created were not absolute. The history of mental retardation might have evolved differently if more had followed Howe's advice in his acknowledgment of fallibility: "It must not be supposed that all idiotic persons can readily be ranged in one or other of these classes. The highest of the lower class of Idiots can hardly be distinguished from the Fool; the least stupid of Fools can hardly be distinguished from the Simpleton; and the highest among the Simpletons stand very near the level of hundreds who pass in society for feebleminded persons, but still for responsible free agents. . . . This view of the gradation of intellect should teach us not only humility, but humanity."[35] From the earliest attention given to "idiocy" in the mid-nineteenth century to Binet's attempt to provide a solid, scientific basis on which to detect feeblemindedness, there was never a conclusive definition of mental retardation. It is externally heterogeneous insofar as there have always been (and continue to be) numerous competing approaches and descriptions. The early institutions served as an organizing principle for these various types of knowledge, and the multiple roles the institution played—moral, therapeutic, pedagogical, medical—are evidence of this. Throughout its history, mental retardation as an object of knowledge has never had a permanent residence in any one field. It was and continues to be an object of medical, psychological, pedagogical, moral, humanitarian, and political discourse.[36]

Instability

A second feature of this classification is closely related to its heterogeneity: mental retardation is what I call an *unstable* classification. The preceding history indicates that the criteria for defining this condition have been continually in flux, and that the etiology and treatment for it have depended as much on social trends, stereotypes, and discriminatory practices and assumptions as they have on hard science. So what are we to make of this? Is it enough to simply say that the category is highly unstable, or that this evidence points to the fact that it is socially constructed? I think the concepts of stability and instability are valuable but require some elaboration.

The term "instability" has a number of meanings in relation to disability generally. In one sense, disability as a category can be viewed as unstable in that its boundaries are permeable: anyone can become disabled at any point in time.[37] Thus disability is not like eye color, an inherited trait.[38] Rather, it is a category whose membership continues to change over time, not only by virtue of the set of individuals who qualify as "disabled" at a particular time, but also because of the changing nature of definitions, therapeutics, and institutional practices that shape what constitutes a disability. At the level of the individual (given the social model's definition of disability as the interaction between the individual and his or her environment), a disability need not remain static. In other words, aside from the possibility of curing or treating the underlying impairment that causes the disability, it is possible that a radical change in the external environment could lead to an individual's no longer being "disabled" by the impairment.[39]

There is another sense of instability that resonates with certain postmodern critiques of the social model of disability. Drawing on postmodern theories of the fundamental instability of the body and identity, some theorists argue that a definition of disability must expose the dynamic and constructed nature of impaired bodies and minds in order to adequately capture the way in which disabilities and disabled identities are created. As mentioned earlier, Tremain argues that the impairment/disability binary posited by social modelists (who take impairment to be a "real" feature of bodies and see disability as a result of social forces and norms) is as problematic as the sex/gender binary, which assumes that "sex" is the natural underlying substance on which or from which gender is created. Given the difficulties in identifying underlying pathologies in many cases of mental retardation, this concern is particularly relevant to theorizing intellectual disabilities.[40]

Beyond the concept of impairment, the category of disability more generally has been viewed by some as an unstable category that mirrors the instability of identity: "I want to make clear that disability is itself an unstable category. . . . What we are discussing is the instability of the category of disability as a subset of the instability of identity in a postmodern era. . . . Rather than ignore the unstable nature of disability, rather than try to fix it, we should amplify that quality. . . . it can create a dismodernist approach to disability as a neoidentity."[41] But what would it mean to amplify the instability of identity in the context of intellectual disability? Is this a potentially liberatory stance, or might there be reasons (political, conceptual, ethical) that this model does not capture the nature or experience of identity for persons with intellectual disabilities?

Thus a tension emerges regarding the status of "mental retardation" or "intellectual disability" as a category: on the one hand, philosophers and parents of persons with severe disabilities contend that to speak of the profoundly disabled as socially constructed fails to capture the realities of their conditions; on the other hand, there is a push to reject the very notion of impairment as something that can be abstracted from social processes, power relations, and the construction of other concepts (e.g., incompetence, intelligence).[42] In many ways this debate is nothing new. These tensions are contemporary incarnations of the conceptual pairs that have defined the history of mental retardation from its inception: organic versus non-organic, static and dynamic. Though it would be inaccurate to suggest that these pairs map directly onto these newer conceptions of disability, it is interesting to recognize certain broader patterns that prefigure the specifics of these newer models. History teaches us that there is unlikely to be a quick or tidy resolution. Nor should we, perhaps, hope for one, as the category of mental retardation may be too complex to demand or expect one.

I think that Hacking's notion of interactive kinds is particularly helpful in navigating these positions and explaining the precise *ways* in which mental retardation continues to be such an unstable category. Hacking makes a distinction that recasts this question in terms of what he calls "interactive" and "indifferent" kinds. An indifferent kind is something that remains unaffected by our definition of it as such, for example, rocks, bacteria, and viruses.[43] To claim that these are indifferent does not suggest that they do not interact or are unchanged by their environments; however, they are not aware of or challenged by what he calls "classificatory looping," the idea that classified individuals are affected by and affect their classification.[44] Unlike many of the kinds that are the objects of the hard sciences, *human* kinds like schizophrenia, childhood autism, and hyperactivity are interactive kinds. They are applied to self-conscious individuals who are aware of these labels and may act and react in such a way that in turn affects the nature of the classification itself; and they are affected by the discursive practices and institutions in which these labels are defined and maintained.

One question that immediately arises regarding this concept in relation to intellectual disability is whether someone who is severely disabled (and may be unaware of the label, and may lack a certain level of self-consciousness) qualifies as an interactive kind. Hacking speaks to this: "by interaction I do not mean only the self-conscious reaction of a single individual to how she is classified. I mean the consequences of being so classified for the whole class of individuals and other people with whom they are intimately connected."[45] Take the example of hyperactive children: "The classification *hyperactive* did not interact with the children simply because the individual children heard the word and changed accordingly. It interacted with those who were so described in institutions and practices that were predicated upon classifying children as hyperactive."[46] Given this example, it is certainly possible to speak about mental retardation (or intellectual disability, more broadly) as an interactive kind that affects even those members who are least able to be *consciously* affected by their membership in this group.

Yet if we define mental retardation as an interactive kind, then we must contend with the question of its relationship to indifferent kinds, and this takes us back to the organic/non-organic distinction. Aren't certain categories like autism and mental retardation both interactive *and* indifferent kinds insofar as there is some underlying pathology (he calls this P) that itself is an indifferent kind? He writes, "Pathology P is itself not conscious or aware, so how can 'autism' be both an interactive kind and an indifferent kind?"[47] He resolves this dilemma by distinguishing between the underlying biological or neurological pathology and the concept, idea, or individual that is classified (in our case, mental retardation or the mentally retarded child).

If we think about the tension between the social construction of mental retardation *as an impairment* and the social construction of mental retardation *as a problem,* we see that it has been a contested classification as both an indifferent kind and an interactive kind since its inception. Certainly the shifting criteria that emerge historically (based on various diagnostic techniques, and the permeability of this category with respect to moral, ethnic, and class-based concerns) suggest that the definition of this condition has been highly unstable. And still today, the nature of pathology P is not clear in all cases. We have organic definitions of mental retardation based on identifiable genetic defects (e.g., fragile X syndrome, Down syndrome), yet we also define it according to the ability to function in a particular setting and admit that in a substantial percentage of the cases, there is no known etiology, no identifiable pathology P: "More than one possible cause is suggested in as many as 50% of cases. The causes may include genetic factors, prenatal influence, and environmental factors following birth. For 75% of children with mild symptoms and 30–40% of those with severe symptoms, no specific cause is apparent. Psychosocial issues have also been implicated in the development of mental retardation."[48] This highlights not only the internal heterogeneity of mental retardation as a category but points to its profound instability, insofar as the underlying impairment or pathology (i.e., the indifferent kind) remains unknown for so many cases.

In light of this, then, there are three levels at which we can say that mental retardation is an unstable classification. As an *indifferent* kind, the underlying pathology or impairment is by no means resolved or clear in all cases. Because it is internally heterogeneous (e.g., made up of so many subcategories), then, we cannot say that any single impairment associated with mental retardation is obvious. As a category of persons, as an interactive kind, we see many examples in the past of how classificatory looping has shaped and reshaped the boundaries and contours of this category. And finally, the debate itself points to the instability of this category at the professional level. As long as it continues to be defined in multiple settings by multiple "experts" with very different heuristic schemes in which to make sense of this category, I think it is valuable to discuss intellectual disability, and perhaps disabilities more generally, in terms of *degrees* of stability.

Prototype Effects

The third feature of mental retardation arises from its instability: its ability to generate *prototype effects*. George Lakoff discusses this notion, first introduced by Eleanor Rosch, in his book *Women, Fire, and Other Dangerous Things*. He proposes an alternative to the classical theory of categorization. In classical theory, no member of a category has special status, the properties defining the category are shared by all of its members, and "all conceptual categories must be symbols that can designate categories in the real world."[49] Lakoff argues, instead, that the way we formulate categories depends on features of our human cognition and experience, and that our categories are often asymmetrical. This last quality can be explained in terms of prototype effects. In a number of experiments, Rosch found that subjects judged certain members more representative of a category than others. For example, a robin was more representative of the category BIRD than a duck; desk chair more representative of CHAIR than rocking chair.[50] Contrary to the classical view of categories, there are often "asymmetries among category members and asymmetric structures within categories."[51] She also found asymmetry in generalization, where "new information about a representative category member is more likely to be generalized to non-representative members than the reverse."[52] Clearly certain kinds of asymmetries have developed in the case of mental retardation.

Insofar as it is a heterogeneous and unstable category, mental retardation has been open to multiple interpretations and definitions. Discourse about mental retardation took place at the level of etiology, description, and treatment, and because of the complex relationship between them, no one explanatory level achieved permanent dominance. At certain moments, however, the focus on one level has allowed a particular portrait of mental retardation to dominate. For instance, during the eugenics movement, there was a great emphasis on etiology. The hereditarian explanation of feeblemindedness became the dominant one, and the prototypical feebleminded individual came from a long line of defectives and threatened to perpetuate his or her bad stock. (Two prominent examples that we have seen are the feebleminded woman and the moron.) However, in the early days of the institution, the idea of cure and treatment gained prominence. The belief in the curability and improvability of idiocy overshadowed most talk of cause, and it was less important to give a precise definition of idiocy than it was to place as many idiots as possible in schools and begin their education and amelioration. The emphasis placed on each particular level— etiology, definition, and treatment—at certain times, then, fueled the creation of certain prototype effects.

Another source of asymmetry can be found in the tensions between the organic/non-organic, qualitative/quantitative, static/dynamic, and visible/invisible. These conceptual pairs have always been present in the classification of mental retardation; however, certain sides of these oppositions have been stressed, resulting in the perception of one type of mental retardation as the best representative of the category. Perhaps the clearest prototype was the moron, who symbolized feeblemindedness in the early decades of the twentieth century. In this case, we find a quantitative, organic (intelligence was considered an innate quality), static, invisible case of mental retardation. The combination of these characterizations resulted in the representation of feeblemindedness as, above all, high-grade, hereditary, and dangerous.

We also find the phenomenon of asymmetry in generalization, where information about a particular prototypical member gets generalized to the whole group. In the mid-nineteenth century, the evidence that some idiots were improvable and perhaps curable was transferred onto the whole population. Mild and severe cases alike were placed in the new schools so that they could benefit. Similarly, once the moron was viewed as the prototypical example of feeblemindedness, his or her incurability was attributed to the entire population. For example, one prominent superintendent, Walter Fernald, "emphasized the irreversible aspects, insisting that 'all degrees of congenital mental defect' resulted from 'permanent brain abnormalities'. This meant that a mentally handicapped person lived with an irremediable condition and Fernald argued that little could be done to improve it [emphasis mine]."[53]

The actual terminology attests to this shift in prototypes. Initially, "idiot" was the generic term for all forms of mental retardation, though it was also the lowest of three subgroups: idiot, imbecile, and feebleminded. As the high-grades became prototypical, the general term changed to "feebleminded" which, like "idiot," was both a generic term as well as a subgroup (in this case, the highest).[54] The fact that the officers of the association decided, in 1891, to designate all state institutions as "Institution for Feebleminded Children" (whereas they had previously used the term "idiot") is also indicative of this shift in prototypes.[55] These two prototype effects help explain why historians have discussed this history in terms of the shift from optimism (in the mid-nineteenth century, when the educable idiot was prototypical) to pessimism (the early twentieth century, when the incurable moron symbolized feeblemindedness).

There is ample evidence (much more than there is room for here) that mental retardation, as a classification, is still prone to prototype effects (including in philosophical discourse, as we shall see). Yet prototype effects are just that—effects. They are not indicative of fundamental changes to the category as a whole; hence, we find the copresence of both sides of the conceptual pairs, and mental retardation continues to be discussed at the levels of etiology, description, and treatment. No one picture has ever entirely eclipsed the others.

Power Relations

As we saw in the previous chapters, there are complex power relations evident in the history of mental retardation. The most obvious relationship emerges between the *non-disabled* and the intellectually disabled, yet the exploration of mental retardation as a gendered category highlights complex power dynamics that emerge in more specific locations. We find these between object of knowledge and expert, between classified individuals and those in positions of power (parents, advocates, institutional figures, physicians, psychiatrists), between groups of the intellectually disabled themselves, between the experts and reformists vying for authority and professional legitimacy, and between disabled and non-disabled *within* the broad category of "woman." The second half of this book will highlight certain reincarnations of these dynamics in contemporary scholarly discourse about disability. But before leaving the historical world behind, I will further explicate the nature of these power relations with some theoretical help from Foucault.

Foucault defines power in terms of action: the exercise of power "is a way in which certain actions may structure the field of other possible actions."[56] He then identifies five points that must be established in an analysis of power. First, power involves *system of differentiations,* differences in status, privilege, economics, culture, competence, which are put into operation by a particular power relationship.[57] The foregoing historical analysis of mental retardation reveals the numerous ways in which persons with intellectual disabilities were differentiated from other individuals (e.g., the distinction between madmen and idiots; feebleminded and able-minded women; animals and the mentally retarded). Moreover, within the category itself it is evident that the intellectually disabled have also been differentiated from each other, and that the subdivisions within this category were drawn according to various criteria (e.g., hierarchically divided by severity; moral and immoral kinds).

Second, power can be analyzed in terms of the "*types of objectives* pursued by those who act upon the actions of others."[58] We have seen the various objectives of the authorities within institutional structures, and the underlying objectives of non-disabled women with respect to their feebleminded counterparts. Though Foucault acknowledges that personal objectives can play a role in the functioning of power, his notion of objectives goes beyond the problem of motive. He does not wish to reduce power to the intentions of those in power. The complex and insidious ways in which the institutions and broader social forces defined and determined the evolution of mental retardation as a category reflect Foucault's claim that power is both intentional and non-subjective.[59] The third point of analysis is "the means of bringing power relations into being." This might be called the *how* of power: what is involved in exercising power (e.g., systems of surveillance, according to certain rules, etc).[60] By closely examining the various forms of oppression at work both within and beyond the walls of the institution, we see how various forms of power relations were brought into being and perpetuated. Foucault also argues that the *forms of institutionalization* that allow power to function must be analyzed.[61] Much of this historical analysis was devoted to examining the predominant site of power from the mid-nineteenth century to the early decades of the twentieth century: the institutions for the feebleminded.[62] During this period, institutional buildings took various forms. They were transformed from educational structures to custodial facilities, and then to medical asylums and hospitals, and their internal structure often reflected the dominant classificatory structure at the time (e.g., as the feebleminded woman became a separate type, institutions became increasingly segregated by sex).

The final point of analysis is to examine *degrees of rationalization*. Power relations depend on "the effectiveness of the instruments and the certainty of results."[63] By rationalization, Foucault means the ways in which power relations are transformed and adjusted to the exigencies of particular situations. The use of unpaid inmate labor under the guise of education and training, which ultimately served the economic needs of the institution, is one example of this dimension of power. Another can be seen in what Foucault calls the tautological nature of the institution: "I think we should talk of an asylum tautology, in the sense that, through the asylum apparatus itself, the doctor is given a number of instruments whose basic function is to impose reality, to intensify it, and add to it the supplement of power that will enable the doctor to get a grip on madness and reduce it, and therefore, to direct and govern it."[64]

This is directly connected to the superintendents' authority, and the fact that the institution was a means by which they legitimized themselves. Foucault's observation regarding the French asylum applies equally to American institutions for the feebleminded. "Medical authority functions . . . as power well before it functions as knowledge."[65] Though the institutions clearly functioned as a way of producing knowledge about this new object of study, Foucault points to a gap between the medical knowledge that was actually utilized and the physician's day-to-day role in the asylum. This "discrepancy between medical theory and asylum practice" is evidence of the disciplinary nature of the institution. Though the institution produced theoretical knowledge regarding nosology and etiology, the treatment for idiots and madmen can also be read as a form of disciplining bodies.[66] The rationalization for the institution's existence and the role of the medical expert (the superintendent in the case of American schools for the feebleminded) ensured both the effectiveness of the instrument and the possibility of obtaining results.[67]

What is fascinating about mental retardation as a classification is its persistence. Perhaps it is precisely *because of,* not in spite of, its heterogeneity, instability, ability to generate prototype effects, and its place within various constellations of power that it survived for so long. As long as there are experts in different disciplines to define them, institutions to house them, schools to teach them, scientists to study them, psychologists to test them, educators to classify them, people to judge them, and theorists to debate the validity of the label itself, persons with intellectual disabilities will continue to be objects of knowledge. It is to the philosophical expert that we now turn.

Part Two

The Philosophical World of Intellectual Disability

4

The Face of Authority

> Feminist and other liberatory epistemologies . . . cannot only
> be correctives to standard epistemologies, but must also at
> times separate or withdraw from dominant ways of making
> sense of the world. If current standards of epistemic credibility
> are embedded in systems of oppression, then epistemic respon-
> sibility requires that we remove ourselves from those practices.
>
> —NANCY TUANA

> Genealogy is, then, a sort of attempt to desubjugate histori-
> cal knowledges, to set them free, or in other words, to enable
> them to oppose and struggle against the coersion of a unitary,
> formal, and scientific theoretical discourse. The project of
> these disorderly and tattered genealogies is to reactivate lo-
> cal knowledges . . . against the scientific hierarchalization of
> knowledge and its intrinsic power-effects. To put it in a nut-
> shell: Archaeology is the method specific to the analysis of
> local discursivities, and genealogy is the tactic which, once it
> has described these local discursivities, brings into play the
> desubjugated knowledges that have been released from them.
>
> —MICHEL FOUCAULT

Institutions for the feebleminded and the rise of mental testing demarcated two
fields in which knowledge claims about intellectual disability could be made.
Physicians, psychologists, and legislators had a profound impact on how intellectual disability was defined and managed, and both the external and internal

heterogeneity of this category speaks to the difficulty of isolating a single object of knowledge amid competing and changing conceptions. The glimpse at the complicated story of disabled and non-disabled women reveals that in addition to the physicians, psychiatrists, and psychologists involved in defining, detecting, and diagnosing idiocy and feeblemindedness, there were other experts who gained prominence and wielded a significant amount of power and authority: women field-workers, feminist activists, and reformists. Thus we can affirm that idiocy and feeblemindedness were interactive kinds in Hacking's sense of the term: they were classifications that were part of interesting looping effects, with permeable and amorphous boundaries that shifted with the professional, social, and political tides of the day. If we map this constellation of experts from the mid-nineteenth century (when idiocy emerged as a distinct object of knowledge) to the present day, even more groups emerge from their respective disciplinary corners to lay claim to knowledge about this group. And as Foucault and Hacking both remind us—the former with his notion of resistance and the latter in his idea of classified subjects transforming the very meaning of categories—there can be significant power coming "from below."[1] Though I haven't focused on this dimension of the institutional world, there is evidence of significant moments when classified individuals and their allies challenged the institutional structure and practice.[2] As the twentieth century progressed, advocacy groups and self-advocates made an indelible mark on the understanding of intellectual disability and its treatment by medical and institutional experts. Where, then, do we find philosophers? How and when do they enter the scene, and as they do make their appearance, what authority do they claim in speaking about this topic?

On the surface, the question of intellectual disability has been relatively neglected by philosophers. A brief survey of the history of philosophy turns up a few examples: references to "defective" babies in Plato and Aristotle, a reference to "madmen" in Descartes's first meditation,[3] a discussion of the distinction between madness and idiocy in Locke, Rousseau's *Emile,* and Adam Smith's discussion of "wretched" creatures who lack reason.[4] There is no sense in which intellectual disability is a canonical area of inquiry in philosophy; it does not seem to be of great importance to many philosophers.[5] One possible approach, then, would be to map the exclusion of intellectual disability from the philosophical scene.[6] While this would be a worthy project, I choose to focus on more recent philosophers who *have* spoken about this topic.

If we move from the institutional world at the turn of the twentieth century to the contemporary world of philosophy, we see that in the past half century philosophers have said quite a bit about intellectual disability. In what follows, I will critically examine epistemic authority and privilege in relation to the philosopher and intellectual disability. While I do not offer a comprehensive review of all that philosophers have said about the subject, I map out certain broad features of traditional philosophical discourse about intellectual disability and point to a series of potential dangers that can befall even the most earnest and well-meaning philosopher interested in entering into this rich area of inquiry.[7] In focusing on the face of the philosopher as moral expert and gatekeeper, I examine practices that contribute to the assertion of epistemic authority, including naming and defining intellectual disability, and determining what kinds of knowledge count in making certain moral claims about intellectual disability. At the end of the chapter I take a genealogical turn away from the archaeological analysis of these local discursivities and begin to uncover how certain forms of subjugated knowledges can emerge when the face of authority is problematized. This process of unmasking is both critical and productive. As I examine how some philosophers have remained entrenched in old terminology, concepts, and questions and seem unaware of the political and conceptual changes that have taken place in the past century, it will become evident that, in certain respects, the philosophical world of intellectual disability harks back to the historical world we have just left behind. I hope this analysis will yield a better understanding of *why* some philosophers speak about intellectual disability in the ways that they do, and point to new paths that we philosophers might travel accompanied by others who might actually lead the way.

The Moral Expert

Naming

Much has been written about the politics of language, naming, and labeling in relation to disability generally, and intellectual disability in particular.[8] Within the self-advocacy movement there is the call to "label jars, not people," and the problematic nature of the term "mental retardation" came to the public eye when the AAMR decided to do away with the term and rename itself the American Association on Intellectual and Developmental Disabilities. The problem of naming is a complicated one, however, particularly in the case of a category like mental retardation. In addition to the heterogeneity of the category (wherein as we have seen there may be mild and severe cases, educable and uneducable individuals, instances where mental retardation is the primary diagnosis and others where it is a condition that accompanies a disability like Down syndrome), there are other factors that complicate the question of how to refer to individuals who are considered to be intellectually/cognitively/developmentally disabled.[9] In her article "Terminology and Power," Ruth Luckasson explores the many complexities involved in naming "mental retardation," including questions of personal, cultural, and social contexts, received and intended meaning, ownership, ideology, and power. She writes, "Naming or terminology in intellectual disability are likely to remain problematic for an extended time because although many of the scientific and practice aspects of the term are relatively resolved, the issues of power are only beginning to be understood."[10] The analysis that follows will attempt to address the question of power, discourse, and naming in the context of philosophical work on mental retardation. Though the problem of power and terminology is being articulated in more concrete ways on the front lines—in the self-advocacy movement, by parents and caregivers, by professional associations and individuals, and by activists and academics associated with the disability rights movement and disability studies—it is precisely *because* of these discussions and debates, and because of the authority assumed within philosophical and bioethical discourse, that philosophers must attend to the question of naming. In looking more closely at how some philosophers speak about this group, however, I will not be evaluating the arguments themselves; rather, I hope that certain epistemological and political implications will emerge through an analysis of the use of language.

Increased attention to mental retardation in philosophical literature coincides with the increased social concern regarding the treatment of this group of individuals in the 1960s and 1970s. As parent advocacy groups and the disability rights movement were emerging, as the Kennedy family brought mental retardation into public discourse, and legal battles were redefining the rights of those labeled as mentally retarded in relation to housing and education, as the push toward deinstitutionalization was taking shape, some philosophers took notice. However, for anyone aware of the debates in the past decades by advocacy and professional groups surrounding the use of the terms "mental deficiency" and "mental retardation," it may come as a surprise to find that philosophical discourse remained entrenched in even older terminology. Though the terms "idiot," "moron," "imbecile," as we saw earlier, were actual scientific subclassifications of mental retardation at an earlier point in history, they persist in certain philosophical discussions. It is unclear whether the presence of this language in philosophical arguments about mental retardation is simply a careless appeal to the colloquial sense of these words, or whether philosophers intend them in the more technical sense, as demarcating levels of mental retardation, and believe them to be in current use. Either way, their appearance in philosophical literature at least a half century after they were abandoned as scientific labels is surprising, puzzling, and worthy of attention.

In his 1974 article "All Animals Are Equal," Peter Singer raises the issue of the "permanently retarded" in his discussion of the possibility of distinguishing morally between human beings and non-human animals. He points to one philosopher's attempt to address the issue of the retarded: Stanley Benn's "clear and honest article . . . [that] argues for equality of consideration as the only possible basis for egalitarianism."[11] The following passage he quotes from Benn is meant to illustrate speciesism[12] in contemporary philosophy: "Not to possess human shape *is* a disqualifying condition. However faithful or intelligent a dog may be, it would be a monstrous sentimentality to attribute to him interests that could be weighed in equal balance with those of human beings. . . . This is what distinguishes our attitude to animals from our attitude to *imbeciles*. It would be odd to say that we respect equally the dignity or personality of the *imbecile,* and of the rational man . . . but there is nothing odd about saying that we should respect their interests equally, that is, that we should give to the interest of each the same serious consideration . . . [emphasis mine]."[13] Singer follows by saying that "Benn's statement of the basis of consideration we should have for imbeciles seems to me correct, but why should there be any fundamental inequality of claims between a dog and a human imbecile? . . . That the *imbecile* is not rational is just the way things have worked out, and the same is true of the dog."[14] Here the term "imbecile" is interchangeable with "permanently retarded humans" (as Singer called them initially). This term is used unproblematically in the article, and Singer later confirms this. He engages in a mental exercise where he substitutes terms in the above passage to make it about race and IQ, and then points to how offensive the statement sounds. He states, "*If the original did not, at first reading, strike us as being as outrageous as the revised version does,* this is largely because although we are not racists ourselves, most of us are speciesists [emphasis mine]."[15] The fact that the language used in the Benn passage is taken as acceptable, and that using the term "imbecile" to refer to the "permanently retarded" is not considered outrageous, is a sign that this terminology is thought to be acceptable.[16]

A more extreme example can be found in Vinit Haksar's book *Equality, Liberty, and Perfectionism.* In his study of the how the notion of perfectionism "is needed to provide the foundations of egalitarianism," the author gives ample attention to the status of "idiots."[17] Throughout the book, this is the term he uses to refer to individuals labeled mentally retarded (we can only assume this is the group he means, for he never explicitly defines "idiocy"). The text is littered with references to "idiots," their distinction from animals, and various descriptions of their worth. In fact, an entire section is devoted to "Some Perfectionist Presuppositions, and Idiots." A few examples will suffice to take us back to the historical world described in previous chapters: "If differences of intrinsic worth between human beings were well marked, then it would be feasible for political principles and policies to take such differences into account. But in fact the differences are not well marked—except perhaps in the case of *idiots and their like* [emphasis mine]."[18] And "if one takes the individualistic line, the *congenital idiot* may appear as a parasite. As an individual he is a very miserable specimen. If all others were like him, the human species as a whole would not be any better than some of the animal species. The *congenital idiot is a parasite;* for people claim for him privileges because he is a member of the human species, yet he does not (unlike normal people) contribute to the true grandeur of the human species, neither now nor (as normal babies will) in the future [emphasis mine]."[19] The only distinction he makes is between congenital idiots and other "mental defectives" who were born with some potential and then lost it: "It is true that the *congenital idiot* falls short of the standard of his species. But it does not follow that any injustice was involved, and so it does not follow that compensatory treatment is due to him. But I admit that in the case of many mental defectives, they have been victims of neglect or of injustice. . . . And in *these* cases compensatory treatment may be fitting. . . . But the problem with congenital idiots is that they never had the relevant potential, they were such degenerate specimens that one doubts if they ever qualified for membership of the egalitarian club."[20]

Though I will not evaluate the actual arguments that Haksar makes in his book, the above passages give a sense of the moral status often accorded to "idiots" in philosophical discourse. For the purposes of this discussion, I include them to illustrate that this kind of language was considered acceptable in philosophical discourse. It is not uncommon to find "idiots," "imbeciles," and "morons" in articles written by philosophers at a time when the clinical, legal, and political world was trying to change the negative perceptions and treatment of people labeled mentally retarded.[21]

Fast-forward to the 1990s. The Americans with Disabilities Act has been passed, the disability rights and independent living movements are in full swing, and the self-advocacy movement among persons with intellectual disabilities is gaining prominence as more institutions are closed and the horrific abuses and marginalization of this group are being recognized. Still, some philosophers retain outdated terminology. In Jeff McMahan's 1996 article, "Cognitive Disability, Misfortune, and Justice," he generally uses the term "cognitively disabled" to refer to the individuals whom he discusses. However, he departs from this language a number of times. In his discussion of whether the "severely cognitively disabled" are entitled to compensatory justice (he concludes that they are not), he offers a thought experiment inviting the reader to compare the relative misfortune of a number of individuals:

> Imagine that a person with extraordinarily highly developed cognitive and emotional capacities—for example, Bertrand Russell—suffers a stroke and is reduced to a state of *idiocy,* with a level of well-being comparable to that of a contented dog. His conditions, clearly, would be terribly unfortunate. Next, consider a congenitally severely cognitively impaired adult (the *"Congenital Retardate"*) whose level of well-being is comparable to that of Russell after the stroke. . . . Finally, consider an extremely dim and stolid man (the *"Dullard"*) who also suffers a stroke that reduces him to the same level as Russell and the Congenital Retardate. While he is more unfortunate than the Congenital Retardate, he is less badly off than Russell. For it is worse for Russell to be a contented *idiot* than it is for the *Dullard.* [italics mine][22]

Leaving aside the merit of this comparison, it is striking that terms like "dullard" and "idiot" appear in his examples. He clearly needs to name each individual by condition, but one is left wondering whether his use of terms is a deliberate appeal to everyday, unreflective assumptions about dullards and idiots. In another thought experiment later in the article, he adds the term "moron" to his list: "Suppose, for example, that one were to wake up one morning to find that during the night the psychological capacities of every human being other than oneself had been mysteriously increased. Relatively speaking, one would suddenly have become a *moron*."[23] Again, the fact that this term is used without qualification leaves one wondering whether he is unaware of the historical significance of these words, and why they are present in an article that otherwise refers to the "cognitively disabled."

In one of the few articles on mental retardation that draws attention to the way philosophers have marginalized this group, Paul Spicker points to other examples: "The case of 'mental handicap'—or 'idiocy'—is something of a paradigm in political philosophy. Writers refer to 'idiocy' or 'mental deficiency' as if it were an obvious exception to the moral canons they apply in other cases. . . . [Joel] Feinberg refers to 'human vegetables'. [Isaiah] Berlin, perhaps a little carelessly, credits Bentham with the 'last word' in writing: Is not liberty to do evil, liberty? If not, what is it? Do we not say that it is necessary to take liberty from idiots and bad men, because they abuse it?"[24] Spicker is pointing to these passages as evidence of the fact that persons with mental retardation have been considered marginal cases.[25] However, even Spicker, in his critique of this marginalization, fails to critically discuss the language used by these philosophers.

What is really at stake here? Yes, the language that philosophers apply to those labeled mentally retarded is reminiscent of the institutional world of mental retardation at the turn of the century. But why should this be cause for concern? The fact that philosophers are uncritically and perhaps unconsciously speaking this language indicates that they are either unaware of or unwilling to acknowledge the historical weight of the words they choose. In earlier chapters I demonstrated that terminology of types of mental retardation was more than incidental. Terms like "idiot," "imbecile," "moron," and "feebleminded" had the status of scientific classifications and were imbued with social and political significance, and there is no reason to think that the weight of these terms and their impact are any less heavy for those to whom they refer.[26] Though these terms now seem to have disappeared from the philosophical scene, this gap between philosophical discourse and professional and political discourse surrounding intellectual disability points to a number of potential dangers that should be acknowledged. Though there is by no means a clear consensus about terminology, to continue to use offensive and/or problematic language without recognizing it as such can perpetuate discriminatory attitudes and erroneous assumptions. It can also be viewed as shirking one's epistemic responsibility to both the reader and the subject, since carelessness in terminology can paint a distorted picture for the reader. It would be interesting to explore the extent to which this language actually taps into the reader's own prejudices and impressionistic knowledge of what conditions like idiocy and imbecility mean. More importantly, however, the uncritical use of such language blatantly ignores the concerns that the subject might have about this language, and the stigmatizing and oppressive effects that perpetuating such terminology could have. Finally, using such antiquated language undermines the philosopher's authority in the eyes of anyone who is familiar with this history, and situates what may be an important analysis or conversation in a space that is undesirable and might in fact alienate others who could prove to be valuable interlocutors.

So what can be done to acknowledge the history and effects of this terminology? Ruth Luckasson offers a set of questions that are helpful to consider in choosing one's words: "Does this term incorporate current knowledge, and is it likely to incorporate future knowledge? Does this term contribute in a desired way to the manner and content of portrayal of people with the disability? Does this term name this and nothing else?"[27] There is no easy solution to the question of terminology, and certainly the categories and accompanying names continue to be contested and in flux. However, asking the critical questions that Luckasson identifies, attending to the dangers of a kind of willful ignorance in this regard, and recognizing the existence and authority of other disciplines and individuals who are invested in the problem of naming intellectual disability is surely a start. The question of language has brought us to the door of this philosophical world; let us now enter and see how the persons with intellectual disabilities are defined, described, and put to work by philosophers.

Defining

Intellectual disability as a classification has always been internally and externally heterogeneous. It is comprised of various kinds of subdivisions and multiple approaches to its definition (e.g., organic and non-organic, static and dynamic), and there has never been a consensus as to its definition, though it has been defined by many "experts" from various disciplines. Both forms of heterogeneity still exist today, and one only has to look at psychology and genetics textbooks, the latest AAMR manual, the DSM-IV, and literature by self-advocates to see that the very nature and status of "mental retardation" is viewed differently in a variety of contexts. If one were to restrict oneself to the philosophical world of intellectual disability, however, a very different picture would emerge: the internal complexities of this classification are rarely discussed and often obscured by the assumption that it is a static, pathological, uniform condition. In this section, I will try to explain the charge by Paula Boddington and Tessa Podpadec that "in the philosophical literature, definitional accounts of mental handicap are either very thin or absent."[28]

The role of philosophers with regard to intellectual disability is far from clear. If we look at the philosophical treatment of intellectual disability in the traditional approach, we get some sense of the scope of problems that are defined: philosophers solve the problem of personhood, discuss what rights might follow from the moral status of the intellectually disabled, address the difficulties this group poses to particular moral theories, and discuss the concrete ethical dilemmas that intellectual disability presents (e.g., paternalism, sterilization, euthanasia). Within the discussion of these difficult issues, however, two epistemic moves regarding authority emerge: in some cases the philosopher asserts the authority to define this group ex nihilo, and in other instances she assumes that she is not expected to define the condition. I will begin by giving a few examples of the first and then move to the second.

In his critique of the treatment of the profoundly disabled in analytic moral philosophy and bioethical literature, Peter Byrne points to the fact that vague definitions seem to be acceptable, if not the norm: "[A] vague reference to the 'seriously retarded' or those with 'profound deficit' is enough to establish that there are at least some human beings (who and how many does not matter) who are no higher than some animals in the way of intellectual attainments. . . . Assertions are being made about fellow human beings which denigrate them in the absence of any attempt to specify to whom the assertions apply and why."[29] In addition to the problems that attend vagueness, there is also the danger that in defining persons with intellectual disabilities, philosophers are misrepresenting them. Eva Kittay critiques Jeff McMahan for his misguided portrayal of individuals with severe intellectual disabilities and for his presumption that hypothetical examples may not have concrete effects. In her extensive response to his use of the term "severely retarded" in his most recent book, *The Ethics of Killing*, Kittay charges that McMahan mischaracterizes the cognitively disabled:

> He says, "The profoundly cognitively impaired are incapable . . . of deep personal and social relations, creativity and achievement, the attainment of the highest forms of knowledge, aesthetic pleasures, and so on." This is seriously misinformed. Most severely retarded people can speak at least a few words and can be and are involved in activities and relationships. Even profoundly mentally retarded individuals are far from being unresponsive to their environment and to other people.[30]

She goes on to rebut the argument that I will call the thought experiment defense: if he has used the label "severe mental retardation" inaccurately, then it is only a matter of mislabeling.

> The misuse of the label does not vitiate the conceptual points. Surely, I cannot gainsay him this. Surely I can. For the case of the CSMR [congenitally severely mentally retarded] is not a hypothetical, purely conceptual case. If the methodological reason for utilizing this group is to have a real-life example against which to test and recalibrate our intuitions, then we must use a group who we know exists to serve the methodological purpose. The label "congenitally severely mentally retarded" does pick out such a group, but seemingly not the one he intended. . . . One cannot use such a term in a stipulative fashion without the

danger of being misunderstood and without the danger of real peril, especially if one advocates a view that says that killing such individuals is morally less serious than killing one of "us."[31]

Should philosophers be expected to define intellectual disability? And in an argumentative context, can they realistically find a way to include all forms or instances within a single term? Would this be too much to ask and might it even hijack the process of considering difficult moral questions related to the intellectually disabled? Some philosophers have taken a more cautious approach and deferred to specialists.

This may be a laudable move, particularly in light of the problems that can accompany certain hypothetical definitions of intellectual disability. However, it can be instructive to examine the ways in which this move is made. Perhaps thinking that it is not their job to define the condition, some philosophers argue that it falls to the "experts" to deal with these difficulties.[32] Despite acknowledging this division of labor, some philosophers do make general statements about the nature of the condition. While recognizing its external heterogeneity (there are plenty of others who can worry about the definition), they often make assertions which belie a lack of appreciation for the internal heterogeneity and complexity of the classification.

Jeffrie Murphy, in "Rights and Borderline Cases," states that the philosopher can only provide a moral framework for discussions about the rights of the mentally retarded, but not an actual "tidy list of rights": "I will plead my philosophical vocation as an excuse for not providing such a list, since it could be compiled only if we leave the world of abstract thought and begin to gather actual empirical information (which I do not possess) on the exact characteristics of . . . retarded persons—*what they are in fact capable of at various stages.* . . . At this point the philosopher must give way to the lawyer, the behavioral scientist, and the physician [emphasis mine]."[33] Though he pleads ignorance as to the actual capabilities of persons with mental retardation, Murphy goes on to make a number of claims that assume some knowledge about their condition. Of individuals who are "more than minimally retarded," he says, "Severely retarded persons normally have little chance of ever becoming autonomous. . . . Here we are dealing with a class of persons who will never be in a position where it could be reasonably claimed that their destinies ought to be determined by their own choices and decisions."[34] The assumption is that the severely mentally retarded lack any decision-making capacity at all. However, he does not indicate the cutoff for severe cases, and the only clarification he has made about the severely retarded is that they are "more than minimally retarded." What does this mean? Has he talked to parents of persons who have been classified as such, or psychologists and/or physicians for that matter, and determined that they are entirely incapable of autonomy?[35] Although he admits that this is not within his philosophical domain, he feels comfortable making general claims about what we can reasonably expect from the severely mentally retarded.

Later, in arguing that the mentally retarded have a right to paternalistic protection, Murphy makes another assertion that assumes an understanding of the capacities and potential of persons with mental retardation: "Here what will be relevant is to guarantee a certain level of security and a certain level, not of education, but of training."[36] He assumes that training is appropriate, though he does not clarify what he means by "training," nor does he explain the distinction between training and education. This is reminiscent of the turn-of-the-century assumption that training was more appropriate than education for the institutionalized feebleminded.

I have no objection to philosophers discussing issues connected with intellectual disability at an abstract level. However, excusing oneself from possessing knowledge about the particulars of the condition while simultaneously making generalized statements that presume such knowledge is problematic. Another example is found in Stuart Spicker's reply to Loretta Kopelman's article "Respect and the Retarded: Issues of Values and Labeling." Spicker admits from the outset that the label "mentally retarded" is both normative and "vaguely descriptive."[37] He goes on to say, "The term itself does not offer more than a clue as to the kinds of cognition and conation at work in atypical individuals, who have profound mental disabilities and are often perceived as socially burdensome. A detailed account of the spectrum of human atypical cognition and conation properly belongs to the disciplines of genetic psychology and genetic epistemology, special variants and extensions of the pioneering work of the late Jean Piaget."[38] Later, in determining whether the "retarded" are proper objects of respect, he again defers to other authorities. "If the retarded individuals can be shown to be capable of such dispositions, knowledge, and rule following (and this is an empirical matter I must leave to the experts—psychologists, physicians and others) then they can be the objects of an *attitude of respect*."[39]

Despite admitting ignorance, he continues to advance generalized statements about "the retarded." In a footnote, Spicker objects to comparisons between children and the "retarded" on the grounds that one is comparing qualitatively different kinds: "The comparison of . . . retarded individuals with children (and the description of their behavior as 'childish') is, to be sure, not only invidious but also in total disregard of the empirical, genetic psychological facts. Retarded individuals, are not just 'slower' to develop then [*sic*] 'normal' children. Rather, they develop in a very specific set of ways qualitatively unlike those of 'normal' children."[40] This is by no means an accepted fact. In their comparison of philosophical and psychological approaches to mental retardation, Boddington and Podpadec discuss the two predominant psychological theories concerning mental retardation. The developmental delay theory assumes that "people with mental handicaps are much the same as everyone else except that they develop more slowly and reach a lower level of development." The deficit theory assumes that they are deficient in some cognitive process that results in intelligent behavior.[41] Here again we see the tension between qualitative and quantitative theories of mental retardation. However, in asserting a clear qualitative difference, Spicker fails to appreciate the complexities that attend these claims.

Thus there is a contradiction between philosophers deferring to "experts" to define mental retardation and making statements that presume "expert" knowledge about the condition. I would like to make one final point regarding these examples. The choice of experts in these two cases betrays a view of mental retardation as primarily a medical condition. If we think back to the history of mental retardation with its complex relationship between social and sexual norms, institutional needs, professional interests, and the complex interrelation between definition, etiology, and treatment, and then consider current moves to reconceptualize disability as a social problem and the increasingly vocal parent and self-advocacy movement, the failure of philosophers to address the conceptually and socially problematic nature of this classification is troubling.[42] Moreover, as I will address later, the fact that the range of experts does not include the parent's or self-advocate's perspective only confirms that, for many, intellectual disability remains entrenched in the medical model.

There is also the danger of falling prey to the fallacy of reification. In his analysis of biological determinism in *The Mismeasure of Man*, Stephen Jay Gould discusses this fallacy—the tendency to convert abstract concepts into entities—as it has applied to the concept of intelligence.[43] He argues that "the attempt to establish a unilinear classification of mental deficiency, a rising scale from idiots to imbeciles to morons, embodies . . . the reification of intelligence into a single measurable entity."[44] The main vehicle for the perpetuation of this fallacy was the IQ test. Binet intended the test to be used as a means to identify mildly retarded children in schools so they could be given the appropriate help for improvement. He did not think the numerical score signified the child's innate intelligence; the test was merely a practical device.[45] However, as we have seen, in the United States one's numerical score on this test came to represent one's level of mental capacity.

While the AAIDD has reconceptualized intellectual disability in terms of the individual's relationship to his or her environment, and the social model of disability has taken root in multiple sites (including special education, psychology, and the law), some characterizations of intellectual disability in philosophy perpetuate this fallacy.[46]

When the heterogeneity, both internally and externally, and the instability of the classification we call mental retardation is overlooked, two assumptions about the category are perpetuated: (1) accepting a pathological or medical model, which assumes that it can be defined solely according to the biological, genetic, or physical traits that constitute the condition; and (2) uncritically assuming that there is a real, identifiable psychological entity (some version of mental ability) whose deficit or lack defines mental retardation. I am not denying the possibility of defining some "pathology P" (e.g., trisomy 21, fragile X), to borrow Hacking's language, in explaining one dimension of what we call intellectual disability in *some* cases. However, this picture does not tell the whole story of this etiologically, socially, and politically complex classification.

There is one aspect of this heterogeneous classification that philosophers do acknowledge, and it is so significant that most of the philosophical literature is structured around it. I am referring to the fact that intellectual disability is a hierarchical category, and there are graded subcategories from mild to severe. Though this is clearly a continuum, philosophers often deal with one end of the spectrum or the other.[47] Thus we find two prototypes in philosophical literature: the mildly retarded person and the severely retarded marginal person or nonperson. The fact that different forms of mental retardation raise distinct philosophical issues is both understandable and expected. What is striking, however, is the polarization of the literature along these lines, resulting in two prototypical kinds that rarely appear together in one text. Lawrence McCullough attests to this and actually warns against conflating the two groups. In his response to Loretta Kopelman, he writes, "I believe she has not always emphasized the importance of *sharply* distinguishing the two lines of argument which an analysis of agency requires when considering, on the one hand, borderline and mildly retarded individuals, and on the other, extremely and profoundly retarded individuals. . . . There are, to be sure, sufficient resemblances between these two extreme groups, but we must be careful that we do not conflate them."[48]

Just as there may be problems that result from conflating these two groups, there are philosophical consequences to the exclusive focus on one of two prototypical cases, as we shall see in greater detail in the next two chapters. Lakoff explains that what makes something a prototypical member of a category is the fact that it is taken as representative of the whole group. The danger is that presenting only one face of intellectual disability (e.g., the severely mentally retarded) will reinforce existing stereotypes and assumptions about persons with intellectual disabilities in general (their supposed lack of autonomy, their inability to be rational, their lack of meaningful relationships with others, and the notion that they can be trained but not educated).

As the chapters on history in part 1 illustrate, there is much analytical work to be done in understanding the implications of the heterogeneity and insta- bility of this category, unraveling the etiologic complexities, and considering the complex relationship between the levels of definition, etiology, and treat- ment. And there is no reason, in the wake of genetic technologies, to think that these complexities are diminishing. In fact, as increasing numbers of genetic anomalies are identified in relation to intellectual disabilities, the question emerges as to what extent mental retardation is efficacious or meaningful as a classification, given that it encompasses organic and non-organic cases, mild and severe, those with biological causes and those without. What unifies this category? Are Boddington and Podpadec correct when they suggest that, at least for philosophers, "what holds the class together is the assumption that they are excluded absolutely or in degree from certain valuable aspects of hu- man life"?[49]

As we begin to unmask the face of authority and go beyond an exclusively moral framework in which to consider intellectual disability, other questions surface. How is the self-advocacy movement reshaping the boundaries of this definition? What possible reverse discourses or looping effects are occurring? How is the reconceptualization of disability as a social product by the disability rights movement affecting the status of this classification? Answers to these questions fall beyond the scope of this volume, but I raise them in order to sug- gest that the philosophical world of intellectual disability is impoverished if it restricts itself to prototypical cases (e.g., the mild and the severe). To illustrate this point concretely, I will examine the construction of two other prototypes in philosophical literature. One emerges through the use of the term "severely mentally retarded" in discussions of the status of non-human animals, and the other relies on the conflation of intellectual disability and suffering. Just as the relationship between oppression and classification became apparent in the examination of the feebleminded woman as prototypical, certain modes of *con- ceptual* oppression will appear as we examine the face of the beast and the face of suffering. Before moving into this, however, I will address a few more episte-mological questions in relation to the nature of the philosopher's authority.

The Gatekeepers

Considerations of how epistemic authority gets constructed must ask what counts as a legitimate knowledge claim and who is granted the authority to speak about the object or subject. The term "gatekeeper" has been used widely in bioethical literature, in regard to the roles that physicians, genetic counselors, and scientists play in relation to these two questions. If we look back through this lens, we find the history of intellectual disability is replete with these gate-keepers: the superintendents of the schools/institutions, the psychologists who implemented mental tests, the women field-workers who determined someone's family pedigree and traced generations, and feminist reformists who had a hand in defining the boundaries of womanhood and motherhood. Yet phi-losophers also can act as gatekeepers when it comes to knowledge of disability. This statement might seem odd, given that discussions of intellectual disability are relatively sparse in philosophy and given philosophers' deference to experts and their reluctance to lay claim to definitional/etiological issues when they *do* speak about intellectual disabilities. Yet philosophers function as gatekeepers in the realm of moral discourse, and this role is worthy of close scrutiny, not only in terms of its theoretical significance but because the philosopher is not, in fact, a mere distant observer.

Peter Byrne writes, "The theorizing of moral philosophers may seem harm-less enough were it not for the fact that such reasoning about the handicapped is reflected in aspects of clinical practice. Indeed, the worlds of contemporary medicine and moral philosophy now interconnect, thanks to the rise of bio-ethics. . . . To an extent which I cannot determine, our society has unsystem-atically and unintentionally embarked on the eugenic policies advocated by some moral philosophers" (e.g., in the pediatric practices toward disabled newborns).[50] In the fields of bioethics, applied ethics, and moral philosophy more generally, then, the stakes are quite high. Beyond the impact of the actual practices and policies that philosophers may endorse, a gatekeeper plays an important part in determining *which* knowledge claims are valued, accepted, and included. Thus it is crucial to explore the mechanisms by which other per-spectives are dismissed, refuted, and excluded. This will require examining how these lines are drawn, specifically through the mechanisms of exclusion, devaluation, marginalization, and distancing. These considerations can be distilled into two fundamental questions: who? and how? Whose voices are included in this philosophical discourse, and how are the parameters of this area of inquiry defined? I will begin with a sketch of how these two questions have been answered within what I have called the "traditional approach" and then move on in the final sections to examples of how the boundaries and configuration of this philosophical discourse about intellectual disability are changing.

Whose perspectives are absent from philosophical discussions of intellectual disability? The most profound silence surrounds persons with the disabilities themselves. While individuals with profound and severe intellectual disabilities may be incapable of entering into the conversation, there is a paucity of work that includes the voices of those with mild intellectual disabilities. In other disciplines there are examples of how these perspectives might be included, but there seems to be little room for such examples in philosophical literature.[51]

Compounding the problem of exclusion are assumptions regarding the lives that persons with intellectual disabilities lead. Just as the testimony of persons with physical disabilities is discounted when they claim to lead lives that are far richer than ones of "minimal satisfaction" and their epistemic authority is challenged even when they themselves make a claim regarding a positive experience of disability, the dominant assumption is that persons with intellectual disabilities do not and cannot experience the same quality of life that a non-disabled person can.[52] Though I will return to this issue more fully in chapter 6 on suffering, I raise it here to point out another way that philosophers can claim epistemic authority in defining the lives of persons with intellectual disabilities. The normative claim that having a condition like mental retardation is "objectively bad" underlies even the most committed work on justice for the mentally retarded from within the traditional approach. In Veatch's words, "Mental retardation . . . is a serious condition, one that any reasonable person would rather not have. In our terms, the disvalue is objective. This means that we cannot cope with the problem of stigma simply by trying to re-educate people into thinking the condition is not inherently bad. Retardation is not like race or gender stigma. Even the most dedicated and sympathetic advocate for the retarded acknowledges that it is a serious problem. . . . The problem is real. It is so clearly a bad thing to have that we can act as if it were objectively a bad condition."[53]

While it is perhaps understandable why the voices of persons with intellectual disabilities are omitted from philosophical discourse (they are consistently defined as lacking the capacities that would render them "knowing subjects" in any sense, making them the paradigmatic case of a group deemed ignorant and epistemically discounted), there is a more complex dynamic with respect to the voices of those who are in a close relation to persons with intellectual disabilities. It is rare to find the voices of parents and those close to persons with intellectual disabilities included in a way that grants them epistemic authority. And when parents/advocates *are* included in the traditional approach, they play a somewhat paradoxical role: they are not granted epistemic authority as experts but *are* deemed important insofar as their relationship to the intellectually disabled person actually *confers* moral status. In exploring this dynamic, the question of *how* one should philosophize about intellectual disability comes to the surface.

In many ethical discussions about intellectual disability, a dissonance is found between the presumed authority of the disengaged moral philosopher and the authority of those who have embodied, concrete relations with persons with intellectual disabilities. Although these two groups are not mutually exclusive, I will keep them separate here because this distinction is central to the positions I am challenging.

This dissonance can be seen most explicitly in statements that dismiss certain attitudes toward persons with intellectual disabilities as overly sentimental and/or misplaced. This often happens in relation to the analogies drawn between the intellectually disabled and non-human animals (a philosophical move I take to be significant enough to merit discussion in the next chapter). In defending the title to his article "Do the Mentally Retarded Have a Right to Be Eaten?" for instance, Jeffrie Murphy says, "Too much well-meaning sentimentality is allowed to pass for thought in discussion of the retarded, and I want to shock my way through this."[54] A more substantive example can be found in Jeff McMahan's book *The Ethics of Killing:* "It seems that our traditional beliefs about the special sanctity of the lives of severely retarded human beings will have to yield. How much they must yield depends on how drastically we are willing to revise traditional beliefs about the permissibility of killing animals with psychological capacities comparable to those of cognitively impaired human beings. Killing animals, and allowing them to die, are morally far more serious matters than we have supposed. But allowing severely retarded human beings to die, and perhaps even killing them, are correspondingly less serious matters than we have believed."[55]

What assumptions lie behind such concerns? First, they erroneously assume that this overly sentimental attitude is widespread. This worry seems misplaced on two counts. First, in concrete terms, one need only look at the disturbing history of intellectual disability and contemporary cases of abuse to see that this is far from the case. The repeated marginalization and dehumanization of this group of non-persons in academic discourse leaves one wondering where, in fact, these heartfelt but "misguided" portraits are.[56] Second, the concern about oversentimentalizing our approach to mental retardation seems to imply a division between a kind of naive, emotional subjectivity and a rational, objective approach to the matter, a distinction which itself is highly problematic. As Sticker suggests, "Whoever addresses disability is engaged in its study in a personal capacity, even if it is only through texts. But even more so if one is close to its acute, living difficulty. Certain affective pre-apprehensions always accompany our efforts to understand its psychological or physical effect and the social space that surrounds and circumscribes it."[57] Calls to distance ourselves from any kind of sentiment or attachment assume that legitimate work in ethical matters rests on the disengaged, detached subject, a point many in feminist ethics and epistemology have challenged. In fact, it is precisely in constructing the Other position as epistemically compromised by virtue of sentiment and proximity that the normative assumptions underlying more "objective" accounts are masked.

In his critique of the ways that Jonathan Glover and James Rachels invoke examples of the severely disabled in their moral theories, Byrne exposes "an implicit, rhetorical contrast between an extant set of moral convictions which is to a large degree made up of inherited prejudices and a new, critical morality which has passed through the mill of rigorous argument."[58] In labeling the Other's position as hopelessly intuitive, however, the normative and intuitive basis for these philosophers' own definitions comes into focus: "On reflection, it becomes evident that the principles and abstract arguments of a Rachels or a Glover depend as much on so-called intuitions as the moralities they oppose. Rachels' decision to base an ethics of homicide on the principle that only those with biographical life deserve protection, while those with merely a biological life do not, would be insupportable unless he had already assumed that his intuition that killing a healthy normal human being was a central example of wrongful death, whereas killing a severely retarded person was a borderline case. . . . His principles have no greater authority than the authority of the initial decision to divide the cases in that way."[59]

The assertion of moral authority on the part of disengaged, unsentimental, level-headed philosophers seems to place scholars who are connected to persons with intellectual disabilities in a sort of double bind, in which their perspectives can be rendered invalid or invisible. In advocating for those close to them and challenging associations made between the mentally retarded and non-human animals, their positions (e.g., the call to recognize the inherent dignity or humanity in that person) may be explained away by virtue of their relation to that individual and thus rendered invalid. Yet if the requirement for participation in moral discourse is a dispassionate, disengaged "objective" stance, then their voices may be silenced or excluded altogether. (This doesn't address the even more problematic exclusion of *non-academic* voices in these debates.) The irony, however, is that while their *voices* may not have a place in moral discourse, the individuals themselves do not disappear.

As we will see in examining the "face of the beast," according to some philosophers the severely mentally retarded (deemed non-persons) are only deserving of moral consideration insofar as they matter to someone else who *is* a person, a feature they share with non-human animals. It is in the wake of these kinds of claims that we must rethink academic authority, grant legitimacy to these other perspectives, and make room for those who are so often presumed to lack a *human* voice. And it is in response to this traditional approach that we can perceive subjugated voices emerging in the critical disability literature.

Subjugated Knowledges and Resistance

Today the traditional approach to intellectual disability is being challenged in many ways. This reflects not only broader changes on the social, legal, political, and academic horizon, but also the increased presence of disability as a legitimate area of philosophical inquiry. Important critiques speak to the question of authority in the context of disability generally. For example, Susan Wendell exposes "the myth of control" to which philosophers and Western scientists subscribe, Anita Silvers calls into question the conceptual moves through which normative and discriminatory assumptions regarding the "objective badness" of disability are made on the part of philosophers and bioethicists, and Ron Amundson interrogates the categories of "normal" and "abnormal" function. In the realm of intellectual disability too we find critiques of the categories themselves, challenges to the very concept of impairment, and perhaps most prominently the disability rights critique of prenatal testing, where the question of the worth of the lives of persons with intellectual disabilities is most acute.

All of this work in the framework of what I have called the critical disability approach is significant, as it constitutes a form of resistance to the epistemic presumptions that are revealed in certain dimensions of the traditional approach. Yet I would like to call on a particular set of voices that occupy an intermediary position if we think about the above/below image: they are philosophers who by virtue of their trade are endowed with a certain degree of epistemic authority, yet they are also closely related to someone with an intellectual disability. In light of the earlier paradox whereby these voices might be silenced (through the assumption that they are too close to their object of study to be objective), it is particularly instructive to examine how they navigate the epistemic waters as both philosopher and advocate.

Some philosophers, in stark contrast to the approaches to defining the personhood (and humanity) of the intellectually disabled that can be found in many philosophical accounts, weave their relationship to a family member with an intellectual disability with their arguments regarding the moral status of these individuals. As they introduce and explore the nature of their relationship with the person, the reader encounters a very different face of intellectual disability. Contrary to the traditional attenuated and abstract visions of the severely disabled, a distinctly human face emerges.

Peter Byrne introduces his son Gareth in the beginning of his book *Philosophical and Ethical Problems in Mental Handicap* as a way of establishing some degree of epistemic authority to speak about this topic. Yet as he identifies his own position, he simultaneously acknowledges the danger that attends the assumption of such privilege: "There is a danger in introducing so personal [a] note into a survey of conceptual and ethical issues. It would be quite wrong to suppose that any of the arguments on matters relating to mental handicap which follow are the sounder or more persuasive because their author has a child with a disability. They must of course stand or fall on their merits. However, Gareth's existence does have a twofold role in the remainder of this story. In the first place, he may reassure the reader that the author has some experience of mental handicap, albeit that it is limited to one, special instance of that category. In the second place, Gareth explains a fundamental ethical commitment underlying the arguments which follow. . . . This book will endorse throughout the notion that those whom we classify as mentally handicapped are just as much persons as the rest of us."[60] In articulating this dual role, Byrne does not intend to let himself off the hook, so to speak, when it comes to the rigor of his arguments. However, he does make the humble claim that his experience may have *some* (though limited) bearing on his knowledge about this topic.[61]

Eva Kittay's work on care, dependency, and disability is even more firmly rooted in her experience as a mother and caregiver to her profoundly disabled daughter. Sesha is a constant presence in Kittay's work as she interweaves her philosophical arguments with rich accounts of her relationship to Sesha.

Though the emphasis in Byrne's and Kittay's work is certainly different (where Byrne's autistic son stands at the entry of his project, Sesha's face shines through Kittay's words throughout her texts), they both claim their child as clearly, unarguably human. They both assert their child's personhood and humanity in the face of arguments that dismiss them. In acknowledging the murkiness of the ethical issues that accompany considerations of intellectual disability, Byrne writes that "the character of my experience with Gareth points me in this direction. That is, I cannot make sense of that experience unless I accept that love and its associated attitudes are revelatory of value and unless the fact of common membership of a community tells morally in the way I suggest."[62]

Kittay develops this idea more fully in her book *Love's Labor,* which explores the nature of dependency and care, arguing that these central features of the human experience are inextricably linked to questions of justice for the severely cognitively disabled. Throughout the book she draws on her experiences with her daughter Sesha and explains her rich and complex relationship to Sesha in such a way that it becomes part of the fabric of her philosophical argument. She writes, "I fear that the stress on independence reinstates Sesha as less than fully human. With every embrace, I know her humanity."[63]

I offer these examples to the reader as evidence of a changing tide within philosophical discourse about intellectual disability.[64] These authors are grounded in what I have characterized as the critical disability approach: they do not take the category of intellectual disability for granted as a "natural kind" (though they differ in the degree to which we can speak about it as socially constructed);[65] they are critically engaging in a dialogue with a philosophical tradition that has marginalized and misrepresented this group of persons; they recognize the history of oppression and abuse to which they have been subjected (thus contextualizing their reflections rather than abstracting them from historical and social realities); and from an ethical standpoint, they assert the humanness of these individuals in a distinctly human space, by grounding their position within the boundaries of a human community and in their own experience and *person*al relationship with them (rather than relying on a comparative look to other species, for example, to explain and defend their moral status). Insofar as these accounts go against common philosophical assumptions about intellectual disability, one can view them as forms of resistance. They are carving out a new epistemic position and bringing "subjugated knowledge" to light in two ways: through the assertion of a standpoint based on a concrete relation to persons with intellectual disabilities (and an interrogation of the complex philosophical concepts and questions that accompany this relationship, including care, dependency, gender relations, and justice); and through the (re)presentation of the face of an Other that has either remained in the shadows or been rendered profoundly foreign to philosophical audiences.

Authority, Privilege, and Standpoints

Drawing on the rich tradition in feminist epistemology of mounting challenges to the Enlightenment ideal of "the view from nowhere" and addressing the necessity for recognizing the unique and valuable standpoint from which oppressed groups and individuals speak, a number of disability scholars have posed the question of whether a "standpoint epistemology for persons with disabilities" is possible. One feature of this conversation is the immediate acknowledgment of the problem of essentializing or generalizing about *all* persons with disabilities. Susan Wendell writes, "I do not want to claim that all people with disabilities, or all women with disabilities, have the same epistemic advantages, or that they all have the same interpretations of their experiences, or even that they all have similar experiences. . . . But . . . I do want to claim that, collectively, we have accumulated a significant body of knowledge, with a different standpoint (or standpoints) from those without disabilities, and that the knowledge, which has been ignored and repressed in non-disabled culture, should be further developed and articulated."[66] Mary Mahowald echoes the concern with difference when she identifies a number of features that differentiate groups of persons with disabilities. She argues that feminists must recognize the fact that "individuals who identify with the culture of persons with disabilities experience significantly different disabilities."[67] These differences include "cause or etiology, time of onset, its expected duration, the severity of its impact on the individual and society, the type of impairment associated with it, and its recognizability or unrecognizability to others."[68] Amid vast differences between disabilities, however, feminist disability scholars like Wendell are still committed to articulating a distinctive standpoint. Given the history of oppression of persons with disabilities of all kinds, the move to give voice to the richness of this history and the insights and knowledge gained from inhabiting this category are well founded.

While the differences between the conditions (attributed to the individual and to her surroundings), perspectives, and experiences of persons with disabilities abound and must somehow find their way into discussions of the possibility of a standpoint epistemology, the question of developing a standpoint epistemology for persons with *intellectual* disabilities presents even greater challenges. For one of the tacit assumptions in much standpoint epistemology is that the marginalized perspective and location of the individual is *articulable* by the individual herself. It is precisely because others have claimed to speak for and about certain groups that the space must be created for these voices to emerge. For persons with mild intellectual disabilities, the possibility of this standpoint emerging is plausible and is increasingly being made possible through the dynamics of self-advocacy and through organizations like People First.[69] As these voices become more vocal, one challenge for persons with non-intellectual disabilities who are engaged in the task of articulating and promoting this standpoint is to practice the inclusivity they ask of the non-disabled world and ensure that these crucial voices do not get lost.[70]

What about persons with significant disabilities who are incapable of articulating their standpoint and reflecting on their location, identity, and surroundings in a meaningful way? Insofar as standpoint epistemology is founded on the necessity of a certain *kind* of knowledge (even if such a theory acknowledges the many forms knowledge might take), what happens to those for whom such knowledge is impossible? If we take the epistemology out of standpoint epistemology, what is left? One way to answer this question is to say that there are other "knowers" who are in close relation to these individuals who might be able to bring this standpoint to the foreground. Assuming that an advocate, caregiver, friend, and/or family member has the possibility of knowing an individual in a way that is not readily apparent to others, he or she may be in a good position to begin to articulate the position of this person. This does, of course, raise significant epistemological questions regarding the potential barriers that may accompany efforts to authentically represent another's standpoint. (I return to this point below.)

Another possibility may be to shift the focus of the discussion. Marianne Janack distinguishes between epistemic authority and epistemic privilege in an effort to examine the ways in which they have become intimately connected. This involves moving away from efforts to "reconstruct an epistemically advantageous standpoint" (built on the assumption that those who occupy these locations are automatically granted this kind of privilege), and "demystifying the process by which epistemic authority is actually conferred. That means unmasking the Enlightenment claim that epistemic authority derives from an epistemically privileged standpoint or position."[71] This approach allows one to focus explicitly on the concrete practices and ways in which epistemic authority is assumed, constructed, or attributed. This task is not antithetical to simultaneously "reconstructing" one's epistemic position and privilege, but it "makes explicit the connection between knowledge production, social and political practices, and the ethical considerations that influence our judgment of a speaker's *ethos*."[72] Janack continues:

> By demystifying the connection between epistemic authority and epistemic privilege, we can push the question of why those of us who are socially marginalized have no say in the kinds of projects pursued, the kinds of evidence taken to be good evidence, and the kinds of evidence taken to disconfirm a given theory. We can focus on the political practices that justify and uphold this exclusion, and on the kinds of political changes necessary for including those voices. . . . This means, in the final analysis, that we cease to argue that social marginalization confers epistemic privilege, and, *by virtue of that privilege,* the marginalized ought to be included in science. We instead turn to the argument that, because the socially marginalized bear as much if not more of the effects of scientific research, our voices ought to be included because it is *right* to include us, or that certain kinds of political changes are made possible by including us.[73]

This approach is particularly promising in the context of persons with intellectual disabilities who cannot speak for themselves. While the basic question of the extent to which someone else can fully "know" and express their standpoint remains (and is worthy of close attention in its own right), the focus on the construction of epistemic authority allows for a critical examination of exclusionary and oppressive practices and assumptions that impact individuals who cannot easily or readily claim epistemic *privilege* that would automatically ensure their inclusion in the purview of standpoint epistemology. In other words, insofar as persons with intellectual disabilities that preclude certain modes of communication fall under the scope of "the socially marginalized" and must "bear as much if not more" of the effects of certain forms of research (and here I will include philosophical along with scientific), their inclusion is equally important and valuable. And while their distinct standpoints may be more difficult to ascertain, it is precisely the critical project of examining how and why they (and those close to them) have been oppressed and discounted that I see as a crucial part of what can be called standpoint epistemology. It is in this sense, then, that I explored some of the ways in which epistemic authority is claimed within philosophical discourse, and the privileges that come with these valued and potentially problematic positions.

The question of authority is not solved by the inclusion of these voices and faces in philosophical discourse about intellectual disability. However, this plurality—methodologically and epistemically—can only lead to a more detailed portrait of intellectual disability and a richer dialogue about the possibility of enlarging the scope of the human community and viewing persons with intellectual disabilities as citizens of a common world: "We cannot seriously maintain that we seek the inclusion of people with ID in their capacity as fellow citizens without considering whether we want to include them in our own lives as our friends. Or can we? The goal of inclusion ultimately raises not only a question for our agencies and organizations, but also for ourselves as human beings: namely, the question of what we think of the good life for ourselves as human beings, and whether there is a place for people with ID in that life. I propose that this is the real challenge that people with ID pose for us, i.e. not so much what we can do for them, but whether or not we want to be with them. Ultimately, it is not citizenship, but friendship that matters."[74] This shared human world cannot be taken for granted, however. As the next chapter will reveal, the face of the beast dominates many philosophical discussions of intellectual disability, thereby placing the severely intellectually disabled in a separate domain.

5

The Face of the Beast

Madness borrowed its face from the beast.
—MICHEL FOUCAULT

By definition, of course, we [normals] believe
the person with a stigma is not quite human.
—ERVING GOFFMAN

They shot quickly. The hand-held camera rapidly panned the
room. . . . The spindly twisted limb was a leg. . . . The blotches
smeared across the wall were feces; the white fabric covering
the figure in the corner was a straitjacket. The crouching child,
back to the camera, was naked and so was the one next to him.
Both of them were on the floor; there was no furniture in the
room save for a wooden bench and chair. The camera focused
for a few seconds on an oddly smiling person, the only one
fully-clothed. That had to be the single attendant. Even as he
stood there, Rivera thought of the Nazi concentration camps.
One could see similar scenes in the news reels of American
soldiers freeing the inmates of Dachau. . . . Was Willowbrook
America's concentration camp? Did we have such horrors too?

In 1951 Willowbrook State School was opened in central Staten Island, New
York, as an institution for the retarded. By 1963 Willowbrook had six thousand
residents living in a space intended for four thousand. Two years later, Senator
Robert Kennedy visited Willowbrook and told the press "that Willowbrook's

wards were 'less comfortable and cheerful than the cages in which we put animals in a zoo. . . . [Willowbrook] was a reproach to us all.'"[1] In 1972 Geraldo Rivera famously exposed conditions at Willowbrook, which housed primarily "custodial cases" (75 percent were profoundly or severely retarded), again alerting the American public to the subhuman conditions prevailing there.[2] Here was a concrete instance of dehumanization that demanded a response. Despite the public outcry, however, change was slow, revealing not only the bureaucratic, political, and economic struggles, but a deeper sense in which concern for this group of persons was lacking.[3] It came eventually, however, and we have witnessed a period of deinstitutionalization and a change in the treatment of persons with intellectual disabilities. Beyond institutional, political, and social changes, however, the question remains: How do we explain why certain human beings are considered so radically other that they are viewed and treated as animals? How can these forms of dehumanization be justified? What allows the "face of the beast," as Foucault writes, to obscure the human face of the madman or in this case, of the intellectually disabled?

The long history of animalized human others is far too complex to trace here. If one focuses exclusively on intellectual disability, it is clear that from its inception, the category of idiocy relied heavily on defining these individuals in terms of their animal nature. In this regard Willowbrook is but one episode in a long pattern of dehumanizing treatment that was both defined and justified by this animalization.[4] The face of the beast that masks the human face of intellectual disability has not disappeared, however. In fact, it can be found in what some might consider an unexpected place: philosophical discussions of justice, rights, respect, dignity, and moral status. It is to this face and this conceptual place that we now turn.

Recall the conceptual tension between qualitative and quantitative notions of intellectual disability. Our historical examination in part 1 revealed both views. Some individuals portrayed "idiots" and the "feebleminded" as lower on a scale of human development, but human nevertheless (e.g., their infantilization by Rousseau and the institution superintendents; recall the term "man-child"). Others considered them to be a qualitatively different kind (e.g., subhuman or animal-like). These two explanations function in philosophical discussions as well. In an article comparing philosophical and psychological discourse about mental handicap, Boddington and Podpadec point to this fact: "Philosophers commonly, although not exclusively, see people with mental handicaps as either non-persons or marginal persons."[5] The former view reflects an interpretation of intellectual disability as qualitatively different, while the latter suggests a quantitative understanding.

According to the quantitative view, individuals with intellectual disabilities are seen as occupying a lower place on the continuum of human abilities. In this sense, they are marginal cases, "only a left-over problem for personhood. It is seen as one of a range of marginal cases to deal with to prevent your theory from leaking round the edges."[6] Boddington and Podpadec go on to say that mental handicap occupies a special place within the group of marginal cases: "Indeed, it could be argued that since, unlike some other 'marginals' such as women and animals, which have been widely written on, mental handicap has been largely overlooked by philosophers, it could, perhaps, be labeled the most marginal of all marginal cases."[7] Rather than examine the depiction of the mentally retarded as marginal cases according to the view that they possess certain capacities or potential to a lesser degree (a quantitative portrait), I intend to look at the more extreme depiction of them as *qualitatively* different from "normal" persons.[8] Often they delineate the very limits of personhood insofar as they constitute a separate category of human *non-persons*. It is striking to find many ways in which individuals with intellectual disabilities have become designated as a *kind* more akin to animals than to other humans in philosophical discourse. Just as nineteenth-century superintendent Isaac Kerlin referred to two of his students as "household pets," I will argue that in many respects, the intellectually disabled have become our philosophical pets.

In order to explain how and why the intellectually disabled have come to occupy such a position in philosophical discourse, we must first examine the nature of the beast, so to speak. First I will explore *how* philosophers speak about intellectual disability in connection with animality, and then turn to a specific and quite common example: the argument against speciesism. Once I have unmasked the face of the beast, I will discuss why these philosophical moves are problematic and, finally, consider whether there may be certain kinds of appeals to animality that can avoid these dangers.

Animalizing Intellectual Disability

When I began researching intellectual disability in the 1990s, I was surprised to find that so many discussions of the intellectually disabled were in animal rights literature. For example, in an anthology called *Ethics in Practice* (1997), all of the references to "deficient humans" are found in the section on animals.[9]

The most obvious association, then, was the fact that the intellectually disabled are a notable presence in philosophical discussions about non-human animals. While intellectual disability received far less philosophical attention in its own right, connections between the mentally retarded and animals also appeared in texts that address intellectual disability explicitly. After looking at numerous examples (only a few of which are mentioned here), I saw a pattern emerge. Generally, the association between the intellectually disabled and non-human animals manifests itself in one of two ways: (1) it can be *comparative,* whereby the condition or status of those with intellectual disabilities is compared with animals, or the relationship between "normal" human beings and the "intellectually disabled" is thought analogous to our relationship with animals; and (2) it can also be *definitional*—the intellectually disabled, by virtue of certain qualities and capacities (or lack thereof) are placed in the same moral category as non-humans.

Let us begin with a few examples of the former case. In his 1984 article "The Rights of the Retarded," Anthony Woozley draws a comparison between the mentally retarded and a dog to illustrate his point that they both lack a sense of justice: "A dog can look at you pleadingly, or even perhaps accusingly; but to say that he is pleading for justice, or accusing you of injustice, is to attribute to him a concept which it would be rash to suppose that he has; the same must be true of many of the retarded."[10] In "Cognitive Disability, Misfortune, and Justice," Jeff McMahan, in addressing the dependent nature of the severely cognitively disabled, states, "As with domesticated animals, if the cognitively impaired are neglected, their dependency will prevent their achieving levels of well-being of which they are otherwise capable."[11]

It is striking that even when philosophers are making arguments *for* the inclusion of persons with (severe) intellectual disabilities in our moral purview, the face of the beast appears. In her defense of the capabilities approach in securing proper treatment and respect for individuals with mental impairments, Martha Nussbaum discusses Eva Kittay's profoundly intellectually disabled daughter, Sesha. In arguing for the possibility of imagining a conception of human flourishing that includes Sesha, Nussbaum makes the following move: "An emphasis on the species norm makes sense even when we are considering a woman like Sesha, who may never be able to attain the whole list of capabilities on her own, and may need to attain some of them through the proxy of her guardians. For what the species norm says to us is that Sesha's life is to that extent unfortunate, in a way that the life of a contented chimpanzee is not unfortunate. People with severe impairments are all too often compared to higher animals. In some ways this analogy can be revealing, reminding us of the complex cognitive abilities of animals. But in other ways it can be misleading."[12]

Animal analogies abound in philosophical discussions, and most authors are uncritical of these moves (Nussbuam is an exception, as she acknowledges there may be something troubling about this).[13] Animals do not serve simply as a means of comparison in discussions of intellectual disability, however. Many philosophers ask whether a distinction can be made between the two groups, thereby suggesting a kinship that goes beyond mere similarity. In his rejoinder to Joseph Margolis, "Do the Mentally Retarded Have a Right Not to Be Eaten?" Jeffrey Murphy admits, "I am no longer confident that this distinction is drawable. . . . I am still revolted at the idea of killing and eating a retarded human; but I believe I am just as revolted at the idea of killing and eating a charming, intelligent gorilla—e.g. Koko."[14] Haksar, in his discussion of idiots, phrases the following question to include an implicit distinction between idiots and human beings, and goes one step further in suggesting that idiots may be less worthy of moral consideration than animals: "It is sometimes thought that human beings, unlike animals, have rationality. But some idiots are less rational than some animals, so why should we give more weight to the interests of idiots than to the interests of animals?[15] Jeff McMahan concludes that the line, in some cases, cannot be drawn: "How a being ought to be treated depends, to some significant extent, on its intrinsic properties—in particular, its psychological properties and capacities. With respect to this dimension of morality, there is nothing to distinguish the cognitively impaired from comparably endowed nonhuman animals."[16] He expands upon this in *The Ethics of Killing,* where he writes, "There are no morally significant intrinsic differences between severely retarded human beings and animals with comparable psychological capacities."[17]

This is by no means a purely intellectual exercise. The concrete consequences of this position are profound, particularly given what McMahan views as a problematic, overly solicitous position toward the severely cognitively disabled. His conclusion inextricably links the discourse of intellectual disability with a consideration of animals: "And if we are specially related to the severely retarded but not to animals, the moral significance of the relation is minimal. . . . it seems that we must revise our understanding of the moral status of *both* animals and the severely retarded. According to this view, which we may call *Convergent Assimilation,* we must accept that animals have a higher moral status than we have previously supposed, while also accepting that the moral status of severely retarded human beings is lower than we have assumed. The constraints on our treatment of animals are more stringent than we have supposed, while those on our treatment of the severely retarded are more relaxed."[18] The association between these two groups appears to ensure the proper treatment of non-human animals: in acknowledging their proximity in the moral community (or at its margins or beyond), we see that we have mistakenly assigned too high a place to the severely retarded human being. Taking this statement in the context of the vast evidence demonstrating the exclusion, marginalization, abuse, and neglect so often accorded to individuals with both severe and mild intellectual disabilities, and the fact that the philosophical tradition has been loath to grant the severely intellectually disabled full moral status, I am left wondering where the source of his concern lies.

Few philosophers have noted this alliance between animals and the intellectually disabled in philosophical literature, let alone critiqued it. Paul Spicker's article "Mental Handicap and Citizenship" is an exception. Spicker argues that comparing the mentally retarded to animals is unfortunate for two reasons: (1) "the moral rights accorded to humans and animals are not equivalent" and (2) "the behaviour of people toward animals is generally different from the behaviour of people toward other people. The identification of mentally handicapped people with animals is liable to change the way in which other people behave towards them."[19] Spicker raises two legitimate concerns here. However, I am going to refrain from discussing the rights of the persons with intellectual disabilities and how they differ from rights accorded to animals, and I do not have data to support the contention that such associations will *necessarily* change behavior toward persons with intellectual disabilities (though I will return to this question later). Rather, I will further explore the reasons for and the implications of philosophical comparisons between animals and the intellectually disabled by critically examining an even more common philosophical move: invoking the intellectually disabled in arguments against speciesism. Do these arguments change hue when viewed in historical context? Is the use of the intellectually disabled in these arguments necessary? What are the implications (conceptual and concrete) of using the intellectually disabled to make the case against speciesism? And finally, must recognition of the human face of intellectual disability inevitably betray a form of speciesism? In considering these questions, I will focus primarily on Peter Singer's seminal work, *Animal Liberation,* and then turn to McMahan's more recent work. These two texts by no means capture the full range of arguments against speciesism, nor is utilitarianism the only platform on which to make such arguments; however, they provide a stark example of a philosophical ethos that continues to pervade discussions of the intellectually disabled in relation to non-human animals.

The Case against Speciesism

In his groundbreaking book *Animal Liberation* (1974), Peter Singer defines speciesism as "a prejudice or attitude of bias in favor of the interests of members of one's own species and against those of members of other species."[20] He goes on to put this form of discrimination on a par with racism and sexism: "Racists violate the principle of equality by giving greater weight to the interests of members of their own race when there is a clash between their interests and the interests of those of another race. Sexists violate the principle of equality by favoring the interests of their own sex. Similarly, speciesists allow the interests of their own species to override the greater interests of members of other species. The pattern is identical in each case."[21] Singer can proudly say that, since the publication of his book, "it is the complacent, unargued assumptions of the moral insignificance of non-human animals which have become scarce."[22] However, in examining both *why* and *how* Singer uses the intellectually disabled as a group to prove his case against speciesism, we must also consider the complacent, unargued assumptions about the intellectually disabled that persist in some philosophical discourse.

It is not surprising that the *severely* intellectually disabled are often used to illustrate examples of speciesism.[23] Take the example of experimentation. Singer presents a possible non-speciesist argument for experimenting on animals but not humans: humans would suffer more than animals because of their higher cognitive functioning. For example, if they were kidnapped and used for scientific experiments their suffering would be greater because they would know what was going on. However, once we take into account the case of the severely retarded, the argument ultimately collapses into speciesism:

> This same argument gives us a reason for preferring to use human infants or severely retarded human beings for experiments, rather than adults, since infants and retarded humans would also have no idea of what was going to happen to them. So far as this argument is concerned non-human animals and infants and retarded humans are in the same category; and if we use this argument to justify experiments on non-human animals we have to ask ourselves whether we are also prepared to allow experiments on human infants and retarded adults;

and if we make a distinction between animals, on what basis can we do it, other than a bare-faced—and morally indefensible—preference for members of our own species?[24]

He goes on to argue that if one considers a speciesist bias morally unjustifiable, then one cannot justify an experiment on non-human animals without also allowing it in the case of a brain-damaged human. Singer appeals to this case to help answer the question, "How do we decide when an experiment is justifiable?" He responds, "We have seen that experimenters reveal a bias in favor of their own species whenever they carry out experiments on non-humans for purposes that they would not think justified them in using human beings, *even brain-damaged ones*. This principle gives us a guide toward an answer to our question. Since a speciesist bias, like a racist bias, is unjustifiable, an experiment cannot be justifiable *unless the experiment is so important that the use of a brain-damaged human would also be justifiable* [emphasis mine]."[25] According to Singer, after we abandon speciesism, we must confront the question of whether any justified experiment on a non-human animal must also be justifiable for a brain-damaged human of the same intellectual level.

Singer also addresses the issue of killing non-human animals. He does this by examining the inherent speciesism in the sanctity of life argument—the belief that human life, and only human life, is sacrosanct.[26] He presents the example of an infant born with "massive and irreparable brain damage . . . so severe that the infant can never be any more than a 'human vegetable', unable to talk, recognize other people, act independently of others, or develop a sense of self-awareness."[27] He then asks whether, if asked by the child's parents, the doctor should kill the infant.[28] For Singer, the fact that many people would object to this but not to the killing of non-human animals puts into relief our speciesist bias: the basis for our outrage in the case of the disabled infant is based on an arbitrary value placed on species membership. Singer argues that there are, in fact, more salient and morally relevant features on which we should base our judgment in the case of killing:

> Adult chimpanzees, dogs, pigs, and members of many other species far surpass the brain-damaged infant in their *ability to relate to others, act independently, be self-aware, and any other capacity that could reasonably be said to give value to life*. With the most intensive care possible, some severely retarded infants can never achieve the intelligence level of a dog. . . . The only thing that distinguishes the infant from the animal, in the eyes of those who claim it has a "right to life," is that it is, biologically, a member of the species Homo Sapiens, whereas

chimpanzees, dogs, and pigs are not. But to use *this* difference as the basis for granting a right to life to the infant and not to the other animals is, of course, pure speciesism. It is exactly the kind of arbitrary difference that the most crude and overt kind of racist uses in attempting to justify racial discrimination. . . . Those who hold the sanctity of life view do this, because while distinguishing sharply between human beings and other animals they allow no distinctions to be made within our own species, objecting to the killing of the severely retarded and the hopelessly senile as strongly as they object to the killing of *normal adults.* [emphasis mine][29]

The implication here is that there are more important features on which to base moral boundaries, which would make the killing of animals equally if not more reprehensible than the killing of brain-damaged infants. It is because of the "arbitrary" boundary drawn between species that those who hold the sanctity of life position (may) condone the killing of non-human animals (it does not follow from this position that one would necessarily condone killing of certain animals under certain conditions) while objecting to the killing of a brain-damaged infant.

In the above examples about experimentation and killing, the severely cognitively disabled serve to illustrate a bias toward our own species which, according to Singer, is both inappropriate and arbitrary. The question of whether drawing a line based on species membership *is* in fact unjustified is a point I will return to later. Before addressing this, however, I will advance three reasons explaining *why* appeals to intellectual disability are so appealing to those making the case against speciesism: (1) the cognitively disabled are viewed as more akin to animals than humans; (2) their condition is portrayed as static, making them an uncomplicated case to examine; and (3) choosing a group that lies at the margins of the definition of humanness helps illustrate the arbitrariness of giving preference to one's own species.

Individuals with severe intellectual disabilities, as defined by anti-speciesists like Singer, are a good group to make the case for redrawing our moral boundaries. Rather than privileging species membership, Singer suggests that there are more important characteristics that determine the worth of a creature. Though Singer wants to promote the utilitarian view that sentience and the capacity to suffer are fundamental to our treatment of both humans and non-humans, he suggests additional criteria which might be taken into account in the case of taking a life. "A rejection of speciesism does not imply that all lives are of equal worth. While *self-awareness, the capacity to think ahead and have hopes and aspirations for the future, the capacity for meaningful relations with others* . . . are not relevant to the question of inflicting pain . . . these capacities are relevant to the question of taking life."[30] He goes on to explain why, based on these criteria, most of us would probably save the life of a "normal human being" over that of an "intellectually disabled" one.[31] Note that he never defines what he means by *normal* or *intellectually disabled,* though one can infer from the passage that a normal human being is one who possesses the "relevant" features, while a person with an intellectual disability does not:

> If we have to choose between the life of a human being and the life of another animal we should choose to save the life of the human; but there may be special cases in which the reverse holds true, because the human being in question does not have the capacities of a *normal human being.* So this view is not speciesist. . . . The preference, in normal cases, for saving a human life over the life of an animal when a choice has to be made is preference based on the characteristics that *normal humans* have, and not on the mere fact that they are members of our own species. This is why when we consider members of our own species who lack the characteristics of *normal humans* we can no longer say that their lives are always to be preferred to those of other animals [emphasis mine].[32]

The relevant features in deciding the worth of a particular life are those which Singer believes "normal humans" possess. However, these features are not limited to humans. He suggests that adults of other species possess the ability to relate to others, act independently, and be self-aware, while the "brain-damaged infant" and the "intellectually disabled" do not (again he conflates terminology, using the terms "brain-damaged," "intellectually disabled," and "mentally retarded" interchangeably). The implication is that these features draw a more accurate and morally appropriate boundary between individual beings (both human and non-human), and that some non-human animals are actually more like normal humans than *abnormal* humans are. It is now possible to classify adult non-humans and normal human adults together, and place the brain-damaged, severely retarded, and hopelessly senile in a separate category, the operative criterion being a certain level of cognitive functioning, from which autonomy, relations with others, aspirations for the future, and self-awareness presumably follow. Singer confirms this when he says, "As long as we remember that we should give the same respect to the lives of animals as we give the lives of those humans at a *similar mental level,* we shall not go far wrong."[33]

Once we draw our moral boundaries according to a different set of criteria, Singer argues, we can see that some of the intellectually disabled may have more in common with animals than they do with normal humans; many non-human animals actually *surpass* the severely cognitively disabled in mental ability. But what assumptions underlie the conviction that the privileging of mental ability is less arbitrary than the decision to give preference to one's own species? To answer this, I turn to the second reason Singer utilizes the intellectually disabled in his arguments: the supposedly uncomplicated nature of this group.

If the capacities outlined above are more morally relevant than species membership, then the problem of normal human infants remains. Insofar as they do not possess self-awareness, autonomy, the ability to have hopes and aspirations, or the ability to have meaningful relationships with others, they too could be grouped with the "severely disabled," the "hopelessly senile" and "brain-damaged" persons.[34] Singer recognizes this and decides to exclude normal infants from his discussion because he views them as a more complicated case: "In case anyone still thinks it may be possible to find some relevant characteristic that distinguishes all human beings from all members of other species, let us consider again the fact that there are some human beings who quite clearly are below the level of awareness, self-consciousness, intelligence, and sentience of many non-human beings. I am thinking of human beings with severe and irreparable brain damage, and *also of infant human beings; to avoid the complication of the potential of infants, however, I shall concentrate on permanently and profoundly retarded human beings* [emphasis mine]."[35] Singer does not address the complication of potentiality, and his preference for the mentally retarded over (normal) infants betrays a static view of mental retardation. The assumption is that while the normal infant has cognitive potential, the "profoundly and permanently" retarded person does not. Singer's choice of this group, rather than normal infants, is based on the assumption that individuals who are born with *no potential for certain cognitive capacities* are more akin to animals than to infants who lack the capacities but supposedly possess the potential for their development. I would argue that to base moral distinctions on some unspecified, undefined *potential* (or lack thereof) is to tread on tenuous ground. Given the historical legacy of static characterizations of mental retardation, as well as the complexities of diagnosis, definition, and treatment surrounding intellectual disabilities, the issue of potential may be even *more* complicated than in the case of a normal infant.[36] Moreover, there is ample evidence to suggest that even the most profoundly intellectually disabled individual can experience some forms of development.[37] The elusive notion of potential cannot be easily dismissed, especially if it is going to provide the moral justification for how this group of people should be treated.

The way that the severely retarded are used in these examples betrays a static view of their condition: it is assumed that they lack the potential for any significant development and that their condition will never change. Even if one could imagine a case like those to which Singer appeals, this would not justify the assumption that *all* cases of profound mental retardation are static and lack all potential. Anyone who has worked with or had a close relationship with a profoundly disabled child would challenge this gross generalization.[38] Even among professionals in the field, there is little consensus. In arguing for an alternative theoretical framework in which to understand and communicate with this complex and varied population of individuals, John Gleason writes, "A comprehensive universal definition of the ability of persons with severe and profound multiple disabilities is difficult to achieve solely through the use of traditional clinical and psychometric measures. The archive records reveal no simple or consistent description of this population."[39]

Despite these complications, in discussions of speciesism the most *severe* (and seemingly unproblematic) cases of intellectual disability seem to be the most useful. Singer never discusses the mildly retarded, presumably because they possess the capacities often considered relevant for moral preference. Thus, in the exclusive focus on the severely retarded, we find another instance of a prototype effect: in the attack against speciesism, the prototypical case of intellectual disability is the "human vegetable" who "can never achieve the intelligence level of a dog."[40] This prototype has a number of features: severe cases are usually compared with animals; this type is often placed in a moral category below normal humans (adults and infants) and many non-humans; and in addition to being viewed as static, the severely retarded individual is designated as a *qualitatively different kind* of being. By virtue of his or her supposed *lack* of potential, the prototypical case of intellectual disability cannot be considered on the spectrum of human development (e.g., like the quantitative picture generated by classification according to IQ score). When the arbitrary boundary of species membership is discounted, the severely mentally retarded individual emerges as a distinct, qualitatively different kind.

The severely intellectually disabled are used in animal rights discourse because they justify replacing speciesism with an alternative set of characteristics, and because they are thought to represent an unproblematic case that does not involve the difficult notion of potentiality. A final reason this group is so appealing in refuting speciesism is that its members lie at the margins of definitions of human nature. As fringe members who, according to some, are only members of our species by virtue of their biology, they can illustrate the arbitrariness

of this boundary. When confronted with the intellectually disabled in this attenuated form, presented as lacking all important human qualities and bereft of
even the *potential* for development, we are reminded of the nineteenth-century
descriptions of idiots as lacking in everything but human form. Today, these
empty "shells of humanity" are used to argue that there are far more important
features than the simple biological fact of belonging to the species *Homo sapiens*. Recall Singer's claim that "to use *this* difference as the basis for granting a
right to life to the [brain-damaged] infant and not to the other animals [adult
chimpanzees, dogs, pigs, and members of many other species who surpass his
or her abilities] is, of course, pure speciesism."[41] By focusing solely on selected
capacities, Singer places individuals with severe intellectual disabilities at the
margins of humanity. Because they supposedly do not share mental capacities possessed by the rest of us, only biology unites us with them. Once these
individuals have been stripped of all relevant human qualities, there is something unjust about preferring them to animals that do possess these qualities,
the argument can be made, simply because they fall on our side of the species
boundary. Only a group so far removed from "us," from "our humanity," could
convince us that *there is only one feature which we have in common* (i.e., we are
all *Homo sapiens*), and that this feature is morally irrelevant.

Consider the following example. At one point, Singer groups the "hopelessly
senile" with the "retarded" and the "brain-damaged." Interestingly, he did not
choose the example of your hopelessly senile grandma to make his case against
speciesism. Arguably, she "can never achieve the intelligence level of a dog."
A "chimpanzee, dog or a pig will have a higher degree of self-awareness" than
Grandma.[42] And we might decide that "an experiment cannot be justifiable unless the experiment is so important that the use of . . . [a hopelessly senile grand-
mother] would also be justifiable."[43] Perhaps we would conclude that it is better
to save the life of a normal human being than Grandma's, or that our choice to
experiment on an animal rather than Grandma is arbitrary and unjustifiable,
and in making it we join racists and sexists in our brand of discrimination.

Why do these examples seem odd or troublesome? Because Grandma, for
many of us, has a human face and a human history, and stands in some kind of
relationship with other human beings, while for many a "human vegetable" or
a brain-damaged infant does not.[44] The example of the severely intellectually
disabled presents us with a case to which many of us have little exposure or
emotional resonance, and draws on our preconceptions and intuitions about
individuals with severe intellectual disabilities. This is evident in McMahan's
claim that speciesism alone cannot justify giving preference to the interests of

the intellectually disabled over "comparably endowed animals." He presents the situation as if, with the exception of close family members, the *only* thing we share with this group of fellow humans is a biological relation: "Bare co-membership in the human species, *which is what we share with the cognitively impaired,* does not involve personal ties, mutual sympathy, shared values, a common commitment to a certain way of life, social cooperation, or any of the other features of relations that are more readily recognizable as legitimate bases for partiality [emphasis mine]."[45] "We" presumably refers to the cognitively able—those of "us" who are assumed to have no connection to this distant group of people. The constitution of the cognitively impaired as a group so radically different from ourselves relies on this us/them dichotomy.

Perhaps the severely intellectually disabled as a group are chosen to refute speciesism not only because its members are often believed to have more in common with animals than with humans, but because they are perceived as radically other.[46] As the discussion of language and definition in the preceding chapter suggests, many philosophers lack familiarity with the history of the classifications and the complexities of this condition (e.g., its internal and external heterogeneity and its instability). Perhaps they have never had contact with individuals who have intellectual disabilities. It is unfortunate that when this socially and philosophically marginalized group does become visible in philosophical literature, it is often in truncated, distorted, or prototypical form. It is equally disappointing that work like Singer's, aimed at dispelling myths and refuting "complacent, unargued assumptions" about one marginalized group, draws on and perpetuates myths and assumptions about another.

One aspect of the philosophical world of intellectual disability, then, is a close relationship between animals and the severely intellectually disabled. While absent from many other areas of philosophy, the presence of intellectual disability in discussions of animal rights is striking, and reveals certain features of the traditional approach to intellectual disability in philosophy. The analysis of this relationship has revealed a number of important patterns in philosophical discourse about intellectual disability. First, the likening of the severely intellectually disabled to animals perpetuates a qualitative view of intellectual disability: they are viewed as qualitatively different than normal human beings, and their similarity with animals suggests that they are closer in kind to non-humans than to humans in certain important ways. The prototypical case of intellectual disability in arguments against speciesism is most often the *severely intellectually disabled* individual—in Singer's words, the "profoundly and permanently retarded." While it may be understandable, given the arguments being made, that other forms of intellectual disability are not addressed, carelessness in terminology can contribute to the erroneous assumption that this subgroup is representative of the whole. (Recall the interchangeable use of the terms "retarded," "severely retarded," "intellectually disabled," "profoundly and permanently retarded," "brain-damaged," "human vegetable.") One might object that since we are philosophers, not doctors or psychologists, the important thing is to have a general sense of the group we are discussing. However, in light of the gravity of the claims being made (e.g., when it is justifiable to *kill*), there is little room for slippery terminology.

Beyond the assumptions and misrepresentations that I have uncovered, are there other reasons to be troubled by this association? If philosophers could be more attentive to language and more scrupulous about defining and explaining intellectual disability, is there good reason to leave this face behind? I suggest that if we consider what is at stake in its preservation and perpetuation, there are compelling reasons to refrain from *animalizing* this group both in arguments devoted to refuting speciesism, and in other philosophical discussions about intellectual disability. To continue to draw connections between non-human animals and persons with intellectual disabilities not only is conceptually unnecessary, but is harmful insofar as it perpetuates certain forms of conceptual oppression while ignoring other concrete forms, and obscures the distinctly *human* face of persons with intellectual disabilities.

Human and Animal Oppression

There are two questions worth differentiating here that I will address in turn. The first is whether it is *necessary* to invoke intellectual disability at all in critiquing speciesism; the second is whether to challenge the associations drawn between non-human animals and the severely intellectually disabled and to assert the moral relevance of speaking about the latter as distinctly *human* beings is a form of speciesism. Let us begin with the first, and perhaps more easily answerable question. When asked recently whether the argument against speciesism needed to invoke intellectual disability, Peter Singer said it did not, but stressed that it was such an *effective* way to make the case.[47] There is no doubt, as we have seen, that there are clear reasons to appeal to this marginal group and its similarities with non-human animals to bring speciesist assumptions into the foreground. However, there may be equally compelling ways to argue against the mistreatment of non-human animals without drawing comparisons with the severely intellectually disabled or constructing examples that appear to pit the interests of one group against the other.

The most obvious point is that it is possible to recognize morally relevant characteristics possessed by non-human animals without using the severely intellectually disabled to make such claims. (And we do this all the time.) Moreover, using the intellectually disabled in arguments against speciesism creates a false opposition that brings the interests of the intellectually disabled into direct conflict with the interests of non-human animals. For example, Eva Kittay, in her extended critique of Jeff McMahan's contention that we must rethink our mistreatment of non-human animals in the context of our misguided solicitude toward the cognitively disabled, argues that it is, in fact, possible to hold the position that "we should treat the CSMR [congenitally severely mentally retarded] as we treat other persons, and also that we should treat animals better than we do now."[48] Peter Byrne echoes this when he argues that it is a false opposition to set the interests of the intellectually disabled against the interests of animals, or to imply that the recognition of one necessarily precludes the other: "The proposition 'if you are human, you have special worth' does not entail 'Only if you are human, do you have special worth.' . . . It seems entirely reasonable to suppose that someone might be absolutely committed to the truth that all our fellow human beings are worthy of the same fundamental respect, because they are our fellow human beings, but consider that the question of how we should regard animals is still open and should be explored on its merits."[49]

To simply say that it is *unnecessary* to marshal examples of intellectual disability to articulate arguments against speciesism and in favor of improving our treatment of non-human animals is not reason enough to stop utilizing such a powerful and effective strategy. However, the fact that the continued association between these groups perpetuates certain forms of oppression while masking others makes the case against these philosophical moves much stronger.

If we recall the discussion of the faces of oppression in part 1, the history of intellectual disability betrays numerous ways in which persons with intellectual disabilities were victims of oppression. However, it is also possible to view the associations between intellectually disabled and non-human animals in philosophical discourse as perpetuating certain forms of oppression at the conceptual level as well. These include instances of exploitation, cultural imperialism, and marginalization.

What would it mean to claim that the severely intellectually disabled are being exploited in arguments against speciesism? Young defines exploitation as the process by which an unequal distribution of benefits results from the transfer of energies from one group to another.[50] We saw an example of this historically in the use of inmates as an institutional labor force. I would argue that at the conceptual level, the severely intellectually disabled are being exploited insofar as they are used in arguments against speciesism, yet reap no benefits from their philosophical labor (and as we will see, may be arguably *worse* off). Peter Singer proudly confirms that in the time since the first edition of *Animal Liberation* (1975), there has been a growing body of philosophical literature and awareness about non-human animals: "Fifteen years ago I had to search hard to find a handful of references by academic philosophers on the issue of the status of animals; today I could have filled this entire book with an account of what has been written on this topic during the past fifteen years. Articles on how we ought to treat animals are included in virtually all the standard collections of readings used in applied ethics courses."[51] There is no question that the philosophical discourse surrounding intellectual disability in its own right continues to grow. However, given the prominent role that the intellectually disabled have been conscripted to play in animal rights literature, it is unfortunate that the face of the beast continues to dominate many philosophical discussions of intellectual disability. Though many other faces of intellectual disability have emerged as the issue of disability generally becomes a more distinct focus of philosophical inquiry, the roots of this association run deep as evidenced by the persistence and unproblematic appeals to non-human animals.

Young says that to experience cultural imperialism is to have one's particular perspective obscured by the dominant culture and to be marked out through stereotypes as other.[52] As we have seen in the above examples, this is precisely what philosophers do at the conceptual level when they rely on and perpetuate stereotypical beliefs about individuals with lower cognitive capacities and present them as radically other in all respects except their species membership. McMahan's claim that "bare co-membership" in the species and Singer's claim that we may have more in common with an intelligent Martian than with an individual with severe intellectual disabilities are just two examples of the ways that these non-persons have been relegated to the sphere of profound otherness. Some might object that in the case of the severely intellectually disabled, their cognitive impairments preclude them from experiencing (in any conscious sense) this form of oppression and that they would be unable to contribute their particular perspective even if they had one. There are two responses to this objection. First, it is problematic to assume that all individuals who have been labeled "severely intellectually disabled" are incapable of conscious experiences and articulation. Furthermore, even if they are not able to understand their being defined as other at the conceptual level, there is reason to be concerned that this will have concrete effects on the treatment they receive. Second, even if the failure to incorporate their perspective into philosophical discourse were justified in regard to individuals who lack the ability to articulate or to experience their oppression self-consciously, excluding the experiences of those who have directly observed and/or have relationships with them, using unfounded generalizations, and dismissing the outrage expressed by some at the associations with animals as an "overly sentimental" or invalid response are indicative of a form of cultural imperialism.

We also see multiple forms of marginalization in this discourse. First, by so often relegating the interests of the intellectually disabled to discussions of their fellow non-persons (i.e., non-human animals) and placing them in the same category, in the literal sense, philosophers constitute them as marginal cases in their moral and political theories. As Peter Byrne observes, "[The cognitively disabled] are treated as marginal from the standpoint of strands of contemporary moral philosophy—utilitarianism, pure and impure, and modes of contractarian thought."[53] They are also of only marginal *importance* as compared to other groups that receive philosophical attention, in this case non-human animals. Finally, in their close association with animals, they are presented as only *marginally human,* reduced to bare fellow-species status, thus placed not only at the margins of the moral community but at the margins of humanity itself. Of course, this is of little concern to those who think that the concepts of the *human* or *humanity* are of no moral relevance in these discussions, which inevitably raises the question, Do such challenges to the animalizing of persons with intellectual disabilities and the argument that their *humanness* must be recognized simply beg the question by lapsing into a kind of speciesism? For to say that the severely intellectually disabled are not profoundly other, that they should not be placed at the margins of our moral boundaries alongside non-human animals, or that we should recognize some *shared* humanity with them seems to imply that there *is* something distinctive and morally relevant about being human. So can one make these claims without being speciesist?

The Relevance of Being Human

Some philosophers have argued that the distinction between human and non-human is central to moral arguments about the mentally retarded. Joseph Margolis, in his 1984 article "Applying Moral Theory to the Retarded," argues that since there is no "principled defense of the humane treatment of the retarded that all rational agents would recognize as correct or conceptually compelling," the best approach is to recognize their species membership. "I confess I still do not see *what* could possibly provide a stronger foundation for humanizing disputes about the retarded." He believes that "blurring the distinction between the retarded and non-human animals is a conceptual disaster."[54] But is Margolis right? If one believes, as Singer and McMahan do, that we must use criteria like cognitive capacities to draw our moral lines, then "blurring the distinction" is not simply a conceptual move but points to a more fundamental position regarding moral status. Thus their argument is that to *maintain* the human/non-human distinction as relevant to defining the moral status of the severely intellectually disabled is to perpetuate a form of speciesism. Regardless of one's position on the moral status of the severely intellectually disabled (e.g., whether they are considered persons or not, whether they are placed on a par with non-human animals who have a similar cognitive abilities or not), I maintain that there may be other reasons to preserve the distinction.

One of the conceptual moves in arguing against speciesism, as we have seen, is to juxtapose the mistreatment of non-human animals and the severely intellectually disabled as a way to challenge our assumptions that the former is somehow more justifiable than the latter.[55] If one analyzes the treatment of animals, there is no doubt that they are oppressed in certain ways. They suffer tremendous violence (as Singer chillingly documents) and exploitation (e.g., they are experimented on to benefit human beings). Singer would argue that they have been unduly marginalized within philosophical discourse insofar as they have been excluded or thought to be morally unimportant. Yet there are important differences between the case of abuses to non-human animals and the forms of conceptual and concrete oppression experienced by persons with intellectual disabilities. In asserting this I do not mean to suggest that one is *worse* or *less serious* than the other; rather, I think that if one is interested in seriously responding to the abuse and oppression of *either* group, there are good reasons to address them separately. With respect to the severely intellectually disabled, I will argue that their membership in a *human* social group is both morally relevant and crucial to recognize in theorizing the oppression of even the most severely disabled individuals.

Young discusses social group membership in terms of the Heideggerian notion of *thrownness:* "one finds oneself as a member of a group, which one experiences as always already having been. For our identities are defined in relation to how others identify us, and they do so in terms of groups which are always already associated with specific attributes, stereotypes, and norms."[56] Insofar as persons with intellectual disabilities are members of a distinct social group in relation to other social groups, they experience concrete consequences from this group membership.[57] Sadly, for many labeled "intellectually disabled," these have amounted to concrete forms of violence, abuse and stigmatization and neglect, as well as conceptual marginalization and exploitation. And it may be important to view these as distinctly *human* forms of oppression.

First, the oppression that Young discusses happens to individuals as members of social groups. Recall her definition of a social group as "a collective of *persons* differentiated from at least one other group by cultural forms, practices, or way of life."[58] One important feature of a social group is the notion of self-identity; Young explains that group membership is partially responsible for constituting individual identities: "A social group is defined not primarily by a set of shared attributes, but by a sense of identity. . . . Though sometimes objective attributes are a necessary condition for classifying oneself or others as belonging to a certain social group, it is identification with a certain social status, the common history that social status produces, and self-identification that define the group as a group."[59] The intellectually disabled have been classified and assigned a particular status within society, though their treatment has clearly not been uniform (as I have shown, institutional life was very different for the less disabled caregivers and the severe custodial cases). This issue of self-identification applies to persons with intellectual disabilities, as evidenced by the growing self-advocacy movement; however, this feature of group membership is arguably more complex for the severely disabled, insofar as their sense of identity is in question. Even if one believes that some members of that group are incapable of self-identification, it is arguable that they still suffer forms of oppression by virtue of their membership in that group.[60] Furthermore, the simplistic and prototypical representations of the intellectually disabled can negatively affect the identities and treatment of those who *do* identify themselves with that group.

Another important feature of group membership is that identities are in part shaped and constituted by virtue of belonging to a particular group. Here I have in mind what Ian Hacking calls "looping effects": the nature of the classification itself can be altered and shaped by the responses of individuals to their classification.[61] Similarly, Young stresses that, though we are "thrown" into preexisting social groups, "it does not follow from the thrownness of group affinity that one cannot define the meaning of group identity for oneself; those who identify with a group can redefine the meaning and norms of group identity."[62] This highlights one difference between human beings as members of social groups and non-human animals, and points to another reason to take seriously the fact that individuals with intellectual disabilities are indeed part of these human groups.

But why is it important to recognize a distinctly *human* social group? Clearly animals exhibit forms of social behavior and group identification, and I do not mean to suggest otherwise. However, I do think that there is an important sense in which human beings should be treated *as human,* in view of their membership in the human community.[63] This is an idea that is obscured by the conflation of the severely intellectually disabled with non-human animals in discussions of what kind of treatment may be justified. As we have seen, non-human animals and the severely intellectually disabled are often compared when discussing the justification and effects of a particular practice. However, examples such as experimentation and killing (which are usually chosen because they directly affect animals) do not highlight the important differences between the intellectually disabled and non-human animals; rather, they reinforce the perception that, in severe cases, the only arbitrary difference between the two groups is species membership. Consider the title of Jeffrey Murphy's article: "Do the Mentally Retarded Have a Right Not to Be Eaten?" He says that his title is not meant to offend, but "to raise the issue of rights for the retarded in its hardest context—namely, do they really differ in any significant way from those animals which we feel free to kill and eat? Too much well-meaning sentimentality is allowed to pass for thought in the discussion of the retarded, and I want to shock my way through this."[64] Other philosophers choose similarly extreme examples. Frank De Roose says, "It is certainly no more than reasonable to require from moral theories that they explain to us why, to give a very crude example, it would be morally repugnant to put mentally-retarded children in front of a bulldozer in order to crush them."[65] The history of intellectual disability is replete with instances of horrific and repugnant treatment; however, it is telling that philosophers formulate their own extreme examples. If one relies solely on these admittedly crude and shocking examples, or practices such as killing and experimentation in the context of the treatment of animals, it is not surprising that philosophers can find little difference between animals and the "severely intellectually disabled." Murphy, for instance, concludes that he is equally morally repulsed by the thought of killing and eating a severely mentally retarded child and Koko the gorilla.[66] However, if we choose a different practice, of which our past offers us plenty, it becomes clearer why the case of non-human animals and the severely intellectually disabled are different in ways beyond their species membership. Consider an alternative example.

Imagine placing a group of beings in a building and keeping them there, unclothed, without a bed, furniture, or toys, forcing them to defecate on the concrete floor, depriving them of any human contact, and only occasionally letting them outside. Is the injustice of doing this to an animal (say a pig or a dog, to use Singer's examples) on a par with treating children with severe intellectual disabilities this way? I think most of us would say no. This is not to say that there are not forms of harm and treatment that are or would be equally deplorable for animals. The point of this example is to illustrate that, when we consider other practices (which in this case are historically accurate) we see that the difference between a dog and a severely intellectually disabled child is not an arbitrary line drawn between species.[67] We are not outraged at keeping animals unclothed, depriving them of bathrooms, or depriving them of loving human contact. When we recognize persons with intellectual disabilities as members of our social, *human* world who are directly and indirectly affected by our institutional practices, and recognize that the treatment (e.g., institutionalization) of certain individuals is often justified by extension to other members of that same social group, the difficulty of distinguishing between non-human animals and the most severe cases of intellectual disability in human beings disappears.[68] By discussing only the severe cases, generalizing about their condition (to the point that they are stripped of all actual and potential human capacities), and choosing examples that do not reflect their actual historical treatment (e.g., eating them), it is easy to divorce persons labeled intellectually disabled from our concrete human world. Their ostracism in the abstract world of philosophy is difficult to reconcile with the fact that persons with intellectual disabilities are members of families, communities, and a social group with a distinct history.

At this point, one could argue that the critique of speciesism in no way suggests that we cannot speak to *particular* forms of treatment as they affect a specific group, and that there is nothing in challenging speciesism that *precludes* one from engaging in an analysis of oppression or the treatment of certain individuals in a way that attends to their membership in a particular group. In fact, McMahan recognizes that there may be reasons to address the oppression of the severely retarded as distinct from the abuse of non-human animals. However, the way he goes about making his case only serves to further dehumanize and marginalize the severely intellectually disabled and, once again, relies on an unnecessary and problematic analogy with non-human animals.

McMahan recognizes that "each severely retarded human being is someone's child."[69] Because of this, he goes on to say, "we [presumably those of us with no connection to them] have indirect or oblique moral reasons to be specially solicitous about the well-being of the severely retarded that we do not have in the case of comparably endowed animals."[70] Though being *human* alone fails to confer any moral status on the most severely disabled, being in a special relation to a *person* does. Even when the fact that the intellectually disabled *are* in some relation to others is recognized, however, the face of the beast does not disappear. McMahan argues that the relationship that the severely intellectually disabled have with family members may be morally significant (i.e., indirectly according the disabled individual some moral standing). In imagining the nature of this relationship, however, he draws a comparison between the severely intellectually disabled and pets. Though he recognizes that this move is potentially offensive, in the end he cannot help but see some value in drawing the parallel:

> Just as it is only respect for other people that forbids us to treat a person's pet in ways that it would be permissible to treat wild animals, so it is mainly this same consideration that forbids us to treat a severely retarded human being in ways in which it would be permissible to treat a comparably endowed animal. But people who are specially related to severely retarded human beings would surely be right to be offended by the suggestion that the individual to whom they are specially related has the status of a pet. This, however, is to misunderstand the claim that I have made. I have not suggested that the severely retarded are *like pets*. I have claimed only that they have an enhanced moral standing—or merit a wider array of protections—by virtue of their being specially related to certain people. In this respect there is a *parallel between the situation* of the severely retarded and that of pets.[71]

This formulation raises a number of questions. First, given the fact that McMahan rejects "bare species membership" as being morally relevant, and assuming that one's pet, according to his own definitions, shared the same cognitive capacities as one's severely disabled child, in what meaningful sense can he argue that the disabled child is *not* like a pet? I assume the answer would have something to do with the differences in the relationship between a parent and child and a pet and its owner; however, how can this difference be articulated without viewing the fact that the severely intellectually disabled are *human* (since according to McMahan's own definition, many of them would not qualify as *persons*)?

Moreover, if one accepts McMahan's claim that the moral standing of the severely retarded non-person is "enhanced" simply by virtue of its relation to another being who *does* have some intrinsic moral status, what does one make of the fact that many of the children at Willowbrook and the countless other institutions dating back to the mid-nineteenth century had been abandoned, and had no such family members or advocates with their well-being in mind? McMahan acknowledges that there may be such cases (though he claims they are rare), and that these may be equally morally troubling. However, once again, they are problematic *only insofar as there may be someone else* for whom these practices are distasteful: "There are, of course, rare cases in which a severely retarded human infant is an orphan, with no one who is specially related to it. It might still be appropriate not to treat it in ways in which it would be permissible to treat a comparably endowed animal, if to do so would be distressing to other people who feel an affinity for the human child that they do not feel for an animal. This is an appeal to a contingent side effect, but it cannot be dismissed as utterly irrelevant."[72] It seems, then, that the dehumanization of children with severe intellectual disabilities (who qualify based on McMahan's definition of these most severe cases) is objectionable only if this practice is "distressing to other people" who somehow feel an affinity for this child. This seems to point to a far deeper question that such theories fail to answer, and that gets at the heart of the problem of viewing the severely intellectually disabled as part of a shared community: What is the nature of this "affinity" and what is it that *allows* or *obscures* us from feeling it?

Some have argued, persuasively I think, that this affinity can be articulated in terms of an affinity between *fellow human beings.* This is a more robust conception of the human than mere species membership, however. Peter Byrne writes, "The concept of human being introduces a way of seeing others which then makes a range of attitudes and responses appropriate. 'Human being' means more than 'member of a certain species'. . . . To deprive us of the concept of human being in reflecting on the cognitively disabled is to banish the memory of the ways we can view and respond to them as fellow human beings."[73] Eva Kittay echoes this when she writes of her daughter Sesha that with "each embrace, I know her humanity."[74]

But isn't an appeal to seeing this *human* face speciesist? I maintain that it need not be.[75] Recall that speciesism is rooted in an *arbitrary privileging* of species membership. However, in keeping the notion of being human at play in our discussion of intellectual disability, it is neither arbitrary nor must it imply *preferential* treatment of human beings over animals. If we move beyond the most basic conception of species membership (biologically defined) to a broader conception of what it means to be a fellow human being, it no longer becomes difficult to see morally relevant differences between non-human animals and the severely intellectually disabled, and the idea of being human no longer seems arbitrary. This case has been made in a number of ways. For example, Loretta Kopelman speaks to this in her discussion of respect and persons labeled mentally retarded: "I will defend the view that *all humans merit some respect* as fellow beings."[76] She goes on to explain that the profoundly retarded are owed respect as our *fellow beings* because they possess three features: sentience, their treatment by us affects our institutions, and they are members of families and communities.[77]

Cora Diamond argues that challenging the connections between non-human animals and the disabled does not entail a speciesist position, and that it is possible to assert the "importance of being human" without diminishing the moral status of animals.[78] Diamond states, "I have tried to argue that in live moral thought there may be a sense of human life, and that that sense of human life may be expressed in what we understand by a human fate, and in how we see the connectedness of human lives. To treat the notion of *human beings* as important in moral thought, as I have, is not to treat animals as outside the boundaries of moral concern, because it is not any kind of attempt to determine the limits of moral concern. A human being is someone who has a human life to lead, as do I, someone whose fate is a human fate, as is mine."[79] It is evident from this passage that Diamond does not see this as a speciesist position, insofar as she is not arguing *against* extending moral consideration to non-human animals. I too would argue that recognizing the humanity in a *human being* and identifying injustices in the failure to do so need not make one guilty of speciesism—the *arbitrary* preference of the interests of one's own species.

But in what is the source of this identification of another's human fate to be found? Diamond says that it is grounded in our imaginative capacity: "They [the severely retarded] are seen with us in being human, where that is understood not in a biological sense, but imaginatively."[80] To further clarify how the recognition of a shared *human fate* can enter into the realm of moral concern, Diamond offers the example of moral outrage one might feel at the ridicule or violence against a human being who may not possess the capacities that certain moral theories might deem necessary for personhood: "In that outrage there may be our imaginative sense of what it is to be human."[81] This sense of outrage has been at the root of the many significant movements to reform our treatment of persons with intellectual disabilities, an outrage at the injustices against *human* beings, an outrage at treating them as *less than human*. Diamond argues that it is this solidarity and outrage that may be lost in a kind of moral discourse that takes the notion *human being* to be irrelevant, an approach that teaches that "we may dispute which human traits have moral relevance, but shared humanity . . . merely *being human* is nothing."[82] This approach, she argues, can lead to a kind of alienation that I think is evident in certain forms of philosophical discourse about intellectual disability.

I maintain that to ignore the fact that the severely intellectually disabled are *human* beings or to claim that it is morally irrelevant cannot but impoverish our discussions of them. As the examples of distinctly dehumanizing forms of violence, neglect, and abuse reveal, there may be important ways in which human beings are capable of experiencing a *particular* kind of oppression that may be obscured and even perpetuated when we make facile analogies with the mistreatment of non-human animals or literally *de-human*ize them in philosophical discourse.

That said, there may be important ways in which the critique of speciesism can be instructive in the context of intellectual disability. Singer makes the point that we value certain characteristics in human beings and have *failed to recognize that·some non-human animals possess them too,* and for this reason, we should refrain from killing and experimenting on them. Yet if we move beyond a view in which the interests of persons with intellectual disabilities and animals are viewed as in conflict, it seems we can simultaneously recognize and valorize certain features of both groups by accurately representing them. This is precisely what I have tried to do in pointing to some of the problematic conceptual and definitional assumptions that underlie philosophical discussions of intellectual disability. In assuming that the severely intellectually disabled lack *all* potential for capacities deemed essential to personhood, this static view of intellectual disability denies any possibility of change or development. This is in stark contrast to the broad range of dynamic theoretical models discussed and debated in most other disciplines that address intellectual disability (and the 2002 AAMR definition) which recognize the condition as both mutable and influenced by the individual's interaction with his or her environment. Moreover, assuming a sharp dichotomy between bare species membership and full personhood suggests that we can easily divide individuals into those with potential and/or actual capacities that make us persons, and those who possess neither potential nor actual features. Rather, if we view this as a continuum of potentialities and abilities, and broaden the range of features that are relevant to a meaningful moral discussion about the intellectually disabled (e.g., membership or thrownness in an already existing social group, member of a familial and social community), it becomes clear that we (the non-intellectually disabled and those with mild or moderate intellectual disabilities) share more with the severely intellectually disabled than just our biological label.[83] This recognition neither necessitates nor is helped by a discussion of non-human animals, nor does it imply anything about animals' moral status, capacities, or treatment.

My purpose here was to begin to outline the way in which arguments against speciesism rely on ableist assumptions and arguments. This is not a new phenomenon. For example, racism has often informed arguments against sexism, and many women with disabilities have pointed to the ways that mainstream feminism has perpetuated certain forms of ableism.[84] In addressing the objection that he is simply privileging animals over humans, Singer himself points to the close relationship between movements against speciesism, racism, and sexism:

> It is often said, as a kind of corollary of the idea that "humans come first" that people in the animal welfare movement care more about animals than they do about human beings. No doubt this is true of some people. Historically, though, the leaders of the animal welfare movement have cared far more about human beings than have other humans who cared nothing for animals. Indeed, the overlap between leaders of movements against the oppression of blacks and women, and leaders of movements against cruelty to animals, is extensive.[85]

If we acknowledge that the distinct forms of oppression and discrimination experienced by both non-human animals and the intellectually disabled can be recognized without perpetuating them in the process, what might it mean, then, to forge an alliance between the disability rights and animal rights movements? Are there new ways in which we can envision a rapprochement, a way to argue against multiple forms of oppression wherein the intellectually disabled do not become our philosophical pets? Might there still be a place for the face of the beast in discussions of intellectual disability?

Reasserting Animality?

The preceding analysis of the ways that non-human animals and the intellectually disabled have been juxtaposed in philosophical literature is by no means exhaustive. Yet while these few examples do not represent the only ways that these associations can be made, I think they reveal a number of features of what I have called a "traditional approach" to intellectual disability: it is viewed as a static, unproblematic kind; it is discussed without reference to the history of the classification; and in its most severe forms, it must be considered at the margins of, or beyond, what we consider to be a "normal" human existence. Hence the ease and frequency with which we find the face of the beast masking any morally significant human face in these prototypical extreme cases.

There is a very different appeal to animality that has emerged recently in connection with intellectual disability, one that can be viewed as leading to the opposite conclusion: it is in recognizing certain animal features in the disabled individual that we are able to view them (and ourselves) as most clearly human. In his book *Dependent Rational Animals,* for example, Alisdair MacIntyre argues that in addition to the virtues of independence, we must acknowledge "the virtues of acknowledged dependence."[86] For MacIntyre, it is precisely in recognizing that "we never completely transcend our animality"[87] that we might more fully realize an ethical relationship toward individuals with intellectual disabilities and broaden our conception of human flourishing.[88] Thus it is in our dependence and vulnerability that we recognize that we are *human* animals, and insofar as all human beings experience these conditions (to a greater and lesser extent), there is an important way in which the line between able-bodied and disabled begins to disappear.

The notion that "reasserting our animality" can both serve to critique certain problematic conceptions of disability and offer a liberatory philosophy in which to attend to the moral status and respect owed to persons with intellectual disabilities is powerful. It resonates with Eva Kittay's work, which argues for a more robust conception of care (fashioned on the principle that we are all dependent, that all human beings are in need of care) in connection with disability.[89] And it suggests that one can attend to the forms of oppression and marginalization experienced by persons with disabilities without lapsing into a kind of speciesism. Rather, as MacIntyre defines his project, it is an attempt "to generally undermine the cultural influence of a picture of human nature according to which we are animals and in addition something else."[90] In one sense, then, when compared to the previous ways in which the link is made between the intellectually disabled and non-human animals, we see here an *inclusive* rather than an *exclusionary* approach: far from the margins, the individual with severe intellectual disabilities represents what is most centrally human: vulnerability, dependence, and our animal nature.

These new directions speak to the possibility of theorizing disability and animality together, and there are intriguing new approaches within phenomenological and ecofeminist work on animality that open up other horizons.[91] However, there may be reasons to proceed with caution and adopt both a retrospective and a prospective approach so that neither the history of this group's associations with non-human animals nor the potential consequences of these theoretical moves are ignored. With respect to the former, Foucault's work can provide a rich starting point.[92]

Beyond mapping historical resonances between the animal-madman and the animal-idiot, how might Foucault's work on the relationship between the human and non-human animal be relevant in responding to these contemporary philosophical examples? When considered from a Foucauldian perspective, the associations between the intellectually disabled and non-human animals should, at the very least, give us pause.

First, Foucault's work on madness emphasizes the historical and epistemological importance of tracing the roots of our present classifications, and the necessity of viewing them as contingent incarnations rather than as atemporal, ahistorical, self-evident categories. The "severely retarded" and the "madman" are not unproblematic human kinds about which certain ethical and political questions can be posed. Foucault's efforts to trace "the archaeology of the silence" that resulted in the split between Reason and Unreason prompts philosophers interested in intellectual disability to consider the silences and dichotomies that underlie contemporary definitions and perceptions of intellectual disability. Foucault's work also leads us to consider the possible continuities and discontinuities between the historical and contemporary discourses that bring certain human others and non-human animals into close proximity.

This question of continuity raises the possibility that the persistence of such associations may perpetuate the dehumanization of people with intellectual disabilities. Though Foucault famously resists being prescriptive in his texts and rarely provides his readers with any explicit normative claims, I read his texts as sites of resistance in themselves and thus view his *History of Madness* as a polemic against the effects and justifications of dehumanization.

In drawing out the complexity and dynamism of the connection between the human and non-human, exposing the "savagery" that accompanied the treatment of the madman through the Classical period, and calling into question the "truth" about the liberatory intentions of the new methods employed in the asylums, Foucault reveals the complex processes by which a *human other becomes animal.* His work, then, leaves us to consider whether philosophical discourse is able to maintain a gap between the intellectually disabled and the non-human animal that is wide enough to ward against further forms of dehumanization.[93]

This takes us back to Spicker's concern, that the appeal to animals in discussions of the intellectually disabled may in fact change the way we treat these individuals. Though I do not have any direct evidence to support the fact that such discussions and examples might lead one to think differently and act accordingly, there is certainly historical precedent (for many different groups) that to view another human being as an animal is precisely the basis on which the most horrific atrocities are justified. Wolf Wolfensberger examines the subhuman, animal-like status that persons with mental retardation have historically been accorded, and explains that believing the retarded were insensitive to heat and cold justified their being denied heat in their cells in the winter. Of the use of the electric cattle prod on the severely retarded, he says, "One can still ask the question why such stimuli are not administered in a fashion which strips the symbolism of animal-handling and particularly of 'dumb cattle.'"[94]

In a contemporary context, we must ask to what extent the justification for killing the severely intellectually disabled relies, explicitly or implicitly, on the same logic of animality. In critically responding to one such example, Byrne writes, "Seeing the cognitively disabled as fellow human beings will remind us, for example, that like the rest of us they were born of human parents. And that fact will in turn bring to our attention that, as human beings rather than cattle on the farm, they were given names not numbers. Their having a name is bound up with the fact that a Down's baby or an autistic three-year-old is still someone. They are still members of the human community."[95]

Critically examining the differences between an inclusive philosophy of animality and disability that preserves the *human* face of intellectual disability (such as MacIntyre's) and arguments that rely on animal analogies to exclude certain severely disabled individuals from the moral or human community is a worthy project. Rather than asking to what extent is it *useful* or *necessary* to draw connections between non-human animals and the intellectually disabled, it may be more fruitful to consider what effect these philosophical moves have on our conception of the human community, disability, and our definition of ourselves as human animals. Why is it that certain human faces call forth the face of the beast more readily than others? Can we speak broadly of a "reassertion of animality" without attending to whose animality has or has not been emphasized or exploited? Without considering the fact that for some, it may be their humanity rather than their animality that needs to be (re)asserted? In the opening to *Madness and Civilization,* Foucault says, "We have yet to write the history of that other form of madness, by which men, in an act of sovereign reason, confine their neighbors, and communicate and recognize each other through the merciless language of non-madness."[96] This leaves us with a final question: May there be other forms of animality or madness that explain why the face of the beast masks the human face of certain others? If we return to Rivera's harrowing images of Willowbrook, it may be wise to keep this Foucauldian question in mind, even as we assert and celebrate our human animality.

6

The Face of Suffering

I will begin by focusing on a modern paradox: Even in the best settings and with the best physicians, it is not uncommon for suffering to occur not only during the course of a disease but also as a result of its treatment. . . . How could it be otherwise, when medicine has concerned itself so little with the nature and causes of suffering? This lack is not a failure of good intentions. None are more concerned about pain or loss of function than physicians. Instead, it is a failure of knowledge and understanding.

—ERIC CASSEL

The means by which attention is brought to suffering may prolong or deepen rather than alleviate it.

—ELIZABETH SPELMAN

The relationship between disability and suffering is one of neither necessity nor sufficiency.

—STEVEN EDWARDS

Given some of the arguments in the preceding chapter, one might wonder to what extent the question of the suffering of persons with intellectual disabilities has been given philosophical attention, as many of these concerns seem to be overshadowed by or subordinated to the suffering of non-human animals. The history of intellectual disability is replete with examples of suffering, many revealed in the horrific conditions exposed through repeated calls for institutional reform. Though one rarely finds references to this history (or contemporary instances of abuse and violence, for that matter), discussions of suffering *do* figure prominently in bioethical and philosophical discourse about intellectual disability. Like the face of the beast, however, the face of suffering functions in complex ways to create and organize this discourse about intellectual disability, to characterize certain forms of intellectual disability, and to perpetuate assumptions and widely held beliefs about the kind of life one must inevitably live with an intellectual disability. Thus it is important to identify and unmask the various faces of suffering so that we can better understand the nature and significance of suffering in philosophical discourse, identify its theoretical and extra-theoretical functions, and make room for other faces to appear.

Just as connections between animality and disability have persisted, the face of suffering has long been associated with disability. A primary objective of many disability rights activists and theorists has been to challenge the conflation made by the non-disabled world between having a disability and suffering. As noted earlier, the disability rights movement has worked to shift from the medical model of disability to the social model. Whereas the former defines disability as a feature of an individual, an unfortunate pathological abnormality in the person, the social model defines disability as an interaction between individuals and their environment. Thus the distinction is made between an impairment (any biological, physiological, or psychological pathology) and a disability, which is the result of having such an impairment. In addition to challenging the definition of disability, the social model calls into question the assumption so often made by non-disabled persons that people with disabilities, by virtue of their impairments, *necessarily* suffer. This has been challenged on multiple fronts, and what has come to be known as the personal tragedy model of disability has been refuted by many who insist that their condition per se is not the cause of their suffering. This is not to deny that some impairments cause pain (physical or psychological); rather, it points to the fact that many persons with disabilities and parents of those with intellectual disabilities claim that the more significant cause of their suffering is living in a society with discriminatory views about disability, a society that presents concrete barriers to leading fulfilling disabled lives.

This critique of the conflation of suffering with having a disability targets three dimensions of suffering: the cause, the inevitability, and the degree of suffering. It challenges the assumption that the *cause* of the suffering that disabled persons experience resides in their condition and not external factors, it refutes the claim that one will *inevitability* suffer simply by virtue of having a disability, and it challenges misrepresentations of the *degree* of suffering experienced by persons with disabilities because of their impairments.[1] In the context of these critiques I will consider a series of distinct issues that arise when the question of suffering is considered in relation to intellectual disability specifically. In light of the complex features of a category like "mental retardation" (e.g., its internal and external heterogeneity, prototype effects) it will become clear that the claim "all intellectually disabled persons will inevitably suffer" is simply untenable, unless it is intended only insofar as all human beings suffer. The differences between mild and severe cases, social and economic circumstances, physical and/or mental illnesses that may affect some but not others point to the difficulties in making generalizations in this regard. Yet like the face of the beast in discussions about non-human animals and intellectual disability, the mask of suffering often obscures the realities and specificities of these cases and can render them insignificant or invisible. As Elizabeth Spelman observes in her book *Fruits of Sorrow,* "The means by which attention is brought to suffering may prolong or deepen rather than alleviate it."[2] Taking this insight as a starting point, I will problematize how philosophical attention is paid to suffering in relation to intellectual disability. As common as the associations are between non-human animals and persons with intellectual disabilities, discussions of intellectual disability rooted in the problem of suffering are even more pervasive. I do not intend to suggest that suffering is not relevant to a discussion of intellectual disability; rather, I hope to trace certain patterns of thought that are potentially problematic, and at the same time reveal new avenues of inquiry that may both alleviate some forms of suffering and change the philosophical face of intellectual disability.

Prenatal and Philosophical Prototypes

Whereas intellectual disability and its various subcategories used to be relatively obscure in philosophical literature, the growing literature in bioethics and the increasingly complicated debates surrounding reproductive technologies and genetic advances have cleared a new place for discussions of intellectual disability. Of course these discussions address disability more broadly, but because so many of the conditions for which techniques like prenatal genetic testing and selective abortion are offered and defended on moral grounds are cases of *intellectual* disability, it merits its own discussion. The association between suffering and intellectual disability is frequently found in bioethical discussions surrounding decisions to reproduce, genetic prenatal testing, and selective abortion. One of the central arguments put forth in defense of these practices is preventing the life of a child who will suffer because of disability. These arguments vary with respect to the particulars of the conditions, the force of the moral argument (e.g., ranging from claims that these techniques are morally permissible to claiming that there is a moral obligation to use them), and the context in which they are made. Yet they share a commitment to the alleviation of suffering and, in doing so, reveal certain underlying assumptions about intellectual disability that require critical consideration. As Deborah Kaplan writes, the primary reason that disabled lives are judged to be not worth living rests on the notion of suffering: "The most appealing and satisfying reason for permitting abortions based on genetic characteristics is altruism. We believe we are saving potential future children from pain and harm. Perhaps it is this justification that is most troublesome to disability rights activists."[3] I will not argue for or against these practices and the arguments that justify them; rather, I intend to point to certain ways that the face of suffering dominates discussions of intellectual disability.

In reexamining the history of intellectual disability, I found that certain kinds and techniques have emerged simultaneously. For example, the use of IQ testing allowed the "moron" to emerge as the prototypical case of feeblemindedness in the early twentieth century. If we turn to contemporary practices concerning intellectual disability, it becomes clear that the advances in genetics and prenatal testing have effected a similar shift in the kinds of knowledge that can be produced about intellectual disability. These new techniques of observation and testing and the knowledge they generate have led to the creation of a new kind of prototypical case of intellectual disability: the prenatal prototype. As we shall see, the creation of this prototype involved a series of assumptions regarding the cause, inevitability, and degree of suffering.

A number of factors contribute to the creation of prenatal prototypes, and the prototype effect is strengthened by its presence in multiple discourses. Thus, while the purpose of this chapter is to unmask the face of suffering in *philosophical* discussions, it is important to recognize the ways in which the face of suffering is supported, fueled, and perpetuated by the intersection of bioethics with genetic, medical, social, and clinical discourses. Bruce Jennings recognizes this in his discussion of what he has termed the "genetic imaginary": "Genetic tests provide a highly charged and theory-laden form of knowledge that structures our perception of our physical bodies, our social selves, and our temporal futures in selective and distinctive ways. And this form of knowledge also structures the perception of the bodies, selves, and futures of our unborn children.... The kind of active, shaping knowledge that genetic testing provides creates a world within the human mind, a world validated by the leading intellects, scientists, and professionals of our time."[4]

Looking at the discourse surrounding prenatal genetic testing in clinical, philosophical, and social contexts, we find that the attribution of suffering is a key component in the development of these perceptions and worlds. The multiple mechanisms by which these portraits are formed are worthy of closer scrutiny because the prototypes that are generated, insofar as they obscure the depth and complexities that attend these products of the genetic imaginary, often amount to only attenuated sketches. As Jennings points out, though this imaginary creates the very possibility of conceiving of this future person, it is also inadequate: "The genetic imaginary is the basis for the possibility of conceiving the reality of the future child at all. In this sense it has more in common with the art of caricature than it does with portraiture. It is a selective focus on certain traits to capture the essence of the self."[5] What, then, allows these prototypes to be constructed, and how do assumptions regarding suffering play a role?

In order to fully understand the construction of these prototypes, it is helpful to focus on the three dimensions of suffering that many disability theorists identify in their critiques: the inevitability, degree, and cause.[6] The first assumption that is often made in discussions of the "potential" or existing disabled fetus is that it is necessarily doomed to a life of suffering; that suffering in the case of a child with an intellectual disability (e.g., fragile X or Down syndrome) is inevitable. In some cases, the very definition of disability implies suffering: John Harris defines disability as a "harmed condition," suggesting that the prospect of life with a disability is one that "any rational person" would rather avoid.[7]

While many disability theorists have challenged the conflation of disability and suffering, the prototypical case of intellectual disability functions in distinct ways. First, because the risk of Down syndrome and other conditions that involve intellectual disabilities is highlighted as a reason for women to undergo prenatal screening, there is a way in which intellectual disability (and the fears and assumptions surrounding it) occupies a central place in the construction of the prenatal prototype. Yet unlike some conditions, where the inevitability and severity of the suffering are not in question (e.g., Tay Sachs disease), the severity and thus the potential for suffering is unknown in many cases. This indeterminacy contributes to the creation of prenatal prototypes, insofar as it is often assumed that the child will inevitably suffer by virtue of the condition itself, despite the severity. For example, in the case of a condition like Down syndrome, the degree of severity cannot be ascertained. Thus to assume that the child will lead a life of suffering by virtue of this condition is erroneous, not only because there is no guarantee that children with Down syndrome will suffer any more than other children by virtue of their condition, but because it is not discernible how severe the child's disability will be.

Just as many disability theorists have challenged this conflation between disability and suffering in general, many have called into question the assumption that the intellectually disabled will *necessarily* suffer. Steven Edwards responds to what he calls the "suffering claim," namely, that "a life with a disability *inevitably* involves suffering, or harm of some significant level. 'Significant' can be taken to mean a degree of harm or suffering above that which might reasonably be expected to befall a typical healthy person during their lifetime."[8] He goes on to argue that if we consider the case of persons with intellectual disabilities, this assumption can be challenged on empirical grounds: "Several counterexamples could be found, for example, of people with moderate intellectual disabilities. It seems perfectly plausible to suppose that many such people lead lives with no more suffering than is endured by a typical non-disabled person. Moreover, it is plausible that significant numbers of moderately intellectually disabled people living in Western countries live lives with very considerable less degrees of suffering than non-disabled people in many poorer parts of the world."[9]

Considerable evidence suggests that persons with varying intellectual disabilities do not *necessarily* lead lives of profound suffering.[10] As Pekka Louhiala notes in his analysis of the moral discourse surrounding the prevention of intellectual disabilities, there may be good reason to consider this case separately: "Intellectual disability is a special case. While we can assume that many syndromes or conditions causing gross physical handicaps certainly bring about suffering, this is not so with conditions causing intellectual disabilities."[11] Supported by research on individuals with a wide range of intellectual disabilities, he concludes, like Edwards, that the conflation of intellectual disability with suffering is fundamentally flawed for a number of reasons: "Firstly, it has not been shown that the intellectually disabled in general have a considerably lower quality of life than the rest of the population. . . . Secondly, it may be that it is not meaningful to refer to the quality of life of the *whole* intellectually disabled population. Thirdly, even if a subgroup or an individual can be shown to have a markedly low quality of life, we must be careful with conclusions about causality, since the low quality may not be a necessary consequence of ID but of environmental origin."[12]

Louhiala's last point raises the question of the *cause* of suffering, which is central to the difference between the prototypical case that is often constructed and discussions of suffering from a critical disability perspective. Any claims regarding the inevitability of suffering must address the nature and source of the suffering.

Consistent with assumptions that underlie the medical model of disability, the inevitability of suffering attributed to the prenatal prototype is grounded in the assumption that the cause of suffering is the condition itself. However, proponents of the social model of disability argue that the suffering that attends disability *cannot* be assumed to be intrinsic to the condition itself. While this has been articulated more fully in relation to persons with physical disabilities, the same argument can be made for persons with intellectual disabilities. As Anita Silvers contends, "Close examination has disclosed the weaknesses of the claim that anchors the medical model—namely, the contention that because impairment is intrinsically bad, or culminates in extreme neediness or dependence that is intrinsically bad, whoever is physically, sensorily, or cognitively impaired should be indemnified for his heightened suffering. What we have learned is that, although disadvantage is tightly tied to disability, the connection does not lie in the inherent inferiority of life with a disability."[13]

The case of intellectual disability poses particular questions and challenges when one considers external causes of suffering. First, one cannot make blanket assertions regarding the social causes of suffering and disadvantage when speaking about intellectual disabilities, as the causes of suffering may be profoundly different for individuals depending on the degree of the disability and the particular environment. For example, many individuals with mild intellectual disabilities indicate that the dynamics of social exclusion, marginalization, and inability to lead a "normal life" contribute significantly to the suffering they experience.[14]

Individuals who are more severely affected may experience heightened forms of suffering. The potential for abuse, the danger of physical needs going unmet because of limited communication, and the danger of neglect are no less acute now than they were in the days of institutionalization.[15] Moreover, certain environmental factors can exacerbate the *condition itself.* From a developmental perspective, the assumption that these lives are not worth living, or that these individuals do not require certain forms of support, care, love, and attention can lead to greater intellectual disablement because the proper environment is not conducive to development and flourishing. Thus, while having an intellectual disability does not *necessarily* suggest that one will suffer (and depending on the nature of suffering, one may arguably be less likely or able to experience certain forms of psychological pain and suffering), the history of the treatment of persons with severe disabilities and their continuing marginalization in our society can contribute to a distinct form of suffering (by virtue of neglect, abuse, and oppression) that can in turn further disable the individual.

What I have outlined here is nothing new. Extensive research in multiple disciplines documents the external, social causes of suffering for persons across the spectrum of intellectual disabilities.[16] I raise these concerns in order to point out a corresponding *conceptual* or theoretical neglect of these external and environmental causes of suffering in bioethical and philosophical arguments that conflate suffering and intellectual disability. In the spirit of Spelman's and Cassel's work, we may ask to what extent the attention paid to suffering and intellectual disability in the creation of this particular prototype (i.e., the disabled child who will inevitably suffer due to the intrinsic nature of her intellectual disability) only serves to deepen the dynamics that contribute to other forms of suffering at the hands of the rest of society.[17]

Thus far we have been focusing on the suffering of the disabled individual. However, there is another face of suffering: the suffering of the family. Interestingly, the conflation of suffering and the family with an intellectually disabled child has the same form as the one we have just examined: the prototypical family will *inevitably* suffer because of the *intrinsic* nature of the disability.

Consider Jeffrey Botkin's argument that "the standard of disclosure for prenatal information should be designed to prevent harms to parents."[18] He says parents might reasonably expect significant harm in conditions that are fatal in childhood, cause chronic illness or repeated hospitalization, that will not allow the child to achieve adult independence, and those that "are of such severity that there are constant demands on the parents for time, effort, and financial resources."[19] He presents Down syndrome as the prime example of a condition that causes parents to suffer, not because their child is suffering but because of the support, time, and effort required of them.[20] Despite the fact that the severity is unknown at the time of diagnosis, 75–90 percent of persons with Down syndrome are capable of living independently of their families and are employable as adults; less than 5 percent are severely to profoundly mentally retarded.[21] Nonetheless, the prototypical future person with Down syndrome is presented as the severe case who is a drain and burden on his or her parents (echoing the personal tragedy model of disability to which many disability theorists object).

In his book *The Future of the Disabled in Liberal Society,* Hans Reinders challenges what he calls the "presumption of suffering" in relation to parental burdens and concludes that "in many instances it is not true that people suffer from being disabled, nor is it true that people necessarily suffer from being the parent of a disabled child in such a way that makes their life unbearable. If so, the conclusion stands that the decision to accept such a child is certainly not an irrational thing to do. This is especially true if the child itself will not necessarily live an unbearable life. In that case the cause of suffering does not so much reside in what nature does to these people but in how they themselves, their relatives, as well as the community in which they live are capable of responding."[22] Reinders then goes on to explore parent accounts confirming that although hardships accompany having a child with an intellectual disability, their experience with them is profoundly enriching. Because this notion is so counterintuitive to many (and clearly challenges the prototypical portrait of the burdened family), Reinders goes to great lengths to explain *how* and *why* parents can make these assertions. Steven Edwards echoes this idea as he recasts Reinders's arguments in the context of his own discussion of the justifications for prenatal genetic screening: "The presumption that the birth within a family of a child with ID jeopardizes the parents' prospects for leading a good life stems from viewing a good life solely in terms of the maximization of autonomy."[23] Ultimately the same question regarding *cause* can be posed to the family prototype: Is the cause of suffering that families experience due to the child's condition or the lack of social support they experience?

Once we unmask the face of suffering that so often accompanies discussions of intellectual disability, other important and radically different questions emerge, prompting a reevaluation of the assumptions made regarding cause, severity, and inevitability of suffering. In an effort to both critically interrogate and move beyond these prototypes, I will explore two additional avenues of philosophical inquiry into suffering and intellectual disability: one historical, the other epistemological.

Contextualizing Suffering

Intellectual disability is rarely contextualized historically in philosophical and bioethical discourse. One might ask, particularly in the context of prenatal testing and selective abortion, why the history of this group matters. I think it does for a number of reasons. First, as with the face of the beast, it allows us to trace the proximity that certain contemporary faces of intellectual disability have with older prototypes. Second, it raises questions about the gendered nature of suffering and intellectual disability. Finally, in some cases it has direct bearing on the assumptions that philosophers make in arguments about suffering and persons with intellectual disabilities.

As we have seen, the creation of prototype effects is nothing new in the history of intellectual disability, and looking back at the conceptual underpinnings of earlier cases can be useful in critiquing and resisting contemporary prenatal prototypes. One such dynamic was found in the relationship between visibility and invisibility. Recall that before intelligence tests were accepted, doctors relied on physical symptoms and other visible manifestations of "idiocy" and "feeblemindedness" to guide their diagnoses. One might say that the notion of invisible idiocy was not yet developed. Whether it was a strange outward appearance, behavioral abnormalities, speech difficulties, unresponsiveness, the inability to perform particular tasks, or animal-like qualities (the list goes on), idiocy was a visible spectacle. The IQ test inverted that visibility: it both allowed for an invisible human characteristic (some form of intelligence) to be assessed and created the ability to pick out high-grade cases of feeblemindedness that had thus far remained undetected (hence the "moron" becomes the prototypical invisible case).

We are currently experiencing another inversion of visibility. Historically, etiology has always been a riddle to be solved. Before the turn of the century, numerous etiologic explanations circulated though consensus was never reached, in part because there was never any concrete *thing* or *feature* to which doctors could point as the cause of idiocy. Hereditarian explanations dominated during the period of eugenic fervor, and pedigree charts tracing one's family history were an attempt to make feeblemindedness visible (though they relied on the recollections of the living about their no-longer-visible dead relatives). However, the *cause* of idiocy and feeblemindedness (defective germ plasm) remained invisible; etiology was inferred from symptoms, behavior, environment, and family trees.

This is no longer the case. The cause of *some* forms of mental retardation is now identifiable at the genetic level: scientists can detect particular genetic anomalies (e.g., trisomy 21, or the "fragile site" on the X chromosome). The triple screen test for Down syndrome (which includes the serum alpha-fetoprotein test usually performed to detect neural tube defects) marked "another major step in genetic screening. . . . Rarely, if ever, has such universal screening been offered and marketed for a single fetal anomaly. . . . The triple screen for Down syndrome is the first universal screening effort for a single disorder with nonlethal prognosis."[24] We now have the triple/quad screen, a test that the American College of Obstetricians and Gynecologists has argued should become a routine procedure for *all* pregnant women.[25] It is likely that as more conditions associated with mental retardation are detected, screening procedures will proliferate, and our perceptions of persons with mental retardation will change.[26] Already there has been an increase in the internal heterogeneity of this classification. Though there are many individuals labeled mentally retarded for whom no genetic etiology is determined, there are subclassifications based on genetic etiology that have become categories in their own right (e.g., Down syndrome, fragile X syndrome).[27]

In the context of prenatal prototypes, it is important to recognize that while the genotype or chromosomal anomaly is visible prenatally, its phenotypic manifestation remains invisible until the child is born or reaches later childhood (depending on the condition). Because the severity of the condition may be unknown, the decision is often based on an imagined picture of the future child, a portrait that can be based on stereotypes and uninformed assumptions rather than actual possibilities. Moreover, as we continue to find more genetic explanations for certain kinds of intellectual disabilities, their heterogeneity as a category is further increased. This suggests that if we are to give an accurate and adequately complex account of the nature and causes of suffering associated with these many conditions, it is important to resist making general statements about suffering and intellectual disability.

This point has been made in the context of genetic counseling and clinical practice. Rayna Rapp's study of women's responses to the process of prenatal screening and decisions regarding selective abortion is a marvelous illustration of how these prototypes are created and sustained by clinicians and clients alike. In addressing Down syndrome, for example, she exposes the profound effect that assumptions and fears associated with mental retardation have on the perception of the prenatal prototype: "Children with Down syndrome may be mildly, moderately, or profoundly retarded, and most fall into the middle range; they run heightened risks of heart and esophageal problems, hearing loss, and increased risk for leukemia. 'Mental retardation' provides an iconic description which blurs differences among children with Down syndrome, even as it categorizes them."[28] This dual function of mental retardation as a classification, obscuring heterogeneity while simultaneously dividing and categorizing, should be explored in a philosophical context as well, since "mental retardation" is no less iconic in the domain of ethical and bioethical arguments. Though one might argue that the concrete effects of these prenatal prototypes may be more pronounced when employed by genetic counselors and clinicians, I would submit that their presence in bioethics, as an institutionalized form of discourse, can have an equally profound impact on both the perceptions and practices surrounding the management and treatment of intellectual disability.[29]

The wealth of research, like Rapp's work, that has been done on the construction of disability in genetic discourse and practice and the voices from below, of clients, patients, and disability activists and advocates, are important resources and reality checks for philosophers who are engaged in constructing models, examples, and prenatal prototypes as they discuss and evaluate the moral dimensions of these practices. Although familiarity with the long history of conceptual divisions and complexities that accompany intellectual disability as a category is no guarantee against prototype effects, one may be less inclined to generalize and rely uncritically on available cultural and social stereotypes in imagining the "disabled child."

A second way in which a return to the past can inform our present discussions regarding suffering and intellectual disability is to reconsider the interesting and complex ways in which intellectual disability has been gendered. Three specific groups of women come to mind here: women as mothers/prospective mothers, women as gatekeepers, and women with intellectual disabilities. In what ways do these roles complicate an analysis of suffering in the context of intellectual disability?

Historically, both mothers and prospective mothers were seen as responsible for intellectual disability in a number of ways. If we look at our contemporary landscape, this has not necessarily changed. It is a widely acknowledged fact that mothers are usually the primary caregivers for children with disabilities, and there is a burgeoning conversation surrounding the gendered nature of care in the context of disability.[30] This inevitably raises the question of suffering if one interprets the disproportionate burden placed on women as caregivers as a source of suffering. Though it is beyond the scope of my analysis here, work like Eva Kittay's suggests that the concept of familial burden cannot be theorized without taking gender into account, nor can it be addressed independently of a careful and critical analysis of our conceptions of care, dependence, and independence.[31]

Similarly, when we examine the ways in which prenatal screening, selective abortion, and other reproductive technologies are placing women in the position of deciding *whether to have* a child with a disability, a very different kind of parental burden emerges in the context of suffering and intellectual disability. This is not to suggest that all women who are engaged in these practices suffer. However, work like Barbara Rothman's exploration of how women respond to the "tentative pregnancy" (that time between genetic testing and deciding whether to keep the child), as well as Rapp's examination of the broad range of emotions and responses women have had to the moral weightiness of the decisions they must make, suggest that this new gatekeeping role has a significant impact on women's lives.[32] Rapp argues that this is an enormously complex role that can offer new possibilities of challenging dominant conceptions of disability and suffering: "Ending a pregnancy to which one is already committed because of a particular diagnosed disability forces each woman to act as a moral philosopher of the limits, adjudicating the standards guarding entry into the human community for which she serves as normalizing gatekeeper. She must make conscious the fears, fantasies, and phobias she holds about mothering a disabled child. And she frequently thinks in a vacuum, lacking much social context for what a particular medical diagnosis of a disability might really imply. Thinking about selective abortion requires women to enunciate and sometimes interrogate their own stereotypes and biases."[33]

While there is now a sense in which all women who avail themselves of these technologies are gatekeepers, I cannot move on without pointing out the striking parallels between the female field-workers of the early twentieth century and the current field of genetic counseling, where 90 percent are women. Genetic counselors have a profound effect on the ways in which prenatal prototypes are constructed and thus play a powerful role in shaping perceptions of intellectual disability and suffering.[34]

There are numerous other ways in which a gendered analysis of intellectual disability, specifically with regard to claims about suffering, might be articulated. For example, in challenging the assumption that the suffering associated with intellectual disability is exclusively due to the condition itself, one can explore the many ways that women with intellectual disabilities experience gendered forms of oppression and abuse, and show how assumptions about femininity and sexuality have dictated certain forms of "treatment" for girls and women with disabilities.[35] Moreover, in the wake of compulsory sterilization during the eugenics movement and the continued debates surrounding sterilization, women with intellectual disabilities face a distinct set of stereotypes and assumptions regarding their ability to become "good mothers."[36]

Feminist bioethicists are uniquely poised to address such issues. And yet the example of Margaret Sanger should remind us that the problem of power and the danger of a certain kind of conceptual exploitation are ever-present. As we have seen, there are numerous historical examples of early feminists building cases for women's reproductive freedom and rights that explicitly employed eugenic rhetoric regarding the undesirability of "feebleminded offspring," thereby drawing a sharp line between "normal" women deserving of reproductive autonomy, and "defective" women who should not be allowed to reproduce more of their kind. Though the terms of the debate have changed, many women with disabilities have pointed to a similar dynamic in contemporary feminist discussions. In the name of preventing suffering, certain erroneous and harmful assumptions are often perpetuated regarding the nature and undesirability of having a disability. As in the case of animal rights discourse, it is important to critically consider whether such conversations are attuned to the interests of persons with intellectual disabilities, or whether the intellectually disabled merely function as a foil for the rights of non-disabled women, thereby perpetuating the oppression and marginalization of persons with disabilities.

I offer one brief example of how feminist discourse might contribute to the creation of prototypes in the context of intellectual disability. Often the "disabled fetus" functions as the morally unproblematic case when it comes to prenatal screening and selective abortion, in stark contrast to the use of sex selection based on gender preference or choosing other non-disability/disease–related features (e.g., length of limb, eye color). In their discussion of the ethics of sex selection, Dorothy Wertz and John Fletcher argue that one of the strongest reasons to oppose prenatal testing for the purposes of selecting the sex of the child is that "it undermines the major moral reason that justifies prenatal diagnosis and selective abortion—the prevention of serious and untreatable genetic disease. Gender is not a disease."[37] The assumption is that in the case of diseases that are "serious and untreatable," prenatal testing is morally justified. Yet, given that the severity of some conditions is unknown, what counts as a "serious disease," or *potentially* serious condition? Adrienne Asch points to the relative acceptability among feminists of aborting fetuses with disabilities, as opposed to the vehement objection to sex-selective abortion: "I know of no feminist who countenances abortion for sex-selection. An overwhelming number, along with at least 80 percent of the nation, condone abortion for fetal 'deformities', 'defects' or 'abnormalities'."[38] This speaks to the tendency in moral arguments about selective abortion to conflate disability with profound suffering and pain and, in doing so, to reinforce the prototypical case of the disabled fetus. As feminist bioethics takes a critical disability approach to many of these advances, the power dynamics between non-disabled women and women with intellectual disabilities witnessed in the early emergence of this category can be instructive in pointing to the many ways in which, as Spelman reminds us, the attention to certain forms of suffering can perpetuate other forms of oppression and discrimination.

As we unmask these multiple faces of suffering that have characterized persons with disabilities and the dynamics that construct and perpetuate them, new questions emerge. Rather than simply conflating disability and suffering, we can ask, How have these particular forms of attention to suffering precluded the analysis of and response to *other* causes of suffering? To what extent does emphasizing prevention, elimination, and cure of intellectual disabilities divert attention and resources away from the many ways in which persons with intellectual disabilities and their families suffer at the hands of a society that devalues them, economically disadvantages them, and subjects them to social stigma and discrimination? How will suffering be increased in promoting practices that are purportedly aimed at eliminating it? And to what extent does the tragic portrait of the inevitable life of suffering obscure other dimensions of disabled existence?

These questions lead us into a deeper epistemological tangle regarding the nature and place of suffering in human lives. How does one determine the nature and scope of another individual's suffering? This becomes particularly difficult when that individual has limited means of expression, and perhaps signals the need to move to a view of persons with intellectual disabilities *in relation* to others who are best equipped to speak about their experiences. Conversely, how might we understand the nature and significance of human flourishing for persons with intellectual disabilities, and what epistemological challenges does this line of inquiry pose? In the spirit of these questions, I would like to consider three specific epistemological problems: the problem of knowing intellectual disability, the problem of epistemic authority, and the problem of doubly negating the worth of intellectually disabled lives.

Epistemological Barriers

> The issue is not whether the women were capable of giving answers to questions about their inner lives, but that the possibility of them having an inner life was not considered at all in formal terms. . . . The pain which the women had experienced in the past was not considered in attempts to understand their current behaviour—sometimes because it was not known, but more often because of an assumption that their intellectual disability would preclude the effects of such experiences and because the women were not viewed as able to learn from them.[39]

Knowing Disability

From its inception, intellectual disability emerged as an *externally* heterogeneous classification: it has always been and continues to be defined by multiple disciplines. With advances in genetics and biotechnology, a new arena has opened in which intellectual disabilities are diagnosed, discussed, and addressed through various technological means (these will potentially grow as the possibilities of genetic enhancement and fetal surgery become more realistic both scientifically and ethically). Yet intellectual disability is also an object of psychological, psychiatric, pedagogical, and philosophical knowledge. In all of these fields questions remain regarding the definition of intellectual disability and what knowledge claims can be made about living a life with an intellectual disability and the suffering it may or may not entail. It is an interesting, almost paradoxical, feature of the prototype we have been examining—the severely intellectually disabled individual doomed to a life of suffering—that in constructing this as the obvious case where disability and suffering are conflated, knowledge about the nature and degree of suffering may be the most difficult to ascertain.

C. F. Goodey explains that this epistemological quandary arises in both the philosophical and genetic domain: "The problem of certain knowledge and the problem of ethics here cannot be disentangled from each other. In epistemological terms, the problem is: how do experts in biotechnology or indeed in bioethics or genetic counseling really know about ID [intellectual disability]? What are the foundations of their knowledge? At least they can know the physical suffering of my toothache by empathy, as something they must have experienced themselves. They have never been intellectually disabled (in the sense that they and most of us construct the term), so this is not something they can know by empathy."[40] When it comes to making knowledge claims about suffering, then, there are definite epistemological obstacles, and it is likely that they are greater for persons who cannot express themselves verbally. It may be useful to identify a spectrum of certainty here, for not all knowledge claims regarding the suffering of a person with an intellectual disability are on equal footing, as they depend on the position of the knower. For instance, parents and those close to an individual (including infants, elderly persons, and many other cases where the "sufferer" cannot express himself or herself) may be far better positioned to make this kind of knowledge claim than a clinician who has little experience with an individual. At the very least, individuals who have direct contact with persons with intellectual disabilities will have a kind of knowledge that the distanced philosopher constructing her thought experiment in order to make ethical claims about the severely intellectually disabled will not have.[41]

Goodey goes on to make an interesting point that even "knowers" of intellectual disability (individuals who have actual contact with persons with

intellectual disabilities) do not have a kind of a priori knowledge about life
with an intellectual disability; they only know intellectual disability against
the backdrop of the division between able and disabled.[42] He explains that "one
cannot claim that arm's-length knowledge of intellectually disabled people is
sufficient while having the advantage of a constant stream of empirical knowledge of the able category."[43] This has implications for knowledge claims about
intellectual disability in all these discourses and raises critical questions for
philosophers who have never had direct contact with the individuals about
whom they speak. Goodey goes on to say that while one could claim that it is
not important in a philosophical context to know persons with intellectual disabilities directly from experience, it is "not an equal contest" insofar as they are
intimately knowledgeable about the "intellectually able": "It is not and cannot
be the case that philosophers, geneticists, bioethicists or genetic counselors do
not know intellectually able people. They *do* have empirical knowledge of such
people, whether they like it or not. . . . Experts in ethics, like geneticists and
genetic counselors, have been in contact with supposedly 'able' humans every
day of their life. . . . The same is not normally true of their relationship with
intellectually disabled people who on current definitions are scarce, around 1%
of the population."[44]

A number of important points can be gleaned from these passages. First,
there is a sense in which to make claims about the intellectually disabled is
already to assume a binary between able and disabled that has a discursive
and concrete history which shapes the nature of the boundary that is drawn.
In the context of suffering this becomes evident when considering the cause
of suffering: to discuss in philosophical terms the certainty and degree of suffering a person with a severe intellectual disability will inevitably experience
by virtue of his or her condition, without any direct knowledge of the lives
about which one is speaking, is to invoke a series of assumptions that have
become entrenched but may not be justified when examining the lived realities
of these individuals more closely. From a lack of intellectual ability and/or the
fact that these individuals are a radical departure from a kind of norm (defined
as species-typical function or some kind of cognitive standard), it does not
necessarily follow that these will be lives filled with suffering, a fact to which
many parents, activists, disability theorists, and persons with intellectual disabilities have pointed.

Moreover, the emphasis on the intrinsic causes of suffering (i.e., the assumption that the condition itself will be the primary cause of suffering) can serve
to obscure more egregious, exogenous causes of suffering. Thus, while a lack of

exposure to the realities of persons with intellectual disabilities may account for some of the problematic assumptions philosophers make about the nature of the condition itself, treating the problem in a historical vacuum ignores the many forms of suffering that result from dehumanizing and oppressive practices, attitudes, and institutions. Recall Jeff McMahan's argument that the severely intellectually disabled have moral standing by virtue of the fact that they matter to another person. In the course of teasing out his argument, however, he acknowledges the possibility of "rare" instances in which these individuals do not have someone for whom they matter: "There are, of course, rare cases in which a severely retarded human infant is an orphan, with no one who is specially related to it. It might still be appropriate not to treat it in ways in which it would be permissible to treat a comparably endowed animal, if to do so would be distressing to other people who feel an affinity for the human child that they do not feel for an animal."[45] If we consider these "rare cases" in historical context, however, we find no reason to assume that they are in fact rare. Thousands of institutionalized children were left behind and abandoned by their families.[46] McMahan does add a caveat to what he views as a "contingent but important example." Even if they are orphaned, the fact that their mistreatment offends *any person's* sensibility may be enough to justify censuring it. Given that these horrific conditions and abuses spanned decades, we are still faced with the question of why so many were not sufficiently offended by such treatment. I am not convinced that McMahan's position can *necessarily* deem certain conditions and treatments as immoral for the most severely intellectually disabled, given the moral status he accords to them. More to the point, however, is the fact that these cases are treated as rare contingencies rather than a fairly common practice until recently that undoubtedly contributed to the suffering of this population.

Even when philosophers do explicitly address external causes of suffering, there are often troubling implications in their continued commitment to preventing these disabled lives. For example, Laura Purdy acknowledges the social roots of suffering for persons with disabilities though ultimately she wants to affirm that disability itself causes suffering. She argues that while arguments to improve social conditions are justifiable and urgent, "it seems to me that some of the arguments intended to further that goal can be . . . inadequate and counterproductive."[47] One reason for this claim is Purdy's belief that we are not moving fast enough to lessen the negative social consequences of disability.[48] Thus, whether they suffer from the condition itself or social obstacles, Purdy assumes that persons with disabilities will inevitably face hardships that could be ameliorated by improved social conditions for the disabled (a variant of the personal tragedy model that relies on the conflation of disability and suffering).

At least two responses can be made to this position on the current inevitability of the suffering of the disabled. First, despite Purdy's pessimism regarding how quickly the climate can and will change, the fact that certain types of suffering have exogenous (e.g., social) rather than endogenous causes means that they are by no means immutable or inevitable. Second, by maintaining that the cause of suffering is irrelevant to her position, Purdy is forced to make extreme claims with which I (and many others) would take issue. Following her analysis to its logical conclusion, she is forced to admit that even for certain females or African Americans, who "can be expected to live especially difficult lives . . . where we can be certain about [the degree and inevitability of the suffering], there is at least a prima facie case against reproduction in these cases too."[49]

Statements such as this one call into question the place of suffering in our human lives, and the extent to which we will attempt to avoid bringing into the world children who will suffer. They also raise the question that Anita Silvers poses in regard to Purdy's arguments, one which has implications for "preventative" measures such as selective abortion: "Which of these sources of possible suffering is it so pressing to nullify as to recommend as the means of doing so the prevention of the lives of possible sufferers?"[50] In attending to the problem of suffering for people with intellectual disabilities, the stakes are high in determining the causes of suffering. And as Purdy's position illustrates, it is by no means clear that even exogenous causes of suffering would prompt some to change their minds about the "tragedy" of disabled lives enough to view them as worthy of being brought into the world.

While the evaluation of another human being's suffering will always involve serious epistemological issues, the internally and externally heterogeneous nature of intellectual disability has indicated that the question of suffering for both future and existing persons with intellectual disabilities is by no means straightforward. Moreover, the construction of prenatal prototypes that rely on conflating intellectual disability and suffering masks important questions regarding alternate causes of suffering in the lives and families of persons with these disabilities. Though one might justify exclusive attention to the severe case because of the need to imagine the worst-case scenario, its predominance runs the risk of obscuring other faces of intellectual disability that are equally important to address in the context of suffering—for example, milder forms that clearly do not necessitate a life of suffering.[51] The prototypical severe case may also divert attention away from a discussion of the many complex ways in which persons with less severe forms of disability suffer at the hands of society.[52] In the case of persons with severe or profound disabilities, the problem of knowing another's suffering can be compounded when the individual is not capable of verbal expression. However, there may be other ways of knowing and attending to the suffering of these individuals. In his discussion of dementia, Bruce Jennings calls for a conception of semantic agency that recognizes modes of communication that exceed verbal discourse: "Semantic agency is the capacity for engaging in the activity of making and experiencing meaning, where meaning taps a level or circuit of communication between human beings that goes beyond unilateral sensation or sensate experience. . . . Touch, gesture, posture, eye contact, even control of body movements to prolong physical closeness like sitting together, can conceivably be media of semantic agency."[53]

A broader conception of the relationships and modes of communication between non-disabled persons and those with intellectual disabilities should figure more prominently in philosophical inquiries that purport to name the source, degree, and certainty of suffering in cases of severe intellectual disability, particularly when such designations are the basis for justifying concrete policies and actions regarding prevention, treatment, and the inclusion of these persons in our communities.

Epistemic Authority

Elizabeth Spelman points to the problem of authority in attending to the suffering of others in the following way: "Feeling for others in their suffering can simply be a way of asserting authority over them to the extent that such feeling leaves no room for them to have a view about what their suffering means, or what the most appropriate response to it is."[54] We have seen examples of the assertion of authority and the silencing of the voices of those suffering or those closest to them in philosophical discourse about intellectual disability. And in light of the epistemological tangles that the complexities of mental retardation as a category and a lived reality reveal, the role of the philosopher as "expert" in this context becomes even more problematic. Given what I have said thus far, it is clear that I think there *is* a place for such discussions in philosophy; however, the dynamics through which certain claims are acknowledged and others dismissed must be critically examined.

First, in relation to disability *generally,* it is important to recognize that the perspectives of persons with disabilities regarding their own suffering and/or well-being are often dismissed.[55] In discussions of genetic prenatal testing and selective abortion, for example, disability theorists' objection to the suffering argument is that by relying on the prevention of suffering, it is assumed that living with a disability necessarily involves suffering or is undesirable in some way.[56] This view is often perpetuated despite claims to the contrary by persons with disabilities. Purdy admits that many people do not experience their disabilities as disadvantages and do not necessarily face tremendous suffering. However, she is quick to dismiss these accounts as either limited or overly optimistic, and is ultimately "skeptical about whether the lessons learned justify the suffering they require."[57] Though there are clearly a wide range of experiences, it is imperative that these accounts be taken seriously. While Purdy charges that Asch and Saxton denigrate the value of healthy bodies, I would argue that they are simply pointing out the way in which the non-disabled place disability and suffering in stark opposition to health and happiness.[58] Anita Silvers's explanation of the able-bodied response to disability may explain Purdy's dismissal of such claims: "Our aversion to the very idea of being disabled forestalls our understanding the disabled from their perspective."[59] Moreover, the fact that arguments like Asch's and Saxton's appear to be overly positive to Purdy might be attributed to the fact that persons with disabilities are often pushed into downplaying the negative aspects of their conditions. Jenny Morris explains: "In asserting our right to exist, we have sometimes been forced into the position of maintaining that the experience of disability is totally determined by socioeconomic factors and thus deny, or play down, the personal reality of disability. It is difficult to integrate this reality in a positive way into our sense of self when the non-disabled world has nothing but negative reactions to the physical and intellectual characteristics of disability. In this way, an assertion of our worth becomes tied up with a denial of our bodies and an attempt to 'overcome' the difficulties that are part of being disabled."[60] Thus I do not accept Purdy's dismissal of accounts by persons with disabilities that challenge the equation of suffering with disability, nor do I believe that the cause of suffering is irrelevant. Furthermore, we need to further examine the historical and psychological roots of the aversion to disability and honestly assess the extent to which this informs suffering arguments.

In the case of intellectual disability, the problem of dismissing or excluding the perspectives of persons with disabilities becomes even more pronounced. In the case of those individuals who *are* capable of articulating their interests, desires, and experiences, there is the danger that they may have their perspectives discounted by virtue of their intellectual disabilities and limitations.[61]

In the context of philosophical discourse, however, these voices are all but absent, a fact that is particularly surprising given the prominent role that suffering plays in so many ethical and bioethical arguments regarding intellectual disability. Perhaps the assumption is that the rational ability necessary for a philosophical inquiry into suffering is precluded *by definition* for persons with intellectual disabilities. While this may be true in "more severe" cases (a favorite prototype in many of these discussions), it is an unwarranted assumption in cases of persons with mild or moderate intellectual disabilities. Portraits of persons with intellectual disabilities are commonly introduced through parental accounts; yet as we have seen, to the extent that these perspectives challenge the conflation of suffering and intellectual disability (e.g., by pointing to the myriad of ways in which persons with intellectual disabilities can be seen as flourishing), they are often dismissed as being overly sentimental or quaint but misguided.[62]

Double Negation of Worth

These epistemological barriers associated with efforts to determine the suffering of persons with severe intellectual disabilities lead to a troubling moral consequence: a double negation of their worth. First, the lives of severe cases are often deemed not worth living, assuming that they are doomed to a life of inevitable suffering. But we also find the opposite depiction: the severely intellectually disabled individual can also be portrayed as *incapable of human suffering* by virtue of the fact that she does not possess the same capacities as a "normal human being." In this sense, then, it is precisely because they are *incapable* of suffering (according to certain definitions of suffering) that they are not viewed as fully human or their lives are not accorded moral worth. Thus we are led to a double negation, as it becomes apparent that there are two ways in which these disabled lives are deemed "not worth living." On the one hand, persons with intellectual disabilities, by virtue of their condition, are assumed to be doomed to a life of suffering, and therefore their lives are not worth living. On the other hand, because some individuals are assumed to be so impaired that they *cannot* suffer, their lives are considered to have less value. (Interesting, the problem of suffering does not disappear entirely in these cases but rather accompanies family members, those related to persons with intellectual disabilities, and society at large. These become the new victims of tragedy and inevitable suffering in the context of persons with intellectual disabilities for whom the normal experience of human suffering is precluded.)

Yet given the opacity of the other's suffering and the epistemological challenges of fully knowing or comprehending the other's experience in the context of persons with severe intellectual disabilities, what claims regarding their inability to suffer can be made with relative certainty? While persons with significant intellectual disabilities may not experience certain dimensions of suffering that accompany more sophisticated levels of awareness and intellectual activity, there are reasons to resist making broad generalizations regarding the kind of pain or harm they are capable of experiencing. For utilitarians like McMahan, sentience is a central criterion in moral considerations. Yet in discussing the moral relevance of the degree of pain that the severely cognitively disabled are able to experience, I am again left wondering to what extent his assumptions are well founded. McMahan offers three reasons for considering the pain of animals different than the pain that full persons experience: the fact that the "activities and experiences of persons are generally more valuable than those of an animal"; the potential for and effects of "psychic scarring" are less given the animal's "shorter and simpler" life; and the fact that animals cannot anticipate pain in the way that persons can.[63] He then extends this to persons with severe intellectual disabilities: "These reasons for thinking that the pain of an animal matters slightly less than the equally intense pain of a person are also reasons for thinking that the pain of a severely retarded human being may matter less. For the lives of the severely retarded also contain less of value that is disrupted by pain, and the severely retarded are, like animals, incapable of anticipating future pain or of fretting that pain may be the harbinger of a debilitating or life-threatening illness. If we conclude that the pain of animals in general matters slightly less than the pain of persons, we must draw the same conclusion about the pain of the severely retarded, if other things are equal."[64]

Beyond the problematic normative judgments that are being made regarding what constitutes something of value in a human being's life, I am left to wonder, particularly given the communication barriers that attend many persons labeled "severely intellectually disabled," whether we can so easily assume that these forms of suffering and pain do not apply to them. McMahan goes on to argue that, of course, insofar as they have "special relations" to others, we are not justified in causing them pain. Yet though they are sentient, the fact that they are *not* capable of suffering in a particular kind of way defines them as less valuable, and once again we find them sharing the same moral dwelling place as non-human animals.

It seems, then, that the "severely intellectually disabled" are at once condemned to suffer (recall the prenatal prototypes) and condemned *not* to suffer.

At the heart of this double portrait, however, is a dense epistemological tangle that involves questions of authority, the inclusion and exclusion of certain standpoints, the opacity of the other's experience, and the elusive nature of suffering itself.

Responses to Suffering

If we return to Cassel and Spelman, the question resurfaces: How can we attend to the other's suffering in ways that will not intensify it? In a medical context, Cassel suggests that we need to increase knowledge and understanding; what might this mean in the context of intellectual disability? Here are a few possibilities that emerge from the preceding discussion. First, it seems imperative to examine the discourses of cure and prevention in relation to intellectual disability and consider the ways in which claims about suffering are woven into the fabric of this debate. Second, we might both mobilize the social model of disability with regard to the ways in which it identifies external causes of suffering (in contrast to the medical model's emphasis on intrinsic causes), and critically interrogate the extent to which it adequately captures and represents the varied situations of persons with intellectual disabilities. Third, in order to avoid perpetuating certain prototypes that mask important facets of suffering in relation to intellectual disability, it is useful to contextualize philosophical discussions of suffering, both historically and in relation to the concrete lives of persons with a wide range of intellectual disabilities. This can both ensure against repeating certain dehumanizing and oppressive practices of the past and broaden the scope and the range of voices that participate in the discussion.

Beyond problematizing the ways in which intellectual disability and suffering are conflated, there is room to confront the definitions of suffering on which these associations rely. How and why does the deprivation of experience become synonymous with intellectual disability and suffering, and should we assume that having an intellectual disability intrinsically deprives one of meaningful experiences? As Steven Edwards writes, "I suppose it may be said that a moderately intellectually disabled person misses out on those dimensions of experience which require considerable intellectual acumen, for example doing complex work in physics, math or even philosophy. But of course it may be said of those of average intelligence that they too miss out on such experiences. . . . The point is that it does not follow from the fact that one is constitutionally incapable of experiencing certain aspects of human experience that one is either suffering or in a harmed condition."[65]

Once this assumption is dislodged, there may be new ways to conceive of flourishing and meaningful existence. Hans Reinders speaks to this as he critiques the profound individualism that underlies our conceptions of meaning and suffering: "The prevalent idea in contemporary culture that creating meaning is an individual activity has serious implications for human beings to whom the notion of agency does not apply. It is this very ideal that makes their lives appear to be deficient. Where there is no agent, there must be a deficit of meaning. Where there is a deficit of meaning, it is difficult not to perceive human existence as the cause of grave suffering. If it is merely a cause of great suffering, the question of why these people are kept alive becomes hard to avoid indeed. Not only is it hard to avoid, it also appears to have a definite answer."[66] Both Edwards's and Reinders's words point to another phenomenon in the discourse about suffering: the danger (or perhaps inevitability) of projection, both in defining the nature of suffering and in making assumptions about the degree to which others suffer. Louhiala observes, "When trying to imagine what an intellectually disabled person feels, we may too easily think what *we* would feel if we suddenly developed similar mental and physical characteristics. This, of course, does not tell anything about the feelings of the actual person, who, in most cases, has had the qualities for a lifetime."[67]

In his book *Suffering Presence,* Stanley Hauerwas observes that our view of suffering and retardation inevitably bears the mark of our (the non-disabled person's) own fears and concerns. Yet beyond simply acknowledging *that* this phenomenon exists, he tries to explain *why* the retarded so commonly prompt this response: "We have no way to know what the retarded suffer as retarded. All we know is how we imagine we would feel if we were retarded. We thus often think we would rather not exist at all than to exist as one retarded. . . . For the retarded do not feel or understand their retardation as we do, or imagine we would, but rather as they do. We have no right or basis to attribute our assumed unhappiness or suffering to them. Ironically, therefore, the policy of preventing suffering is one based on a failure of imagination. Unable to see like the retarded, to hear like the retarded, we attribute to them our suffering."[68]

But if, as Hauerwas suggests, we are facing a "failure of imagination," how can we enlarge our imagination without simultaneously projecting ourselves onto the intellectually disabled?[69] What does it mean to imagine the other in a way that escapes the confines that I inevitably place around that very image? It is here that we confront our last face of intellectual disability: the face of the mirror.

Conclusion:
The Face of the Mirror

> [In dreams] Everything says "I," even the things and the animals, even the empty space, even objects distant and strange which populate the phantasmagoria.... To dream is not another way of experiencing another world, it is for the dreaming subject the radical way of experiencing its own world.
>
> —MICHEL FOUCAULT

> I think that it is incumbent upon nondisabled scholars to pay particular attention to issues of their own identity, their own privilege as nondisabled people, and the relationship of these factors to their scholarship.
>
> —SIMI LINTON

In unmasking certain philosophical faces of intellectual disability, I have explored multiple ways in which the "intellectually disabled," the "severely cognitively disabled," the "mentally retarded" have been portrayed as profoundly other. Yet there is another face that is worthy of consideration, one that takes us back to the questions that Foucault posed in defining the task of historical ontology: "How are we constituted as subjects of our own knowledge? How are we constituted as subjects who exercise or submit to power relations? How are we constituted as moral subjects of our own actions?[21] In thinking about these

The "Normal"

Questions to ask

questions, it is important for us to consider what they mean if we interpret the "we" as the non–intellectually disabled.

Chapter 6 concluded with the problem of projection: those who construct certain portraits of persons (or distinctly non-persons) with intellectual disabilities may impute fears, assumptions, and biases onto the other in the attempt to render her intelligible. In this respect, then, one might say that the intellectually disabled function as a mirror for the non-disabled. The more I think about the mirror role, however, the more complex this face becomes, for it seems to work at so many different levels in relation to intellectual disability. In her discussion of how Third World subjects have functioned as mirrors for the West, Uma Narayan says, "To be positioned as a mirror is to be put out of countenance, to lose face."[2] Though I will not explore the possibilities in depth here, I think it is important to point out a number of ways in which the intellectually disabled can lose face if they merely serve as a mirror for the non-disabled.[3]

The first two mirror roles play what might be called an ontological or existential function: they point to some dimension of my own nature, though as we shall see, they do so in slightly different ways. The first is a version of the "there but for the grace of God go I" sentiment. As MacIntyre writes, "Of the brain-damaged, of those almost incapable of movement, of the autistic, of all such we have to say: this could have been us. Their mischances could have been ours, our good fortune could have been theirs. (It is this fact about us that makes our relationships to seriously disabled human beings quite other than our relationship to seriously disabled animals of other species.)"[4] Yet this mirror can become akin to a funhouse mirror in that when I see the intellectually disabled individual, I see myself in a distorted form. This is what Hauerwas sees in Adam Smith's characterization of the non-rational other, an account that powerfully captures the sense in which I construct the other as a projection of my own fears. Hauerwas quotes Smith and then continues in his own words:

"Of all the calamities to which the condition of mortality exposes mankind, the loss of reason appears, to those who have the least spark of humanity, by far the most dreadful, and they behold that last stage of human 'wretchedness' with deeper commiseration than any other. But the poor wretch, who is in it, laughs and sings perhaps, and is altogether insensible of his own misery. The anguish which humanity feels, therefore, at the sight of such an object, cannot be the reflection of any sentiment of the sufferer. The compassion of the spectator must arise altogether from the consideration of what he himself would feel if he was reduced to the same unhappy situation, and, what, perhaps is impossible, was at the same time able to regard it with his present reason and judgment." We thus persist in our assumption that the retarded suffer from being retarded not because we are unsympathetic with them but because we are not sure how to be sympathetic with them. We fear that the very imagination which is the source of our sympathy . . . is not shared by them. To lack such an important resource, we suspect, means they are fatally flawed, for one thus lacks the ability to be the subject of sympathy.[5]

These writers, separated by more than two centuries, speak to the way that the rational, non-disabled individual imagines the "poor wretch" through the projection of the self: as one who is stripped of certain central human powers. This may account for why this human other inspires such fear, as one imagines oneself in this attenuated human form. When the intellectually disabled simply perform this mirror function, however, there is the potential for a double distortion to occur. Not only do I see myself in some disturbing, alien form, but I simultaneously run the risk of distorting the reality of the other precisely because she becomes a manifestation of my own fears as I imagine myself in this condition.

Another version of this ontological/existential mirror does not necessarily lead to this kind of distortion, but is similar in that it allows the intellectually disabled to be the occasion for one's own self-reflection. The boundaries of disability as a category are permeable, and thus there is a sense in which we are all temporarily able. The existential awareness of one's being-toward-disability (to transpose a Heideggerian turn of phrase) may provide the impetus to critically examine one's personal relationship to the possibility of disability and the meaning of disability in a broader social context. This can translate into the idea that "we are all disabled somehow," and lead to a call to abandon the us/them dichotomy that defines so many discussions of intellectual disability.

Many versions of this notion have been put forth for many different reasons. In a theological context, for example, Hauerwas calls for a recognition of all humans' fallibility and "disability" in relation to God, leading us to see in the retarded something of ourselves and our own vulnerability: "Prophetlike, the retarded only remind us of the insecurity hidden in our false sense of self-possession."[6] Robert Veatch echoes this in the opening of his book *The Foundations of Justice: Why the Retarded and the Rest of Us Have Claims to Equality*: "We are all, in some sense, handicapped. . . . By exploring the claim of the retarded we shall really be exploring our own status as human, moral agents, our own rights and obligations as members of the moral community. If all of us in the end are finite, human creatures sadly deficient in some way, mentally, physically, socially, or spiritually, then the problem of the claim of equality for the retarded is really a problem for all members of the human community. Unless we understand the moral foundations of the claims of the retarded, then, neither the retarded nor the rest of us will be treated fairly."[7]

This notion is embodied in various non-theological philosophical perspectives as well. For example, MacIntyre argues for the importance of acknowledging and valuing, rather than devaluing, our dependence, our vulnerability, our need for care. Thus we see ourselves in the individual with a disability, as we are all at certain points subject to such needs: "Those in dire need both within and outside a community generally include individuals whose extreme disablement is such that they can never be more than passive members of the community, not recognizing, not speaking or not speaking intelligibly, suffering, but not acting. I suggested earlier that for the rest of us an important thought about such individuals is 'I might have been that individual.' But that thought has to be translated into a particular kind of regard. The care that we ourselves need from others and the care that they need from us require a commitment and a regard that is not conditional upon the contingencies of injury, disease and other afflictions."[8]

In a similar vein, but from within her capabilities approach, Martha Nussbaum has argued against defining a separate list of capabilities for persons with intellectual disabilities, and in doing so, suggests that the us/them dichotomy is problematic: "Using a different list of capabilities or even a different threshold of capability as the appropriate social goal for people with impairments is practically dangerous, because it is an easy way of getting off the hook, by assuming from the start that we cannot or should not meet a goal that would be difficult and expensive to meet. . . . Such an emphasis on singleness is important not just strategically, but also normatively: for it reminds us of the respect we owe to people with mental impairments as fully equal citizens who are members of the human community and who have the ability to lead a good human life. It also reminds us of the continuity between so-called normal people and people with impairments."[9] The argument for continuity between the disabled and non-disabled does not necessarily entail the belief that we are all disabled; however, it speaks to a similar move whereby the intellectually disabled provide an instructive lesson regarding the vulnerability and limitations that all human beings face.

There may be great value in acknowledging human vulnerability and dependence, and there may be political and moral reasons not to view the intellectually disabled as qualitatively distinct kinds, as radically other. There may also be conceptual, political, and practical reasons to resist proclaiming that

[handwritten margin note at top: Problem of erasing between the line disabled + non-disabled]

we are all disabled. First, there is the danger that the other is obscured, that the intellectually disabled literally lose face, or disappear, if they are simply a means for the non-disabled to recognize their own limitations. If the motivation to examine existing forms of oppression is rooted simply in fearing or acknowledging "that may someday be me," rather than in the realities of the other's oppression, a genuine interest in the interests of persons with intellectual disabilities will be obscured by the fears and assumptions that shape the non-disabled person's reflection. Given the structural nature of oppression and the necessity for recognizing certain forms of difference to secure forms of social and economic support, harmful practical consequences may result from trying to erase these boundaries. As disability theorist and activist Simi Linton argues, "I'm not willing or interested in erasing the line between disabled and nondisabled people, as long as disabled people are devalued and discriminated against, and as long as naming the category serves to call attention to that treatment."[10]

Another feature of the mirror role, as defined by Uma Narayan, is what she terms the "big bad West" syndrome. In discussing the ways in which Western scholars express interest in Third World subjects, she explains that in some kinds of scholarship, the critical examination of colonial practice simply reflects the West's own practices back to itself rather than engage with the specific nature of oppression in these contexts: "The Third World and Third-World subjects function as Mirrors in which the West can engage endlessly in the task of returning to itself, even as it believes it is moving its gaze to an Other place."[11] Though the position of the intellectually disabled in philosophical discourse is not directly analogous here, her concern resonates with one of my own. One reason that philosophers address intellectual disability is to see how acceptable or complete our moral theories are, to answer the question, How well do our theories fare when we consider marginal cases like the intellectually disabled? This is an important question to ask. However, this critical posture is self-defeating if the face of the intellectually disabled becomes eclipsed as attention is focused solely on the theories and on the non-disabled as beneficiaries. If attention is given to marginal cases solely to examine to what extent the theory is complete but fails to attend to the specific moral problems and interests of these marginal cases, I would argue that there is a danger similar to the one Narayan sees in post-colonial scholarship: "To be a Mirror is different from being a Face that looks back at the West, with a range of expression and responsiveness that, while responses to a Western Other, are also the responses of a Subject-in-Its-Own-Right."[12] There is a profound irony in turning to the question of

[handwritten margin notes: West only sees its own inherent in helping Third World — West does not enter into What Third World needs]

intellectual disability in order to critically reevaluate our moral theories, only to distort, efface, or dismiss these individuals in the process.[13]

Another way in which the intellectually disabled can serve as a mirror for the non-disabled, then, is in a broader professional context. The history of institutionalization includes numerous examples of ways in which the feeble-minded provided the fodder for professionals to gain legitimacy and power. In the academic institution, this power can manifest itself through conceptual exploitation, where the intellectually disabled are put to philosophical work without reaping any benefits from their position. We saw this in some animal rights literature, which included the intellectually disabled in moral arguments to bolster the interests of animals. The concern with the mirror role here is twofold: the attention paid to this marginal case can either lead to a critique of the theory (akin to Narayan's big bad West syndrome) that fails to recognize the intellectually disabled subject in any meaningful sense; or the examination of intellectual disability legitimates a kind of cognitive privilege without addressing the complex moral issues and power relations that emerge in connection with this group of individuals. Goodey describes this kind of reflexivity in the context of research more generally: "The search for certainty about [intellectual disability] is conducted largely by the academic and scientific community, that is, a community seen specifically as the bearer of intellectual ability by and on behalf of the rest of society. Not only is it possible to invent and reinvent these concepts at will, the predominant will is that of a group whose self-definition constitutes a vested interest in the argument."[14]

The call to recognize ourselves (the non–intellectually disabled) in the other can be valuable. These moves can allow us to recognize that the severely intellectually disabled individual may be more than an empty shell of humanity and that we share more with them than bare species co-membership. In a broader theoretical context, there is no question that addressing the complexities of intellectual disability holds the potential to critically revisit and perhaps change our philosophical views—to recognize they may not be capacious enough, to affirm that a recognition of sameness, rather than difference, can be powerful in the face of marginalization and other forms of conceptual and concrete oppression. Thus the turn to consider how certain moral theories fare with regard to these marginal cases can be instructive, and I do not mean to cast suspicion over all such attempts. However, when the attention paid to the group serves to render the other invisible, when it does not embody a genuinely critical stance, when it protects against, rather than confronts, the epistemological barriers that intellectual disability raises by maintaining control over the image that is reflected back, the face of the intellectually disabled runs the risk of being obscured or distorted in philosophy.

Continuities and Discontinuities

The presence of the faces of authority, the beast, and suffering and the mirror in philosophical discourse can be traced back to the years when the categories of idiocy, feeblemindedness, and later mental retardation began to gain scientific legitimacy and became fixed by certain conceptual frameworks, moral ideas, institutional practices, and disciplinary claims to knowledge that were in a constant state of flux.

Mapping out the various ways that intellectual disability has been defined and discussed in a philosophical context shows that the conceptual tensions associated with the history of intellectual disability have been transposed and transformed, yet they are present all the same. The tension between viewing the intellectually disabled as both quantitatively and qualitatively different from the non-disabled is evident in the face of suffering and the face of the beast, respectively. In the case of suffering, a universal human experience, the intellectually disabled are assumed to suffer to a far greater extent by virtue of their condition, or, conversely, they are assumed to have a diminished capacity to suffer in comparison to "normal" persons. In associations drawn between non-human animals, however, we find the persistence of the view that the severely intellectually disabled are so profoundly, qualitatively different from "us" that they are understood to be in greater proximity to animals, both in terms of their capacities and their moral standing.

These assumptions, which characterize what I have called the traditional approach, have begun to give way, however, and new questions and faces have emerged. The move to reclaim our animal nature and explore it as a foundation for rethinking our relationship to disability has moved us back to the quantitative portrait, where the intellectually disabled may have certain qualities that are more pronounced or evident, for example, vulnerability, dependence, neediness. Yet these are all viewed as part of what makes us human animals. And the postmodern call to recognize disability as the paradigmatic unstable identity places disability at the center, rather than at the margins, of a conception of human subjectivity.

With respect to suffering, the social model challenges us to examine external causes of suffering that, in the case of intellectual disabilities, may be more damaging than the suffering that arises from the condition itself. This challenge calls into question the static portrayals of intellectual disability as a fixed, organic, easily definable, immutable state of being. As we have seen, new ways of defining forms of intellectual disability in the wake of genetics have recast the ways in which it is made both visible and invisible prenatally. Yet the conceptual terrain is no less complex. The philosophical and theoretical debates regarding the medical, social, and postmodern models of theorizing disability speak to the persistence of the tension between viewing it as organic and non-organic, as both static and dynamic. And as we saw in the historical overview of intellectual disability in part 1, these tensions highlight certain features of this category that also continue to define it: its internal and external heterogeneity, its instability, its ability to generate prototype effects, and its embeddedness within certain power relations.

But I have not mapped these resonances only for the sake of showing some kind of continuity between the past and present, between the concrete institutional world and the academic philosophical world. I have also attempted to make sense of what I have experienced as a profound dissonance in view of a discontinuity between past and present. Things have changed considerably in the ways that intellectual disabilities are understood and addressed: deinstitutionalization, a vibrant disability rights movement, disability studies, vast legislative reform, the AAIDD (the oldest professional institution in this country devoted to "feeblemindedness") removing the term "mental retardation" from its title, parent advocacy, self-advocacy, books co-authored by persons with Down syndrome, autism, and mental retardation. The voices and concerns of persons with intellectual disabilities are now more prominent in discussions of rights, advocacy, and access; the conceptual models that have emerged in philosophy and other disability theories capture the complex relationship between forms of oppression and exclusion, and no longer take "disability" (and intellectual disability, specifically) for granted as a natural human kind; and the growing emergence of a critical disability perspective in bioethics and the more widespread challenges posed to many new reproductive and genetic technologies by disability advocates suggest that the fate of the intellectually disabled in the genetic age is by no means sealed. Surely we have come a long way since the mid-nineteenth century, and since Oliver Wendell Holmes famously decreed in the 1927 *Buck v. Bell* case, "Three generations of imbeciles are enough!"

The dissonance, then, comes from a feeling that these profound changes are not reflected in some of the faces of intellectual disability found in philosophy.

Writing this book has been an attempt to make sense of this dissonance, to outline it, problematize it, and perhaps begin to explain the reasons behind it.

Cognitive Dissonances

> Almost as a form of emotional exercise, I have tried, on occasion, to step back and see him as others might see him, as an instance of a category, one item on the long list of human subgroups. This is a child with Down syndrome, I might say to myself. This is a child with a developmental disability. It never works: Jamie remains Jamie to me. I have even tried to imagine him as he would have been seen in other eras, other places: This is a retarded child. And even: This is a Mongoloid child. This makes for unbearable cognitive dissonance.
>
> —MICHAEL BÉRUBÉ

> We are always ready to find dignity in human beings, including those whose mental age will never exceed that of an infant, but we don't attribute dignity to dogs or cats, though they clearly operate at a more advanced mental level than human infants. Just making that comparison provokes outrage in some quarters. But why should dignity always go together with species member-ship, no matter what the characteristics of the individual may be?
>
> —PETER SINGER

The fact that some philosophers call into question the personhood and dig-nity of individuals with intellectual disabilities and routinely compare them to non-human animals can provoke surprise, bewilderment, and even outrage in non-philosophers and philosophers alike.[15] How can one explain what seems to be such an anomalous and morally problematic way of talking about intellec-tual disability by individuals who, by profession, are engaged with questions of rights, justice, and dignity?[16] In drawing these reflections to a close, I will briefly consider three dissonances within philosophical discourse that may explain why philosophers are able to pose these questions and make these associations with such ease and conviction. They can be found along the three axes that Foucault identifies as essential to historical ontology: knowledge, power, and ethics.

The first dissonance can be found in relation to epistemic authority. As we have seen, there is a dissonance between the presumed authority of the disengaged moral philosopher and the authority of persons who have intellectual disabilities and those persons who are in embodied, concrete relation to them. This authority is expressed in multiple ways: in the dismissal of "overly sentimental" attitudes toward intellectual disability; in the assumption that one who has had no contact or interpersonal relationship with a certain kind of individual may, in fact, be best qualified to make judgments about that individual's nature, capacities, and moral status; and in the many gaps between presumed knowledge about this group and actual evidence to support assertions about the nature and experience of intellectual disability. This leads to a number of questions. First, if in fact there are views about persons with intellectual disabilities that are guilty as charged (i.e., sentimental, solicitous), does this necessarily mean that they should not be a part of rational, moral discourse about intellectual disability? Susan Wendell discusses the importance of acknowledging and integrating the standpoint of persons with disabilities into philosophical discourse. And in the case of those who cannot speak for themselves, who cannot articulate their standpoint, it may be all the more important for those who inhabit their world to begin to give voice to that standpoint. In fact, failing to do so might compromise the scope, depth, and validity of our ethical inquiries.

Second, insofar as these "overly solicitous" advocates are responding to the deeply troubling associations between the mentally retarded and non-human animals, why should expressions of outrage and other charged emotions be discounted? Philosopher Cora Diamond discusses the important place of outrage in the context of the abuses of the mentally retarded, and the powerful words of women like poet Audre Lorde remind us of the essential place that anger and other "unseemly" responses to oppression and violence have in both diagnosing and responding to the problem.[17] Yet beyond the legitimate horror felt at the grave abuses to this group, outrage also has a place in response to certain forms of philosophical or conceptual dehumanization, particularly those that can accompany the associations between non-human animals and persons with intellectual disabilities. Is it not a source of greater concern to respond without outrage to the various forms of dehumanization that can accompany the associations between non-human animals and the intellectually disabled? Peter Byrne gives voice to this in response to one such analogy in an argument about vivisection, and highlights how the author's response to outrage is itself outrageous: "[Frey] begins with a list which starts with the 'very severely mentally enfeebled, the seriously brain damaged, severely handicapped newborns.' So it is clear that the mentally handicapped are the first candidates. Frey acknowledges that there may be . . . outrage caused by his proposal. His response is to appeal to the possibility that such feelings of outrage may be 'susceptible to removal by education, information and careful explanation of the arguments.' He is in effect asserting here that the negative value of outraged feelings is a product of ignorant, non-philosophically informed sentiments within the moral community. Train its members in moral philosophy well enough and the feelings will not arise."[18]

In some cases, the very process by which "legitimate" knowledge surrounding intellectual disability is produced highlights the profound distance between the knowing subject and its object. The creation and maintenance of this space, reminiscent of the gulf between Reason and Unreason uncovered by Foucault, may begin to account for the dissonance between the philosophical authority to call the personhood of certain individuals into question, and the conviction by those same individuals and those who see themselves as part of a shared community with the intellectually disabled that they are people first.

A second dissonance emerges between the commitment to justice for certain groups (e.g., non-human animals, non-disabled women) and a lack of commitment in philosophical discourse to issues of justice for persons with intellectual disabilities. Rather than attempt to quantify this imbalance in the attention devoted to each group, I point to two forms of oppression that underlie and may perpetuate this discrepancy, hence raising the question of power in connection with knowledge.

As we have seen, persons with intellectual disabilities have been marginalized in philosophical discourse in multiple ways. They are literally put aside, placed outside the boundaries of justice concerns when they are denied any form of personhood. When they are addressed, they are almost always defined as marginal cases. The same could certainly be said for non-human animals, as they are generally not defined as persons and are also presented as marginal cases in certain contexts. However, when considering how these two marginalized groups appear side by side, we see another face of oppression, what I have called conceptual exploitation. Young defines exploitation as the process by which an unequal distribution of benefits results from the transfer of energies from one group to another.[19] At the conceptual level, the severely intellectually disabled are being exploited insofar as they are utilized simply to bolster the case for better treatment for nonhuman animals. When these arguments fail to recognize the oppression of persons with intellectual disabilities or use them to challenge species membership as a basis for moral status and thereby strip them of any morally relevant qualities, they are victims of a form of conceptual exploitation. A similar effect can be seen in feminist bioethical discussions that rely on prototypical representations of intellectual disability to guarantee (non–intellectually disabled) women's reproductive rights.

Persons with intellectual disabilities in much of philosophical discourse are both marginalized and conceptually exploited, and often only appear on the philosophical stage to serve as a backdrop for concerns about justice for other groups. Though these two modes of oppression are conceptual, they may be as potentially harmful as concrete forms of oppression. At the very least they uncritically sanction the continual pairing of the mentally retarded and non-human animals, perpetuate stereotypes and prototypes, and deflect attention from the problem of justice for persons with intellectual disabilities.

When Foucault asks how we constitute ourselves as moral subjects, a broader question is implied: How do we draw the boundaries of our moral communities and determine who can be housed within them? This leads to the third dissonance—between the task of constructing conceptual communities and drawing these philosophical lines (e.g., placing non-human animals and the intellectually disabled in the same moral domain), and a lack of attention to the concrete existence of persons with intellectual disabilities in human communities. When the portraits of the intellectually disabled in moral discourse are painted in the most abstract and attenuated ways, a profound distance is implied between the impoverished lives of these "non-persons" and the rich lives that the intellectually disabled share in community with others. Recall McMahan's description of what we share with the severely intellectually disabled. He presents the situation as if, with the exception of close family members, the only thing we share with this group of fellow humans is a biological relation: "Bare co-membership in the human species, which is what we share with the cognitively impaired, does not involve personal ties, mutual sympathy, shared values, a common commitment to a certain way of life, social cooperation, or any of the other features of relations that are more readily recognizable as legitimate bases for partiality."[20]

"We" presumably refers to the cognitively able—those of "us" who have no connection to this distant group of people—while "they" would include both the severely cognitively impaired and their families or people close to them (since these individuals clearly share more with the cognitively impaired than bare species membership). Constituting the cognitively impaired as a group so radically other relies on this us/them dichotomy. And it is this conceptual distance, I want to argue, that may explain the ease with which philosophers can place persons with intellectual disabilities under the same roof as non-human animals. What is lost as a result, however, is the rich tapestry of concrete, embodied lives and relationships that can only come with the inclusion of narrative accounts and the standpoints of persons who inhabit this fully human world that remains relatively unknown to many. When Eva Kittay writes that she can't help but see her daughter in the fullness of her humanness, she is acknowledging a place for Sesha in the human community that is far more robust than "bare co-membership" in the human species.

The failure to recognize and incorporate the lived, human dimensions of these lives gives the conceptual space that non-human animals and the cognitively disabled share in moral discourse greater legitimacy. And it is here that the insistence on and celebration of narrative work and the ethical demand that intellectual disability be included in considerations of justice and moral personhood can begin to challenge a philosophical world in which non-human animals and the severely intellectually disabled are only members of our human communities by virtue of the non-disabled person's affection for them.

Mary Mahowald writes, "It is easier for academics who are currently able to be open to those with physical disabilities than those with cognitive disabilities. In contrast, it may be difficult not only for academics who are currently able but also for those who are physically disabled to be genuinely open to persons who are cognitively disabled."[21] In attempting to redress this distance, I put forth some possible strategies. First, the moral and epistemic authority of those in relation to persons with severe intellectual disabilities must be affirmed. This involves recognizing the importance of narratives as a part of moral discourse. Second, it is imperative to attend to the complex and disturbing history of the associations between animals and persons with intellectual disabilities, and to contextualize any contemporary connections that are drawn. Third, we must ask whether it is necessary to use the severely mentally retarded to make the case for non-human animals, and vice versa. Isn't it possible to make claims to justice for both groups independently, rather than relying on specious comparisons and a framework in which their interests are presented as in conflict? Finally, I think it is crucial to confront the fears and discomfort associated with intellectual privilege and, more importantly, make room for outrage in these discussions.

There is an emergent body of work in feminist epistemology that may offer another way to explain the dissonances I have discussed and a promising strategy in addressing them. Inspired by work in critical race theory, the turn to epistemologies of ignorance becomes particularly interesting when considered in the context of disability and the discourse surrounding intellectual disability in particular. In her article "The Speculum of Ignorance," Nancy Tuana offers a taxonomy of ignorance, identifying six distinct forms. While her analysis centers on examples from women's health (and the creation of "knowledge about women's bodies in the contemporary women's health movement"), a field that is closely linked to the topic of this volume, her categories provide a useful tool in making sense of and challenging certain kinds of philosophizing about disability.[22] I have grouped these into three categories: deliberate efforts to remain ignorant, maintaining the ignorance of other groups, and genuine epistemic barriers.

Two of the forms of ignorance are predicated on a deliberate effort to remain ignorant: "knowing what we do not know, but not caring to know"[23] and willful ignorance.[24] These are qualitatively different because in the latter case, "they do not know and they do not want to know," whereas in the former case, the objects of knowledge are simply "not linked to present interests." The first case has to do with "certain forms of knowledge being beyond the scope of interest" (Tuana gives the example of the scientific community choosing not to work on developing a male contraceptive pill). In the case of intellectual disability, this form of ignorance can help to explain a number of features of the discourses I have examined. First, there is a clear lack of interest among some philosophers in regard to the specific conditions and the lived realities of the individuals they discuss. As we have seen, at times they defer to medical experts in an effort to explain why they do not include the nature and complexities of the condition. The admission that this is not an area of interest or expertise, however, does not deter them from assuming moral authority in making claims about the fate of the individuals in question. There is also an obvious disinterest in the historical basis of this category, as the history of oppression and treatment of people with intellectual disabilities is rarely invoked when they draw connections between this group and the oppression of non-human animals and when they address the question of suffering. Thus one can ask the extent to which the historical context and specific complexities of mental retardation simply fall below the radar of philosophical interest, or whether there is a more palpable sense in which philosophers "care not to know" or find out about such details when comparing the mentally retarded to non-human animals and addressing the ways and reasons that persons with intellectual disabilities suffer.

The second form of ignorance is more intimately connected with maintaining one's own position of power and refusing to jeopardize it by considering the position (and oppression) of others. Tuana cites Marilyn Frye's and Charles Mills's important work on race and the "determined ignorance" on the part of whites who are unfamiliar with "the oppressive conditions experienced by nonwhites, the institutions, beliefs, and practices that underlie such inequities, and the privileges that benefit whites simply because of their racialized position."[25] There seems to be something analogous or related going on in the complete omission in philosophical discourse of the many historical appeals to the animality of the intellectually disabled in justifying their dehumanizing treatment. The horrific conditions at Willowbrook exposed in the 1970s, where children were kept naked in cells, awash in their own feces, and denied all human contact, represent but one example of how the relationship between the intellectually disabled and animals has been more than a mere philosophical exercise. While it is certainly difficult to ascertain the extent to which certain omissions and distortions in philosophical discourse about intellectual disability are clearly forms of active ignorance or simply a question of defining the scope of one's philosophical attention (captured by the first form of ignorance), the question of cognitive privilege must be considered in the context of arguments that dehumanize individuals with severe intellectual disabilities.

Tuana also identifies ways in which ignorance is imputed to groups other than the knower, processes that have to do with assuming and constructing the ignorance of another; it exposes the ways in which those with epistemic authority attempt to strip others of their privilege and authority. This kind takes two forms: "they do not want us to know" and "ignorance produced by the construction of epistemically disadvantaged identities."[26] The first case involves the process whereby the "ignorance of certain groups is systematically cultivated."[27] Here Tuana gives examples of the ways that women were deterred from becoming knowledgeable about their own bodies, and asks how certain groups have been "deemed ignorant." Again, one does not have to look far in the treatment of individuals with intellectual disabilities of all forms to find instances of this. In a philosophical context it is important to consider how the generalizations philosophers make about persons with intellectual disabilities (and a carelessness in attending to specific dimensions of these disabilities) construct certain groups as globally "ignorant" in problematic ways. While this form of ignorance focuses more on how specific forms of knowledge are rendered inaccessible to a group that has been epistemically discounted, the second form seems even more devastating to me insofar as it globally denies certain identities any epistemic authority (though the two are clearly connected).[28] In the context of philosophical discourse about intellectual disability, it is as important to be alert to the ways that certain groups (disabled and non-disabled) are epistemically disenfranchised as it is to critically examine certain forms of willful ignorance about both the history and lived realities of these categories.

The last two forms of ignorance are caused by somewhat more solid episte-mological barriers than the others. The first—we do not even know that we do not know—speaks to my reaction upon reading philosophical work on intel-lectual disability that strips this group of any recognizable human character-istics.[29] Thus we can ask, Are there dimensions to these supposedly impover-ished lives that are inaccessible to those who simply construct abstract thought experiments? It seems so. The epistemological challenge, then, is to find ways that will bring certain forms of knowledge to light and dismantle the barriers that obscure them.

Perhaps there are dimensions of severe intellectual disability that will always lie beyond a philosopher's (or family member's or advocate's) epistemologi-cal grasp. To acknowledge this is to engage in a form of "loving ignorance," whereby we "accept what we cannot know."[30] In some ways, the tension between these last two forms of ignorance may be the space in which to best capture some of the challenges and lessons offered by persons with severe intellectual disabilities. At the very least, the curious fact that those closest to these persons are often most readily able to accept this form of ignorance puts into relief the desperate need for a rethinking of authority, humility, and epistemic respon-sibility.[31] Reclaiming ignorance: what an intriguing and potentially dangerous notion when spoken in the context of fighting oppression and empowering persons with intellectual disabilities. What an odd sounding phrase in a philo-sophical context, what an absurd slogan for epistemologists, yet one that takes me back to Plato, where this journey began.

World Travel

This book has juxtaposed two worlds: the institutional world of the past and the contemporary philosophical world of intellectual disability. Though the institutional world and all its practices may seem more obviously "concrete" than the philosopher's arguments and texts, both the superintendents of the nineteenth- and twentieth-century institutions and the philosopher who takes intellectual disability as an object of study are engaged in what Nelson Good-man has called "worldmaking." As human classifiers or "world-makers," he says, "we are confined to ways of describing whatever is described."[32] He goes on, "Worlds are made and found; knowing is remaking and reporting; discover-ing laws involves drafting them; recognizing patterns is inventing and imposing them; comprehension and creation go together."[33]

The historical development of intellectual disability as a classification is interesting in this regard because it illuminates the complex relationship between finding and making, comprehension and creation, when the object of investigation is a human being. And we find similar incarnations of the category and certain parallels in the ways that contemporary philosophers have created their own world of intellectual disability.

Yet in examining these two worlds, I have not simply hoped to uncover interesting or intriguing parallels between them. Exposing the complex history of intellectual disability as an object of knowledge plays a crucial role in articulating a critique of the traditional philosophical view of intellectual disability. Anita Silvers captures this in what she has called the process of "historical counterfactualizing": "Acknowledging, rather than ignoring, whether social institutions have historically embraced or excluded certain kinds of selves alerts us to how what we take to be essential conceptions of these excluded persons may in actuality be the product of historical contingency."[34] This resonates with the way Foucault views the task of the intellectual, and the relationship between philosophy and history: "I would say also, about the work of the intellectual, that it is fruitful in a certain way to describe that which is, while making it appear as something that might not be, or that might not be as it is. . . . It is also why, in my opinion, recourse to history . . . is meaningful to the extent that history serves to show how that which is has not always been; that is, the things which seem most evident to us are always formed in the confluence of encounters and chances, during the course of a precarious and fragile history."[35]

In traveling between the early institutional world of intellectual disability and the contemporary world of philosophical discourse, and mapping the resonances and distances between them, I have pointed to the possibility of exploring other worlds that have remained distant from and obscured within philosophy. I view this work as both a preface to and a demand for a more inclusive philosophical dialogue. Thus I have challenged certain "ways of worldmaking" that lead us farther away from the worlds of persons with intellectual disabilities, that marginalize or deny the existence of these other worlds, that refuse to entertain the possibility of appreciating the richness of these worlds, or that fail to recognize them as distinct and yet part of a larger shared world.

In sounding cautionary notes about how we philosophize about intellectual disability, however, I am not suggesting that we leave the philosophical world behind altogether. In a now famous exchange, Derrida challenges the very nature of Foucault's project on the history of madness. Derrida argues that Foucault's *History of Madness* was a failed attempt to open a space in which madness itself could appear: "In writing a history of madness, Foucault has attempted to write a history of madness itself. Itself. Of madness itself. That is, by letting madness speak for itself. Foucault wanted madness to be the subject of his book in every sense of the word: its theme and its first-person narrator, its author, madness speaking about itself."[36] The work failed in two ways, according to Derrida. First, it did not, in fact, give voice to the mad themselves; madness did not in this sense "speak for itself." But this fact points to a deeper paradox, as Derrida calls into question the viability of a project that attempts to radically critique Reason by using its own instruments. If we take these charges seriously, is there a sense in which my book falls prey to a similar trap? To what extent have I tried to let intellectual disability "speak for itself"? In critiquing certain modes of philosophizing about intellectual disability, in unmasking and challenging the philosopher's role from within the discipline itself, have I, in Audre Lorde's words, tried to dismantle the master's house using the master's tools?

With respect to the question of whether intellectual disability speaks for itself in this book, I have not intended to speak for persons with intellectual disabilities, nor do they speak for themselves here. I have, however, explored some of the complex dynamics and the mechanisms whereby certain narratives are rendered invalid, particularly in the case of those who speak for and speak with their family members who have intellectual disabilities in an academic context. As we have seen, it is not enough to simply call for inclusion; Henri Stiker reminds us that the way in which certain voices are included can itself be problematic. In problematizing the way intellectual disability has been discussed "from above," I have attempted to clear the philosophical space in which the voices and perspectives of persons with intellectual disabilities may be incorporated and welcomed. One of the challenges, then, is to rethink what such an expansion of our philosophical discourse might require, what it might mean to engage in a genealogical project as defined by Foucault, to emancipate "subjugated knowledges,"[37] to take seriously the powerful self-advocacy slogan "nothing about us without us,"[38] and to consider what these might mean in the context of a wide range of intellectual disabilities.

But what of Audre Lorde's claim that "the master's tools can never dismantle the master's house"? In the most general sense, this book is not a call to put all philosophical tools aside. The deep conviction that philosophy in its many forms has something to contribute with regard to intellectual disability underlies my commitment to take seriously how and why we currently speak about it. If intellectual disability has indeed begun to move away from the margins of philosophy, there is reason to look, far beyond the scope of this book, at the many ways that intellectual disability can inform, challenge, and recast our deepest ethical, epistemological, political, and existential questions, and open new horizons for philosophical inquiry. This kind of work is already taking place, and is having a profoundly transformative effect. Though I express a Foucauldian concern with the way that some techniques and modes of power have come to define the intellectually disabled against the backdrop of certain divisions (e.g. person/non-person, normal/abnormal), I do not wish to imply that somehow rational discourse has no role to play. Nor did Foucault, if we recognize the specificity of his critical project: "I think that the central issue of philosophy and critical thought since the eighteenth century has always been, still is, and will, I hope, remain the question: What is this Reason that we use? What are its historical effects? What are its limits, and what are its dangers? How can we exist as rational beings, fortunately committed to practicing a rationality that is unfortunately crisscrossed by intrinsic dangers? One should remain as close to this question as possible, keeping in mind that it is both central and extremely difficult to resolve. In addition, if it is extremely dangerous to say that Reason is the enemy that should be eliminated, it is just as dangerous to say that any critical questioning of this rationality risks sending us into irrationality."[39]

Maria Lugones captures the riches, the epistemic and political changes that such work can bring about in her concept of world travel: "The reason why I think that traveling to someone's 'world' is a way of identifying with them is because by traveling to their 'world' we can understand what it is to be them and what it is to be ourselves in their eyes. Only when we have traveled to each other's 'worlds' are we fully subjects to each other. . . . Through traveling to other people's 'worlds' we discover that there are 'worlds' in which those who are the victims of arrogant perception are really subjects, lively beings, resistors, constructors of visions even though in the mainstream construction they are animated only by the arrogant perceiver and are pliable, foldable, file-awayable, classifiable."[40]

In some instances of intellectual disability, the desire to fully comprehend what it is to be them and what it is to be ourselves in their eyes may have to yield temporarily to a form of loving ignorance. However, being willing to witness and be a part of another person's world is different from treating her as a mirror in which I only see myself. And it may open up other possibilities for connection, communication, and dwelling together.

The opening chapter owes its title to Georgina Kleege, for it was her characterization of blindness as "the filmmaker's worst nightmare" that spoke to my impression of philosophy's relationship to intellectual disability. Yet I am not unaware of the ways in which visual metaphors permeate my own discussion. The mirror image is the most obvious, but I have couched many other ideas in the language of seeing faces and unmasking ideas. To explore the relationship between philosophy as reason or *logos* and vision, the visible, or the specular is beyond my reach here.[41] However, there would be a sad irony in addressing the problems of ableism without acknowledging the fact that my own language betrays the mark of a certain way of being in the world.

There may be liberatory potential in moving beyond the specular in the context of intellectual disability. I have spoken of the faces of intellectual disability we find in certain historical and philosophical discourses, but the face of the other holds deeper significance. Emmanuel Levinas's work on the "face," on the ethical demand that I experience in its presence, points to one way of imagining our relation to the other in a way that goes beyond a literal interpretation of simply seeing the face of the other.[42] In a more literal sense, apprehending the face of the other means more than simply seeing it. In moving beyond an emphasis on the gaze, on the visual, we may find new dimensions of being beside the other, in the presence of the other, and explore the power of touch, of the embrace—both literally and metaphorically—in relation to intellectual disability.[43]

In discussing what he means by critical ontology, Foucault says that this historico-critical attitude must be "experimental" rather than putting forth a single permanent theory or doctrine: "A critical ontology of ourselves must be considered not, certainly, as a theory, a doctrine, nor even as a permanent body of knowledge that is accumulating; it must be conceived as an attitude, an ethos, a philosophical life in which the critique of what we are is at one and the same time the historical analysis of the limits imposed on us and an experiment with the possibility of going beyond them."[44] It is time to redefine and re-imagine our philosophical ethos in the face of intellectual disability.

Notes

Introduction

The first epigraph is from Michel Foucault, "The Masked Philosopher," in *Foucault Live, Interviews (1966–84),* ed. Sylvere Lotringer (New York: Semiotext(e), 1996), 198–99.

1. Alisdair MacIntyre, *Dependent Rational Animals* (Chicago: Open Court, 1999); Martha Nussbaum, *Frontiers of Justice: Disability, Nationality, and Species Membership* (Cambridge, Mass.: Belknap, 2006); Eva Kittay, *Love's Labor: Essays on Women, Equality, and Dependency* (New York: Routledge, 1999); Ian Hacking, *Social Construction of What?* (Cambridge, Mass.: Harvard University Press, 1999).

A 2008 conference, Cognitive Disability: A Challenge to Moral Philosophy (held at Stony Brook University, Manhattan), assembled a number of prominent philosophers and bioethicists, and is evidence of the growing attention being paid to intellectual disability. A collection of papers from this event can be found in Licia Carlson and Eva Kittay, eds., *Cognitive Disability and Its Challenge to Moral Philosophy* (forthcoming).

2. Peter Singer, op-ed, *New York Times,* January 26, 2007.

3. Henri Stiker, *A History of Disability,* trans. William Sayers (Ann Arbor: University of Michigan Press, 2000), 15.

4. Georgina Kleege, *Sight Unseen* (New Haven, Conn.: Yale University Press, 1999), 57.

5. See, for example, Anita Silvers, "(In)Equality, (Ab)Normality, and the Americans with Disabilities Act," *Journal of Medicine and Philosophy* 21 (1996): 102–11; Silvers, "On Not Iterating Women's Disability," in *Embodying Bioethics,* ed. Laura M. Donchin and Anne Purdy (Lanham, Md.: Rowman & Littlefield, 1999), 177–202; Ron Amundson, "Disability, Handicap, and the Environment," *Journal of Social Philosophy* 23, no. 1 (1992). This brief listing does not begin to capture the extensive literature in this area.

6. See Michael Oliver, *The Politics of Disablement* (London: Macmillan, 1990); Susan Wendell, "Toward a Feminist Theory of Disability," *Hypatia* 4, no. 2 (Summer 1989);

Wendell, *The Rejected Body: Feminist Philosophical Reflections on Disability* (New York: Routledge, 1996); Harlan Lane, "Constructions of Deafness," *Disability and Society* 10, no. 2 (1995); Michelle Fine and Adrienne Asch, eds., *Women with Disabilities* (Philadelphia: Temple University Press, 1988); Jenny Morris, *Pride and Prejudice: Transforming Attitudes to Disability* (Philadelphia: New Society Publishers, 1991); Lennard Davis, ed., *The Disability Studies Reader* (New York: Routledge, 1997); Rosemarie Garland Thomson, *Extraordinary Bodies* (New York: Columbia University Press, 1997); Susan Browne, Debra Conners, and Nanci Stern, eds., *With the Power of Each Breath: A Disabled Women's Anthology* (Pittsburgh: Cleis, 1985); Francis and Silvers, *Americans with Disabilities*. This list is hardly complete, as there are far too many discussions of the social model to include in this list.

7. Francis and Silvers, *Americans with Disabilities*, 210.

8. Peter Mittler, "International Perspectives," in *The Human Rights of Persons with Intellectual Disabilities: Different but Equal*, ed. Stanley Herr, Lawrence O. Gostin, and Harold Hongju Koh (Oxford: Oxford University Press, 2003), 25–48, 29.

9. It was founded in 1876, originally called the Association of Medical Officers of American Institutions for Idiotic and Feeble-minded Persons. In 1933 it was renamed the American Association on Mental Deficiency, and in 1988 changed the term "mental deficiency" to "mental retardation." See William Sloan and Harvey A. Stevens, *A Century of Concern: A History of the American Association on Mental Deficiency, 1876–1976* (Washington, D.C.: American Association on Mental Deficiency, 1976). Just this past year it changed its name from the American Association on Mental Retardation to the American Association on Intellectual and Developmental Disabilities. See www.aaidd.org.

10. Ruth Luckasson et al., *Mental Retardation: Definition, Classification, and Systems of Supports*, 9th ed. (Washington D.C.: American Association on Mental Retardation, 1992), x.

11. Ibid., 1.

12. Ibid., 13.

13. Ibid., x. This is a departure from clinical definitions that still portray mental retardation as a pathological condition. The *Diagnostic and Statistical Manual of Mental Disorders: DSM-IV* defines mental retardation as "significantly subaverage general intellectual functioning that is accompanied by significant limitations in adaptive functioning. . . . The onset must occur before age 18 years" (Washington, D.C.: American Psychiatric Press, 1994), 39. The *ICD-10: International Statistical Classification of Diseases and Related Health Problems* defines it as "a reduced level of intellectual functioning resulting in diminished ability to adapt to the daily demands of the normal social environment" (Geneva: World Health Organization, 1994), 227. Both the DSM-IV and the ICD-10 divide the category into subclassifications of mild, moderate, severe, profound, and severity unspecified.

14. American Association on Mental Retardation, 2002.

15. See James W. Trent, *Inventing the Feeble Mind: A History of Mental Retardation in the United States* (Berkeley: University of California Press, 1994), chap. 7; David Rothman and Sheila Rothman, *The Willowbrook Wars* (New Brunswick, N.J.: Aldine Transaction, 2005).

16. Organizations such as People First, an international self-advocacy group, continue to challenge the notion of mental retardation and have empowered countless individuals in a variety of ways. For literature by and about self-advocates, see Paul Williams and Bonnie Shoultz, *We Can Speak for Ourselves: Self-Advocacy by Mentally Handicapped People* (London: Souvenir, 1982); Gunnar Dybwad and Hank Bersani Jr., eds., *New Voices: Self-Advocacy by People with Disabilities* (Cambridge, Mass.: Brookline, 1996); Dan Goodley and Geert Van Hove, eds., *Another Disability Studies Reader: People with Learning Difficulties and a Disabling World* (Antwerp-Apeldoorn: Garant, 2005); Jason Kingsley and Mitchell Levitz, *Count Us In: Growing Up with Down Syndrome* (New York: Harcourt Brace, 1994).

17. More than seven hundred genetic etiologies have been identified as causes of mental retardation, though genetic disorders probably account for only one-third of all cases of mental retardation. See Elisabeth M. Dykens, Robert M. Hodapp, and Brenda M. Finucane, eds., *Genetics and Mental Retardation Syndromes* (Baltimore, Md.: Brookes, 2000), 3–5.

18. See Mark Rapley, *The Social Construction of Intellectual Disability* (Cambridge: Cambridge University Press, 2004); Richard Jenkins, ed., *Questions of Competence: Culture, Classification, and Intellectual Disability* (Cambridge: Cambridge University Press, 1998).

19. Patricia Ainsworth and Pamela C. Baker, *Understanding Mental Retardation* (Jackson: University of Mississippi Press, 2004), 3.

20. The ICD-10, for example, holds that "levels of intelligence should not be rigidly applied" because of problems of cultural bias. Ainsworth and Baker, *Understanding Mental Retardation*, 69.

21. See Rapley, *Social Construction;* Marian Corker and Tom Shakespeare, eds., *Postmodernity/Disability* (New York: Continuum, 2002).

22. Lennard Davis, *Bending Over Backwards* (New York: New York University Press, 2002), 86.

23. Peter Byrne, for example, makes a case on multiple fronts against the deconstruction of the concept of cognitive disability, arguing that the reality of this condition cannot be ignored and that the creation and application of this label is not the source of oppression for people with cognitive disabilities. See *Philosophical and Ethical Problems in Mental Handicap* (London: Macmillan, 2000).

24. Robert M. Veatch, *The Foundations of Justice: Why the Retarded and the Rest of Us Have Claims to Equality* (New York: Oxford University Press, 1986), 197.

25. Anita Silvers, "Formal Justice," in *Disability, Difference, Discrimination,* ed. Anita Silvers, David Wasserman, and Mary Mahowald (Lanham, Md.: Rowman & Littlefield, 1998); Eva Feder Kittay, *Love's Labor* (New York: Routledge, 1999); Ron Amundson, "Biological Normality and the ADA," in *Americans with Disabilities: Exploring Implications of the Law for Individuals and Institutions,* ed. Leslie P. Francis and Anita Silvers (New York: Routledge, 2000); Susan Wendell, *The Rejected Body* (New York: Routledge, 1996).

26. I will return to the question of social construction later in this chapter.

27. Hacking, *Social Construction,* 20.

28. Ibid., 56, 58. Though in his book Hacking defines unmasking as one form of constructionism, I am using it in a broader sense as I apply it to philosophical discussions of intellectual disability.

29. Ian Hacking, *Historical Ontology* (Cambridge, Mass.: Harvard University Press, 2002), 23.

30. Foucault, "What Is Enlightenment?" in *Ethics: Subjectivity and Truth: Michel Foucault,* ed. Paul Rabinow (London: Penguin, 2000), 316.

31. Foucault, "What Is Enlightenment?" 318.

32. Ibid., 318.

33. Michel Foucault, "The Subject and Power," in *Michel Foucault: Beyond Structuralism and Hermeneutics,* ed. Hubert L. Dreyfus and Paul Rabinow, 2nd ed. (Chicago: University of Chicago Press, 1983), 222.

34. Ibid., 223.

35. Michel Foucault, *History of Sexuality* (New York: Vintage), 1:95–96.

36. Foucault, "What Is Enlightenment?" 315–16.

37. Michel Foucault, *Histoire de la Folie* (Paris: Galimard, 1979), 57. Derrida believes that it is in the evil genius hypothesis that Descartes confronts the possibility of total madness: insanity is welcomed into the most essential interiority of thought.

38. Roy Porter, "Mother Says It Done Me Good," *London Review of Books* 16 (April 1997): 6.

39. Michel Foucault, "Discourse on Power," in *Remarks on Marx* (New York: Semiotext(e), 1991), 174.

1. Twin Brothers

1. For an overview of the histories of mental retardation that have appeared in the past century, see the introduction to Steven Noll and James W. Trent, eds., *Mental Retardation in America: A Historical Reader* (New York: New York University Press, 2004). For other histories, see Peter Tyor and Leland Bell, *Caring for the Retarded in America: A History* (Greenwich, Conn.: Greenwood, 1984); Leo Kanner, *A History of the Care and Study of the Mentally Retarded* (Springfield, Ill.: Thomas, 1964); Richard C. Scheerenberger, *A History of Mental Retardation* (Baltimore, Md.: Brookes, 1983); Scheerenberger, *A History of Mental Retardation: A Quarter Century of Promise* (Baltimore, Md.: Brookes, 1987); Trent, *Inventing the Feeble Mind.*

2. See Michel Foucault, *The Birth of the Clinic: An Archaeology of Medical Perception* (New York: Vintage, 1994); Foucault, *Discipline and Punish: The Birth of the Prison* (New York: Vintage, 1979); Foucault, *History of Madness* (New York: Routledge, 2006).

3. For examples of Foucauldian approaches to the history of disability generally, see Henri Stiker, *A History of Disability,* trans. William Sayers (Ann Arbor: University of Michigan Press, 1997); Shelley Tremain, ed., *Foucault and the Government of Disability* (Ann Arbor: University of Michigan Press, 2005). Moreover, there is interesting work to be done in connection with Foucault's course on psychiatric power, one of the only instances where he speaks directly about the institutions for idiots and intellectual disability (as opposed to madness) more generally. See Michel Foucault, *Psychiatric*

Power: Lectures at the Collège de France, 1973–1974, ed. Jacques Lagrange and Arnold Davidson, trans. Graham Burchell (New York: Picador, 2008).

4. Michel Foucault, *The Birth of the Clinic: An Archaeology of Medical Perception*, trans. A. M. Sheridan Smith (New York: Vintage, 1994), xix.

5. Foucault, *Discipline and Punish*, 255. James Trent's book *Inventing the Feeble Mind* offers a comprehensive account of the mechanisms through which these new types were defined.

6. I am particularly interested in examining Foucault's course on psychiatric power, where he speaks directly to the institutions for idiots. In fact, Foucault accords an even more significant place to idiocy (over madness) in the development of psychiatric power and theories governing the child: "It seems to me that psychiatrization of the child came about through a completely different figure: the imbecilic child, the idiot child, the child who will soon be called retarded." *Psychiatric Power*, 203. In this lecture he examines the development of theories of idiocy from Esquirol to Seguin and analyzes psychiatric power embodied in institutions.

7. See Wolf Wolfensberger, "The Origin and Nature of our Institutional Models," in *Changing Patterns in Residential Services for the Mentally Retarded*, ed. Robert Kugel and Ann Shearer (Washington, D.C.: President's Committee on Mental Retardation, 1976), 48–70; Duane Stroman, *Mental Retardation in Social Context* (Lanham, Md.: University Press of America, 1989), 101–14; Trent, *Inventing the Feeble Mind*, chaps. 1–5.

8. Philip M. Ferguson, *Abandoned to Their Fate: Social Policy and Practice toward Severely Retarded People in America, 1820–1920* (Philadelphia: Temple University Press, 1994), 3.

9. Ibid., 75.

10. Michel Foucault, "Polemics, Politics, and Problemizations: An Interview," in *The Foucault Reader*, ed. Paul Rabinow (New York: Pantheon, 1984), 389.

11. Wolf Wolfensberger, *The Principle of Normalization in Human Services* (Toronto: National Institute on Mental Retardation, 1972), 15–24.

12. John Locke, *An Essay Concerning Human Understanding* (London: M'Corquodale, 1900), 105–106.

13. To trace parallel and intersecting histories of idiocy and insanity is a book of its own, and despite its importance in the development of intellectual disability as a category, I will make only occasional references to it in this chapter. For histories of insanity, see Michel Foucault, *Madness and Civilization: A History of Insanity in the Age of Reason*, trans. Richard Howard (New York: Pantheon, 1965); Gerald Grob, *Mental Illness and American Society, 1875–1940* (Princeton, N.J.: Princeton University Press, 1983); Jan Goldstein, *Console and Classify: The French Psychiatric Profession in the Nineteenth Century* (Cambridge: Cambridge University Press, 1987).

14. See Douglas Baynton, *Forbidden Signs: American Culture and the Campaign against Sign Language* (Chicago: University of Chicago Press, 1996); Harlan Lane, *When the Mind Hears: A History of the Deaf* (New York: Vintage, 1989); Adriana S. Benzaquen, *Encounters with Wild Children: Temptation and Disappointment in the Study of Human Nature* (Montreal: McGill-Queen's University Press, 2006).

15. Foucault, *Psychiatric Power*, 205.

16. Wolfensberger, *Principle of Normalization,* 31.

17. Dorothea Dix, "Memorial to the Legislature of Massachusetts" [1843] in *History of Mental Retardation: Collected Papers,* ed. Marvin Rosen, Gerald Robert Clark, and Marvin S. Kivitz (Baltimore: University Park Press, 1976), 1:5, 15.

18. Despite her concerns, Dix "became one of the earlier supporters of purely cus-todial state asylums for the incurably insane and idiotic." Philip Ferguson, "The Legacy of the Almshouse," in *Mental Retardation in America,* 40–64, 41.

19. Marvin Rosen, Gerald Robert Clark, and Marvin S. Kivitz, introduction to *History of Mental Retardation: Collected Papers,* 1:xvii–xviii; Trent, *Inventing the Feeble Mind,* 12–16.

20. Rosen, Clark, and Kivitz, introduction, xviii. For a thorough examination of the early years of the institutions for the feebleminded, see Trent, *Inventing the Feeble Mind,* chap. 1.

21. Foucault, *Discipline and Punish,* 202.

22. See Trent, *Inventing the Feeble Mind,* 40–59; Mabel Talbot, *Edouard Seguin: A Study of an Educational Approach to the Treatment of Mentally Defective Children* (New York: Columbia University Press, 1964).

23. Edouard Seguin, *Idiocy and Its Treatment by the Physiological Method* (Albany, N.Y.: Brandow, 1910), 32.

24. Samuel Gridley Howe, "On the Causes of Idiocy" [1848] in *History of Mental Retardation: Collected Papers,* 1:37. Trent, in *Inventing the Feeble Mind,* traces the many transformations that these classificatory systems underwent and examines how they reflect the broader aims and exigencies of the institutions and changes in social percep-tions, rather than simply reflecting the objective knowledge about discrete kinds.

25. Seguin, *Idiocy,* 56.

26. Charles T. Wilbur, "Institutions for the Feeble-Minded," in *History of Mental Retardation: Collected Papers,* 1:296.

27. Seguin was a student of Pinel's.

28. Foucault challenges the extent to which the new asylum, despite liberating the insane from their physical shackles, truly "liberated" them.

29. Foucault, *Madness and Civilization,* 270.

30. Sloan and Stevens, *Century of Concern,* 1–2.

31. See Erving Goffman, *Asylums: Essays in the Social Structure of Mental Patients and Other Inmates* (Garden City, N.Y.: Anchor, 1961), 6.

32. Foucault, *Discipline and Punish,* 215.

33. As we shall see, the notion of productivity functioned in complex ways within these institutions.

34. Foucault, *Discipline and Punish,* 235–36.

35. For an example of a description of life within these institutions, see Trent, *Inventing the Feeble Mind,* chap. 4.

36. James Trent does an excellent job of interpreting this history through the lens of the professional authority and the interests these superintendents had in maintaining their legitimacy.

37. Penny Richards, for example, argues that a "far more complicated narrative emerges" when we move beyond the walls of the institution. See Penny Richards, "'Be-

side Her Sat Her Idiot Child': Families and Developmental Disability in Mid-Nineteenth Century America," in *Mental Retardation in America*, 66.

38. I thank Jennifer Clegg for pointing out the dangers in focusing exclusively on the "dark institutional history" of intellectual disability in response to a paper I gave at a conference on philosophy and cognitive disability.

39. Georges Canguilhem, *The Normal and the Pathological*, trans. Carolyn R. Fawcett (New York: Zone, 1989), 41–42.

40. For an extensive discussion of Seguin's view in the context of the American history of intellectual disability, see Trent, *Inventing the Feeble Mind*, chap. 3.

41. Seguin, *Idiocy*, 57.

42. Foucault, *Psychiatric Power*, 205. Here Foucault is quoting the French physician Belhomme (1824).

43. Foucault, *Psychiatric Power*, 209.

44. Seguin, *Idiocy*, 48.

45. Quoted in Trent, *Inventing the Feeble Mind*, 17.

46. Seguin, *Idiocy*, 29. The notion of the mentally retarded as innocent and deserving of moral status despite their deficiencies can be found in philosophical literature on mental retardation that takes a theological approach. Though I will not be discussing this perspective, it is important to note that it exists as an alternative to the kind of discourse that will be examined in chapter 5. See articles in "Section III: Theology and Philosophy of Religion," in *Ethics and Mental Retardation*, ed. Loretta Kopelman and John C. Moskop (Dordrecht: Reidel, 1984), 127–84.

47. Jean-Jacques Rousseau, *Emile, or On Education*, trans. Allan Bloom (New York: Basic, 1979), 61.

48. Ibid.

49. Quoted in Trent, *Inventing the Feeble Mind*, 104.

50. Quoted in Nicole Hahn Rafter, *Creating Born Criminals* (Chicago: University of Illinois Press, 1997), 24.

51. Foucault, *Psychiatric Power*, 209.

52. Though I discuss curability and incurability later, it should be pointed out that both notions are consistent with this picture of idiocy as a quantitative difference. The incurables are "eternal children" who are incapable of moving beyond infancy. As Foucault points out, there are two forms of this developmental failure: arrested development and slowed development. He argues that this distinction is central to the classificatory difference between idiots and the mentally retarded and to Seguin's program for education/treatment of idiocy. See Foucault, *Psychiatric Power*, 207–208.

53. Quoted in Sloan and Stevens, *Century of Concern*, 6.

54. The IQ score is still a component of many definitions of mental retardation. The DSM-IV, ICD-10, and the AAIDD definitions all include the IQ score as a means of determining the level of "subaverage intelligence," though it is worth noting that the AAIDD now defines it primarily in terms of supports.

55. I discuss the relationship between animality and madness in Foucault's *Madness and Civilization* in Licia Carlson, "The Human as Just An *Other* Animal," in *Phenomenology and the Non-Human Animal*, ed. Christian Lotz and Corinne Painter (Dordrecht: Springer, 2007).

56. Howe, "On the Causes of Idiocy," 37.

57. Ibid., 38.

58. Ibid., 39.

59. Ibid., 37.

60. Alonzo Potter, John K. Kane, James Martin, George E. Wood, and Charles D. Cleaveland, "Education of Idiots: An Appeal to the Citizens of Philadelphia" [1853] in *History of Mental Retardation: Collected Papers*, 1:63.

61. Henry Herbert Goddard, *The Kallikak Family: A Study in the Heredity of Feeble-mindedness* (New York: Macmillan, 1939), 66.

62. For some excellent discussions on this, see David Wright, "Mongols in our Midst: John Langdon Down and the Ethnic Classification of Idiocy, 1858–1924"; and Daniel J. Kevles, "Mongolian Imbecility: Race and Its Rejection in the Understanding of Mental Disease," in Steven Noll and James Trent, eds., *Mental Retardation in America*; Anna Stubblefield, "'Beyond the Pale': Tainted Whiteness, Cognitive Disability, and Eugenic Sterilization," *Hypatia* 22, no. 2 (Spring 2007): 162–81.

63. For a comprehensive account of the problem of feeblemindedness in the South, see Steven Noll, *Feeble-minded in our Midst: Institutions for the Mentally Retarded in the South* (Chapel Hill: University of North Carolina Press, 1995). Only two of the ten institutions that opened in the South in the first four decades of this century had inmates of both races (p. 89).

64. Noll, *Feeble-minded in our Midst*, chap. 5; Stubblefield, "Beyond the Pale."

65. Seguin, *Idiocy*, 39.

66. Chris Borthwick, "Racism, IQ, and Down's Syndrome," *Disability and Society* 11, no. 3 (1990), 403–410.

67. See Wright, "Mongols," 103–104. See Kevles, "Mongolian Imbecility," for an interesting discussion of how the relationship between race and Down syndrome persists and transforms as the twenty-first century progresses (120–27).

68. Edouard Seguin, "Origin of the Treatment and Training of Idiots" [1866] in *History of Mental Retardation: Collected Papers*, 1:156.

69. Foucault, *Psychiatric Power*, 208–209.

70. In looking for *qualitative* portraits today, the view that some individuals with severe intellectual disabilities are somehow qualitatively different and closer to non-human animals seems to have survived only in philosophical discourse. I'm unaware of any other discipline or context in which this kind of association is made.

71. Isaac Kerlin, "Our Household Pets" [1880] in *History of Mental Retardation: Collected Papers*, 1:285.

72. By "functional" I do not mean physiological, as contrasted with anatomical. I mean it as a way of defining conditions according to the individual's ability to function in certain ways in a particular environment. This sense of "functional" is contrasted with "biological" or "organic" definitions, which define forms of mental disability in terms of some organic defect, independent of the person's relationship with the environment.

73. Seguin, *Idiocy*, 29.

74. Howe, "On the Causes of Idiocy," 37.

75. Quoted in Trent, *Inventing the Feeble Mind*, 65.

76. Ibid., 80.

77. I discuss the conflation of training and education later in this chapter.

78. See Penny Richards, "'Beside Her Sat Her Idiot Child': Families and Developmental Disability in Mid-Nineteenth Century America," in *Mental Retardation in America*, 65–86. I will discuss the relationship between mothers and causes of intellectual disability more extensively in the next chapter.

79. For a discussion of the roles that families were expected to play, see Richards, "Beside Her Sat Her Idiot Child"; and Janice Brockley, "Rearing the Child Who Never Grew," in *Mental Retardation in America*, 130–64.

80. Foucault, *Psychiatric Power*, 115.

81. Howe, "On the Causes of Idiocy," 35.

82. Ibid., 50–59.

83. Ibid., 34.

84. Ibid.

85. Though I do not explicitly discuss the complex eugenics movement, it directly influenced the classifications and practices surrounding the feebleminded. See Mark Haller, *Eugenics: Hereditarian Attitudes in American Thought* (New Brunswick, N.J.: Rutgers University Press, 1963); Stephen Jay Gould, *The Mismeasure of Man* (New York: Norton, 1981); Daniel Kevles, *In the Name of Eugenics* (New York: Knopf, 1985); Martin Pernick, *The Black Stork: Eugenics and the Death of "Defective" Babies in American Medicine and Motion Pictures* (New York: Oxford University Press, 1996); Diane Paul, *Controlling Human Heredity: 1865 to the Present* (New York: Humanity, 1995).

86. See Rafter, *Creating Born Criminals*, 68–69; chap. 4.

87. There are many counterexamples to this parallel. For example, the fact that Down syndrome, a condition responsible for mental retardation, is caused by an incurable chromosomal defect does not imply that the individuals are incapable of benefiting from education and are impervious to environmental influences. In fact, many suggest that the mental retardation which accompanies this genetic defect is in large part due to environmental deprivation and erroneous assumptions about the child's cognitive abilities (see Borthwick, "Racism").

88. Quoted in Philip L. Safford and Elizabeth J. Safford, *A History of Childhood and Disability* (New York: Teachers College Press, 1996), 168.

89. Ibid., 169.

90. Edouard Seguin, "Psycho-Physiological Training of an Idiotic Hand" [1879] in *History of Mental Retardation: Collected Papers*, 1:163. See Trent, *Inventing the Feeble Mind*, chap. 3.

91. Seguin, "Origin and Treatment of Training of Idiots," 158.

92. Potter, Kane, Martin, Wood, and Cleaveland, "Education of Idiots," 65.

93. The difference between education and training will be addressed later in this chapter.

94. Goddard, *Kallikak Family*, 53.

95. See Trent, *Inventing the Feeble Mind*, chap. 6; and Tyor and Bell, *Caring*, for a detailed account of the "menace of the feebleminded."

96. Goddard, *Kallikak Family*, 101–102.

97. For a history of sterilization, see Philip R. Reilly, *The Surgical Solution: A History of Involuntary Sterilization in the United States* (Baltimore, Md.: Johns Hopkins University Press, 1991); Trent, *Inventing the Feeble Mind*, chap. 6.

98. Ferguson, *Abandoned*, 10.

99. Safford and Safford, *History*, 181.

100. Ibid.

101. There was opposition in the association to integrating the feebleminded into public schools, most likely because the superintendents felt their professional authority threatened. See Sloan and Stevens, *Century of Concern*, 95.

102. Ibid., 26.

103. Potter, Kane, Martin, Wood, and Cleaveland, "Education of Idiots," 64.

104. Ibid., 65.

105. Foucault, *Psychiatric Power*, 212.

106. Ibid., 214.

107. Ferguson, *Abandoned*, 2–3.

108. Ibid., 70. This statement was made by Wilbur.

109. Trent, *Inventing the Feeble Mind*, 80.

110. Trent, *Inventing the Feeble Mind*, 88–90. It is also interesting to note that epileptics were often housed separately. Ellen Dwyer provides a fascinating analysis of the intersections between epilepsy, categories of intellectual disability (e.g., idiots, imbeciles, morons), and institutional practice in her examination of New York State's Craig Colony for epileptics. See "The State and the Multiply Disadvantaged: The Case of Epilepsy," in *Mental Retardation in America*, 258–80.

111. Fernald writes, "In the custodial department are classed also the moral imbeciles and the adults of both sexes who have graduated from the school department, or are past school age, but cannot safely be trusted, either for their own good or for the good of the community, out from under strict and judicious surveillance." "Description of American Institutions" [1893] in *History of Mental Retardation: Collected Papers*, 1:324.

112. Isaac N. Kerlin, "Moral Imbecility" [1889] in *History of Mental Retardation: Collected Papers*, 1:307. For a wonderful discussion of the evolution of this concept, see Rafter, *Creating Born Criminals*, chap. 4.

113. Sloan and Stevens, *Century of Concern*, 26.

114. Rafter, *Creating Born Criminals*, 69.

115. Though I am drawing a distinction between them, I realize that there may not be a firm line between training and education. Learning adaptive and vocational skills can be viewed as a *kind* of education.

116. *History of Mental Retardation: Collected Papers*, 1:323. Here we see a quantitative portrait of feeblemindedness.

117. Burton Blatt, *The Conquest of Mental Retardation* (Austin: Pro-ed, 1987), 178.

118. Fernald, "Description of American Institutions," 323; Trent, *Inventing the Feeble Mind*, 94–95.

119. Fernald, "Description of American Institutions," 325.

120. Trent documents that such training often began as early as age 5 (p. 109).

121. Fernald, "Description of American Institutions," 324.

122. Trent, *Inventing the Feeble Mind*, 109.

123. I examine this paradox more thoroughly in the next chapter.

124. Quoted in Ferguson, 121.

125. Trent, *Inventing the Feeble Mind*, 23. In looking at the training and education of inmates in relation to institutional needs, I do not want to be reductionist and do not mean to suggest that the survival of the institution was the only aim behind such practices. It is important to distinguish between those practices and improvements that enhanced the quality of life of the individuals in the institutions and those that did little to improve their lives but only contributed to the institutional utility. There may also be those that were beneficial for both and might even have had a synergistic benefit. (I thank Eva Kittay for making this point.)

126. What follows does not begin to capture the complexity and richness of the eugenics movement and its relationship to mental testing and to theories and practices surrounding intellectual disability.

127. The moron (as a species of moral as well as intellectual deficiency) was prefigured in the moral imbecile. See Rafter, *Creating Born Criminals*.

128. Goddard's study in the heredity of feeblemindedness tells the story of Deborah Kallikak, a twenty-two-year-old woman at the Vineland Training School where Goddard opened his Department of Research. Goddard traces the Kallikak family's ancestry back to Deborah's great-grandfather Martin Sr. and his fateful union with "the nameless feeble-minded girl" whose illegitimate feebleminded son split this family between the upstanding line of normal offspring Martin had with his wife, and the feebleminded line that produced Deborah three generations later (p. 113). The name, which Goddard invented, is derived from the Greek *kallos* (good) and *kakos* (bad).

129. They were usually southern and eastern Europeans.

130. The campaigns for institutions in the mid-nineteenth century were far less prominent in the public light than the campaign against the menace of feeblemindedness and the eugenics movement of the early twentieth century. See Trent, *Inventing the Feeble Mind*, chaps. 5–6.

131. Goddard, *Kallikak Family*, 56.

132. Ibid., 58–59.

133. Ibid., 101–102.

134. Foucault, *Discipline and Punish*, 255.

135. Quoted in Rafter, *Creating Born Criminals*, 140.

136. Alfred Binet and Theodore Simon, *The Development of Intelligence in Children*, trans. Elizabeth Kite (Nashville, Tenn.: Williams, 1980), 76.

137. Ibid., 40.

138. Ibid.

139. Ibid., 42–43.

140. Seguin, *Idiocy*, 58.

141. Henry H. Goddard, "Four Hundred Feeble-Minded Children Classified by Binet Method," in *History of Mental Retardation: Collected Papers*, 1:364.

142. Binet and Simon, *Development of Intelligence*, 37.

143. Sloan and Stevens, *Century of Concern*, 108.

144. There is a complex story as to why the IQ test proved popular in the United States but not in France: it was administered to army recruits (see Gould, *Mismeasure*,

192–233). For discussions of the eugenics movement in France, see Mark Adams, ed., *The Wellborn Science: Eugenics in Germany, France, Brazil, and Russia* (Oxford: Oxford University Press, 1990); Ian Dowbiggin, *Inheriting Madness* (Berkeley: University of California Press, 1991); Robert A. Nye, *Crime, Madness, and Politics in Modern France* (Princeton, N.J.: Princeton University Press, 1984).

145. Quoted in Gould, *Mismeasure*, 163.

146. These family histories—called pedigree studies—are discussed at greater length in the next chapter.

147. Goddard, *Kallikak Family*, 66.

148. In the preface to *Kallikak Family*, Goddard asks that "the scientist reserve judgment and wait for the larger book for the proof of these statements and an adequate discussion of Mendelism in relation to the problem" (p. x). At the end of his book, although Goddard acknowledges that there may be good reason to think that feeblemindedness is *not* a "unit character" in Mendel's sense (p. 111), he says "enough here is given to show the possibility that the Mendelian law applies to human heredity" (p. 115).

149. Ibid., 12.

150. Ibid.

2. Gendered Objects, Gendered Subjects

The epigraph is from Elizabeth Spelman, *Inessential Woman: Problems of Exclusion in Feminist Thought* (Boston: Beacon, 1988), 14.

1. Foucault, *Psychiatric Power*, 15.

2. Foucault argues that power can come "from above" (one example of this is monarchic power) as well as from below. See *History of Sexuality*, 93–94.

3. Foucault, *Psychiatric Power*, 15.

4. The following represent just a small segment of this burgeoning field: Wendell, *Rejected Body*; Silvers, Wasserman, and Mahowald, eds., *Disability and Difference*; Asch and Fine, eds., *Women with Disabilities;* Linton, *Claiming Disability;* Jenny Morris, *Pride against Prejudice;* Morris, *Encounters with Strangers;* Eva Kittay, Alexa Schriempf, Anita Silvers, and Susan Wendell, "Special Issue: Feminism and Disability," pts. 1–2, *Hypatia* 16, no. 4 (2001); 17, no. 3 (2002); Rosemarie Garland Thomson, *Extraordinary Bodies;* Bonnie Smith and Beth Hutchison, eds., *Gendering Disability* (New Brunswick, N.J.: Rutgers University Press, 2004).

5. Many of the chapters in *Mental Retardation in America* have added to this task. See Nicole Rafter, "The Criminalization of Mental Retardation"; Molly Ladd-Taylor, "The Sociological Advantages of Sterilization: Fiscal Policies and Feeble-Minded Women in Interwar Minnesota"; Karen Keely, "Sexuality and Storytelling: Literary Representations of the 'Feebleminded' in the Age of Sterilization"; Penny Richards, "Beside Her Sat Her Idiot Child"; Janice Brockely, "Rearing the Child Who Never Grew"; Leila Zenderland, "The Parable of the *Kallikak Family:* Explaining the Meaning of Heredity in 1912."

6. I use the term "gendered" in the same sense that Sandra Bem does as she discusses the way persons and practices become gendered. She outlines three lenses, or assumptions that reproduce male power: androcentrism, or male centeredness; gender polarization, meaning that the perceived differences between men and women function

as an organizing principle of social life; and biological essentialism, the justification of inequality by appealing to biological accounts of male-female difference. Sandra Bem, *Lenses of Gender: Transforming the Debate on Sexual Inequality* (New Haven, Conn.: Yale University Press, 1993), 2.

7. Membership in these groups was not mutually exclusive; the overlapping of women's roles is one of the more interesting features of this history. Note that the groups of women I discuss in this chapter were white women who were subject to Victorian stereotypes of femininity that applied to them only (i.e., they did not apply to African Americans or immigrants from eastern and southern Europe). Though there were class differences between them (e.g., many institutionalized feebleminded women were poor, while the researchers and reformists were mostly upper middle class), this chapter focuses on gender, rather than race and class, as a lens of analysis that applies to this specific population of women.

8. See Foucault, *History of Madness; Birth of the Clinic; Discipline and Punish; History of Sexuality.*

9. Foucault, "The Subject and Power," in Hubert Dreyfus and Paul Rabinow, eds., *Michel Foucault: Beyond Structuralism and Hermeneutics* (Chicago: University of Chicago Press, 1983), 222.

10. Foucault, *History of Sexuality,* 95.

11. Foucault, "Subject and Power," 222–23.

12. Foucault speaks to the possibility of "reverse-discourse" in *History of Sexuality,* 1:101. This would be a power relation that is liberating rather than oppressive.

13. Foucault, "Subject and Power," 208.

14. Iris Marion Young, *Justice and the Politics of Difference* (Princeton, N.J.: Princeton University Press, 1990), chap. 2.

15. Ibid., 40.

16. Ibid., 41.

17. Ibid., 9.

18. Ibid., 43.

19. Ibid., 41.

20. Ibid., 42.

21. There is no question that violence played an enormous role in this history. The corporal punishment and abhorrent living conditions in institutions, forced sterilization, and sexual abuse of inmates are only a few examples. However, my discussion here will not address this form of oppression.

22. Young, *Justice,* 49.

23. Ibid.

24. Ibid., 53.

25. Ibid.

26. Ibid., 56.

27. Ibid., 58–59.

28. This is the subject of both Elaine Showalter's book *The Female Malady: Women, Madness, and English Culture, 1830–1980* (New York: Pantheon, 1986); and Phyllis Chesler, *Women and Madness* (New York: Avon, 1983).

29. See *History of Mental Retardation: Collected Papers.*

30. See Sloan and Stevens, *Century of Concern.*

31. Trent, *Inventing the Feeble Mind,* 69–77.

32. Ibid., 23.

33. Kerlin, "Moral Imbecility," 308.

34. See Rafter, "The Criminalization of Mental Retardation," in *Mental Retardation in America.*

35. A quote from Dr. G. H. Knight, one of the founding members of the association, in 1891. Sloan and Stevens, *Century of Concern,* 21.

36. Sloan and Stevens, *Century of Concern,* 26.

37. Ibid., 76.

38. Peter Tyor, "Denied the Power to Choose the Good: Sexuality and Mental Defect in American Medical Practice, 1850–1920," *Journal of Social History* 10 (1977): 473.

39. Quoted in Tyor, "Denied the Power," 482.

40. Tyor, "Denied the Power," 480.

41. By the late 1880s, Pennsylvania, Ohio, and Illinois all had separate cottages, or facilities, for women of childbearing age. Trent, *Inventing the Feeble Mind,* 76.

42. Sloan and Stevens, *Century of Concern,* 65.

43. Letchworth Viliage, a state institution for the feebleminded in Thielles, New York, was opened in 1911, and by 1926 it had two thousand patients. Of the 107 men and 148 women paroled, 14 men and 84 women were returned to the institution (5 percent of the women were returned because they had given birth to illegitimate children). See Howard W. Potter and Crystal McCollister, "A Resume of Parole Work at Letchworth Village," in *History of Mental Retardation: Collected Papers,* 2:137.

44. Ibid.

45. Trent, *Inventing the Feeble Mind,* traces the uses of sterilization and says that by the 1920s it had become a precondition for parole (chap. 6).

46. Potter and McCollister, "Resume of Parole Work," 143.

47. Tyor, "Denied the Power," 477.

48. Goddard, *Kallikak Family,* 11–12. See Leila Zenderland, "The Parable of *The Kallikak Family,*" or a fuller discussion of the way that this case reveals the intersection of various gender roles and conceptions of degeneracy and heredity. In *Mental Retardation in America,* 165–85.

49. Young, *Justice,* 43, 45.

50. Ibid., 41.

51. Seguin, *Idiocy,* 190.

52. Ibid., 193.

53. Ibid.

54. Isaac N. Kerlin, "Manual of Elwyn," in *History of Mental Retardation: Collected Papers,* 1:316.

55. Foucault, *Psychiatric Power,* 115.

56. Fernald, "Description of American Institutions," 324.

57. Ibid., 324–25.

58. Trent, *Inventing the Feeble Mind,* 105.

59. Ibid., 122.

60. Fernald, "Description of American Institutions," 325.

61. Trent, *Inventing the Feeble Mind*, 104.

62. Quoted in Trent, *Inventing the Feeble Mind*, 104–105.

63. William Rhinelander Stewart, *The Philanthropic Work of Josephine Shaw Lowell* (New York: Macmillan, 1911), 100.

64. See Trent, *Inventing the Feeble Mind*; Tyor, "Denied the Power."

65. See Trent, *Inventing the Feeble Mind*, chap. 5.

66. Ibid., 110.

67. Ibid., chaps. 4–5.

68. Young, *Justice*, 54.

69. Though the transfer of benefits of their labor conforms to Young's definition of exploitation, I want to avoid reducing their caregiving labor to a form of exploitation. It is very possible that this work was meaningful and enriched the lives of both the caregivers and the residents in their care.

70. Young, *Justice*, 50.

71. The hierarchical nature of this model (i.e., rulers/ruled) may be seen as at odds with a Foucauldian notion of power as coming from multiple points and with the possibility of resistance. See *History of Sexuality*, 94–96.

72. Trent, *Inventing the Feeble Mind*, 129.

73. See Nicole Hahn Rafter, *White Trash: The Eugenic Family Studies, 1877–1919* (Boston: Northeastern University Press, 1988).

74. For a discussion of mother-blaming as it manifests itself in a series of perfect mother and bad mother myths, see Paula Caplan, *Don't Blame Mother: Mending the Mother-Daughter Relationship* (New York: Harper & Row, 1989).

75. Marouf Arif Hasain Jr., *The Rhetoric of Eugenics in Anglo-American Thought* (Athens: University of Georgia Press, 1996), 81.

76. Quoted in Sloan and Stevens, *Century of Concern*, 76–77.

77. Linda Gordon, *Woman's Body, Woman's Right: A Social History of Birth Control in America* (New York: Grossman, 1976), 122.

78. See Penny Richards, "Beside Her Sat Her Idiot Child"; and Janice Brockley, "Rearing the Child Who Never Grew."

79. Seguin, *Idiocy*, 60, 62.

80. Caplan, *Don't Blame Mother*, 105.

81. Foucault, *Psychiatric Power*, 115.

82. For example, connections were made between women's mental activity and allegedly dangerous menstrual disorders. See Judith Walzer Leavitt, ed., *Women and Health in America* (Madison: University of Wisconsin Press, 1984).

83. Sloan and Stevens, *Century of Concern*, 14.

84. Gordon, *Woman's Body*, 140.

85. Hasain, *Rhetoric of Eugenics*, 83. Janice Brockley points out the ways in which literature around this period invoked and represented conceptions of good parenting by mothers *and* fathers. See "Rearing the Child Who Never Grew," in *Mental Retardation in America*, 130–38.

86. Ibid., 84.

87. Ibid., 81.

88. Brockley, "Rearing," 136.

89. Recall from the previous chapter how the inability of mothers to properly care for and provide a good environment for their disabled children justified the need for institutionalization.

90. Gordon states that the concern with race suicide, the idea that the white population was in decline and that immigrant and degenerate women were the only ones having babies, created a backlash against the women advocating "voluntary motherhood." The feminist arguments that motherhood would be improved if women were more educated and had control over reproduction through birth control were reversed by anti-feminists. As greater emphasis was placed on heredity, the emphasis shifted from motherhood as a skilled labor to viewing women as breeders, whose motherly function was part of nature (*Woman's Body*, 134).

91. Sloan and Stevens, *Century of Concern*, 76.

92. Hasain, *Rhetoric of Eugenics*, 82.

93. See Zenderland, "Parable," 172–78.

94. Rafter, *White Trash*, 74.

95. Ibid., 21.

96. Hasain, *Rhetoric of Eugenics*, 82.

97. It would be interesting to trace the ways in which the field-workers had *less* power than mothers and parents, more generally, insofar as parents were primarily responsible for institutionalizing their children. For a discussion of the nature of this parental power, and the tensions between parents and medical authorities, see Ellen Dwyer, "The State and the Multiply Disadvantaged: The Case of Epilepsy," in *Mental Retardation in America*, 265–66, 273–74.

98. Zenderland, "Parable," 177.

99. There are very interesting parallels between this work and the newly emerging field of genetic counseling which is primarily practiced by women and provides a similar gatekeeping role, which I discuss in part 2.

100. I make this distinction for the purposes of my discussion; I am not suggesting that the two groups are mutually exclusive.

101. Dorothea Dix is another figure worthy of close examination in this regard. See *Voices for the Mad*.

102. For a sense of the debates surrounding interpretations of Lowell, see Nicole Rafter, "Criminalization of Mental Retardation," 233; and Joan Waugh, *Unsentimental Reformer: The Life of Josephine Shaw Lowell* (Cambridge, Mass.: Harvard University Press, 1997), 2–11. For similar discussions of Sanger, see Angela Franks, *Margaret Sanger's Eugenic Legacy: The Control of Female Fertility* (Jefferson, N.C.: McFarland, 2005); and Alexander Sanger, "Eugenics, Race, and Margaret Sanger," *Hypatia* 22, no. 2 (Spring 2007): 210–17.

103. Sanger, "Eugenics, Race, and Margaret Sanger," 213.

104. Rafter, "Criminalization of Mental Retardation," 249. She was widowed, however, and she neither had her child out of wedlock nor belonged to the lower, "undesirable" classes. See Waugh, *Unsentimental Reformer*, 78–91.

105. I will speak to these contemporary challenges for feminism more directly in chapter 4.

106. Robert H. Bremner, *American Philanthropy* (Chicago: University of Chicago Press: 1960), 101. For a comprehensive biography that examines the significance of Lowell's professional life, see Waugh, *Unsentimental Reformer.*

107. Waugh, *Unsentimental Reformer,* 103.

108. Waugh makes the interesting point that despite being the lone woman amid numerous men, "she was always aware that as one of the first women in a high-profile public position, she could advance her policy goals more effectively by being 'every inch a woman' than she could by insisting on equality of the sexes in all areas" (*Unsentimental Reformer,* 123).

109. Stewart, *Philanthropic Work,* 91–92. As I discuss later, the fact that Lowell wanted these institutions to be run by women suggests that she might also be viewed as an early feminist. Unfortunately I cannot fully explore this claim here.

110. Stewart, *Philanthropic Work,* 91–92; Waugh, *Unsentimental Reformer,*134–35.

111. Stewart, *Philanthropic Work,* 101.

112. Waugh, *Unsentimental Reformer,* 118–19.

113. Trent, *Inventing the Feeble Mind,* 74.

114. Ibid.

115. Ibid., 75.

116. Stewart, *Philanthropic Work,* 119.

117. Quoted in Trent, *Inventing the Feeble Mind,* 76.

118. Rafter, *Creating Born Criminals,* 41.

119. Trent, *Inventing the Feeble Mind,* 76.

120. Stewart, *Philanthropic Work,* last chapter; Waugh, *Unsentimental Reformer,* 239–42.

121. Anne Firor Scott, "Women's Voluntary Associations: From Charity to Reform," in Kathleen McCarthy, *Lady Bountiful Revisited: Women, Philanthropy, and Power* (New Brunswick, N.J.: Rutgers University Press, 1990), 35–54, 48.

122. Trent, *Inventing the Feeble Mind,* 74. Waugh, *Unsentimental Reformer,* also speaks of the paradoxical nature of her work: "The more she expanded the scope of her own power, the more she made it possible for other women to consider alternative career choices. From the 1870's on, she promoted female professionalism . . . and tied the benefits of civil service reform to increased employment opportunities for women" (p. 141).

123. Waugh, *Unsentimental Reformer,* 118.

124. Quoted in Stewart, *Philanthropic Work,* 101.

125. See Hasain, *Rhetoric of Eugenics,* chap. 4.

126. Gordon, *Woman's Body,* 144.

127. Ibid., 121.

128. For a sketch of these various interpretations, see Angela Franks, *Margaret Sanger's Eugenic Legacy: The Control of Female Fertility* (Jefferson, N.C.: McFarland, 2005), 5–13.

129. See Franks, *Margaret Sanger;* Alexander Sanger, "Eugenics"; Ellen Chesler, *Woman of Valor: Margaret Sanger and the Birth Control Movement in America* (New York: Simon & Schuster, 2007).

130. Margaret Sanger, *Woman and the New Race* (New York: Brentano's, 1920), 40–41.

131. Ibid., 87.

132. Quoted in Franks, *Margaret Sanger*, 44.

133. Sanger, *Woman and the New Race*, 45. Again, there is a strong connection between the racism inherent in this discourse and disability. Unfortunately this is a broad topic, beyond the scope of this project.

134. Franks, *Margaret Sanger*, 16.

135. Sanger, *Women and the New Race*, 233–34.

136. Franks, *Margaret Sanger*, 188.

137. In examining the power dynamics between these groups of women, I have not meant to demonize these early reformers and feminists. In many cases their intentions were noble and their efforts undoubtedly had significant effects and may have improved the lives of many. However, it is instructive to see how certain assumptions and power dynamics informed and defined their conceptions of disability and their relationship to this group of others.

138. Iris Marion Young, "Lived Body vs. Gender: Reflections on Social Structure and Subjectivity," *Ratio*, December 4, 2002, 425–26.

139. Spelman, *Inessential Woman*, 7.

3. Analytic Interlude

1. Eva Kittay, "When Caring Is Just and Justice Is Caring," in *The Subject of Care: Feminist Perspectives on Dependency*, ed. Eva Feder Kittay and Ellen K. Feder (Lanham, Md.: Rowman & Littlefield, 2002), 265.

2. Hacking, *Social Construction*, 101–102.

3. For the purposes of my discussion in this chapter, I will focus on *mental retardation* specifically, as a historical category of intellectual disability that is still used in certain contexts.

4. The literature on the social construction of disability has grown exponentially in the past twenty-five years, and this is by no means a comprehensive survey or even a representative sample. Amid this enormous body of work that spans many disciplines, I have chosen a few examples that aptly illustrate the distinctions I am drawing.

5. See Angela Licia Carlson, "Mindful Subjects: Classification and Cognitive Disability" (Ph.D. diss., University of Toronto, 1998), 6; Hacking, *Social Construction*, 36–37.

6. See Michael Oliver, *The Politics of Disablement* (London: Macmillan, 1990), 22.

7. Wendell, *Rejected Body*, 35.

8. Ibid., 36–46.

9. Jane Mercer, *Labeling the Mentally Retarded: Clinical and Social Systems Perspectives on Mental Retardation* (Berkeley: University of California Press, 1973), 36.

10. See Rapley, *Social Construction*; Robert Bogdan and Steven J. Taylor, *Inside Out: The Social Meaning of Mental Retardation* (Toronto: University of Toronto Press, 1982); Bogdan and Taylor, "Relationships with Severely Disabled People: The Social Construction of Humanness," *Social Problems* 36, no. 2 (1989): 135–48; Philip Ferguson, "The Social Construction of Mental Retardation," *Social Policy* 18, no. 1 (1987): 51–56; Richard Jenkins, ed., *Questions of Competence: Culture, Classification and Intellectual Disability* (Cambridge: Cambridge University Press, 1998).

11. Harlan Lane, "The Social Construction of Deafness," *Disability and Society* 10, no. 2 (1995): 172.

12. Adrienne Asch and Michelle Fine, "Shared Dreams: A Left Perspective on Disability Rights and Reproductive Rights," in *Women with Disabilities* (Philadelphia: Temple University Press, 1988), 5–6.

13. See Ron Amundson, "Biological Normality and the ADA," in *Americans with Disabilities;* and "Against Normal Function," *Studies in History and Philosophy of Biological and Biomedical Sciences* 31C (2000): 33–53.

14. See Oliver, *Politics of Disablement,* 22.

15. Ibid., 58.

16. He includes it explicitly as an example, though I will not address these passages from the book here. See Hacking, *Social Construction,* 111–12.

17. I borrow this term from James Trent.

18. Hacking, *Social Construction,* 6.

19. See Trent, *Inventing the Feeble Mind;* Rapley, *Social Construction;* Noll and Trent, eds., *Mental Retardation in America.*

20. Hacking, *Social Construction,* 6.

21. See Rapley, *Social Construction;* Dan Goodley and Mark Rapley, "Changing the Subject: Postmodernity and People with 'Learning Difficulties,'" in *Disability/Postmodernity,* 127.

22. Shelley Tremain, "The Subject of Impairment," in Corker and Shakespeare, eds., *Disability/Postmodernity,* 42.

23. Kittay, *Love's Labor,* 180.

24. Byrne, *Philosophical and Ethical Problems.* While I am sympathetic to Byrne's practical considerations, I do not agree with many of his conclusions when he critiques analyses of oppression and the "deconstruction of cognitive disability" in chapter 5. A different approach to the question of whether the category of intellectual disability should be preserved can be found in a recent volume on intellectual disability and human rights. See Stanley Herr, Lawrence O. Gostin, and Harold Hongju Koh, eds., *The Human Rights of Persons with Intellectual Disabilities: Different but Equal* (Oxford: Oxford University Press, 2003).

25. Hacking, *Social Construction,* 12.

26. Ibid., 122.

27. Though I build on certain dimensions of Ian Hacking's discussion of the looping effect of human kinds in what follows, he has recently abandoned talk of "kinds" altogether. See Ian Hacking, "Kinds of People: Moving Targets," *Proceedings of the British Academy* 151 (2007): 285–318.

28. Though the moral imbecile was still thought to be intellectually inferior to a "normal" individual, his or her defining feature was *moral* deficiency.

29. One might argue that my description of internal heterogeneity is really evidence of an external variation; in other words, the vertical and horizontal means of ordering subgroups is simply evidence of different people offering competing definitions. I will maintain the distinction between external and internal, however, given that these multiple subdivisions were often part of one person's classification scheme.

30. Seguin, *Idiocy*, 29.

31. L. P. Brockett, "Idiots and the Efforts for Their Improvement" [1856] in *History of Mental Retardation: Collected Papers,* 1:78.

32. Binet and Simon, "Upon the Necessity of Establishing a Scientific Diagnosis of Interior States of Intelligence," in *History of Mental Retardation: Collected Papers,* 1:335.

33. See Ned Block and Gerald Dworkin, eds., *The IQ Controversy: Critical Readings* (New York: Pantheon, 1976). More recently debates were sparked by publication of Richard J. Herrnstein and Charles Murray, *The Bell Curve: Intelligence and Class Structure in American Life* (New York: Free Press, 1994). See Steven Fraser, ed., *The Bell Curve Wars: Race, Intelligence, and the Future of America* (New York: Basic, 1995); Russell Jacoby and Naomi Glauberman, eds., *The Bell Curve Debate: History, Documents, Opinions* (New York: Times Books, 1995).

34. See the DSM-IV, ICD-10, and AAMR definitions of mental retardation.

35. Howe, "On the Causes of Idiocy," 49. The final words of this passage are evidence of the sense, even among superintendents, that caring for idiots was a benevolent and humanitarian cause.

36. These disciplines have not always held equal status with respect to mental retardation; one rich area of research would be to examine the historical shifts in the authority of various discourses. Medical discourse dominated in the mid-nineteenth century, and with the rise of genetic explanations of mental retardation, is likely to become even more prominent.

37. This insight has led many in the disabled community to refer to the non-disabled as TABs: temporarily able-bodied persons. The same, of course, could be said about the able-minded.

38. AAMR, 1992, 9.

39. Interesting cross-cultural work on mental retardation points to this fact. See essays in Jenkins, *Questions of Competence;* R. B. Edgerton, "Mental Retardation in Non-Western Societies: Towards a Cross-Cultural Perspective on Incompetence," in *Socio-Cultural Aspects of Mental Retardation,* ed. H. C. Hayward (New York: Appleton-Century-Crofts, 1970); Edgerton, *The Cloak of Competence* (Berkeley: University of California Press, 1993).

40. An example of this critique in the context of mental retardation can be found in Mark Rapley's arguments regarding the production of incompetence in *Social Construction.*

41. Lennard Davis, *Bending Over Backwards* (New York: Routledge), 23, 25–26.

42. See Jenkins, ed., *Questions of Competence.*

43. Hacking, *Social Construction,* 104–106.

44. Hacking gives three examples of this: mental retardation, schizophrenia, and autism (109–17).

45. Hacking, *Social Construction,* 115.

46. Ibid., 103.

47. Ibid., 119.

48. Patricia Ainsworth and Pamela C. Baker, *Understanding Mental Retardation: A Resource for Parents, Caregivers, and Counselors* (Jackson: University of Mississippi

Press, 2004), 3. For an extensive discussion of the various kinds and causes of intellectual disability, see James Harris, *Intellectual Disability: Understanding Its Development, Causes, Classification, Evaluation, and Treatment* (New York: Oxford University Press, 2005).

49. George Lakoff, *Women, Fire, and Dangerous Things: What Categories Reveal about the Mind* (Chicago: University of Chicago Press, 1987), xiv.

50. Ibid., 41.

51. Ibid.

52. Ibid., 42.

53. Peter Tyor and Leland Bell, *Caring for the Retarded in America* (Westport, Conn.: Greenwood, 1984), 98.

54. In 1910 Goddard renamed this group "morons" to avoid terminological confusion. But for at least twenty years, "feebleminded" referred to both the entire category and a particular subclassification.

55. Sloan and Stevens, *Century of Concern*, 20.

56. Michel Foucault, "The Subject and Power," in *Michel Foucault: Beyond Structuralism and Hermeneutics*, ed. Hubert L. Dreyfus and Paul Rabinow, 2nd ed. (Chicago: University of Chicago Press, 1983), 222.

57. Ibid., 223.

58. Ibid.

59. Foucault defines power as intentional ("there is no power exercised without aims") yet non-subjective: it cannot be located simply in one individual; it functions through practices. See *The History of Sexuality*, vol. 1, *An Introduction*, trans. Robert Hurley (New York: Vintage, 1990), 94–95.

60. Foucault, "Subject and Power," 223.

61. Ibid.

62. This was not the only institutionalized discourse, however. Mental retardation was also an object of pedagogical and psychological inquiry, which had their own forms of institutionalized knowledge.

63. Foucault, "Subject and Power," 223.

64. Foucault, *Psychiatric Power*, 165. He goes on to discuss the ways in which this tautology was evident in the "schools" for "idiots" (218–19).

65. Ibid., 3.

66. Foucault, *Psychiatric Power*, 180–81.

67. As we have seen, many of these results were aimed at benefiting the institutions more than the individuals housed within them.

4. The Face of Authority

The first epigraph is from Nancy Tuana, "The Speculum of Ignorance: The Women's Health Movement and Epistemologies of Ignorance," *Hypatia* 21, no. 3 (Summer 2006): 14. The second epigraph is from Michel Foucault, *Society Must Be Defended: Lectures at the Collège de France, 1975–1976* (New York: Picador, 1997), 10–11.

1. I will take up this question of knowledge coming from below more explicitly later in this chapter.

2. Foucault provides an interesting analysis of the ways in which the "moral treatment" of madness was actually a response to certain forms of insurrections that could not be contained. This suggests that resistance in various forms was an integral part of the asylum. See Foucault, *Psychiatric Power*.

3. This reference sparked a fascinating exchange between Foucault and Derrida, which I will address in the conclusion to this volume.

4. An important project would be to trace these historical examples. One excellent resource that covers Enlightenment conceptions of idiocy in the context of cases of "wild children" is Adriana S. Benzaquen, *Encounters with Wild Children: Temptation and Disappointment in the Study of Human Nature* (Montreal: McGill-Queens University Press, 2006).

5. Of course, to make such a claim, the very definition of what counts as a proper philosophical topic and what is viewed as part of the discipline itself must be addressed.

6. This could amount to something like the "archaeology of silence" that Foucault hopes to achieve in his history of madness—in his case he is mapping the silence that falls in the gap between Reason and Unreason.

7. Here I have in mind the traditional approach that I defined in the introduction.

8. Ruth Luckasson and A. Reeve, "Naming, Defining, and Classifying in Mental Retardation," *Mental Retardation* 39, no. 1 (2001): 47–52; F. E. Stockholder, "Naming and Renaming Persons with Intellectual Disabilities"; and Gary Woodhill, "The Social Semiotics of Disability," in *Disability Is Not Measles,* ed. Marcia Rioux and Michael Bach (North York: L'Institut Roeher, 1994).

9. I will not address the terms "cognitively disabled," "intellectually disabled," or "developmentally disabled" here; my focus will be on the specific term "mental retardation" and its precursors.

10. Ruth Luckasson, "Terminology and Power," in *The Human Rights of Persons with Intellectual Disabilities,* ed. Stanley Herr, Lawrence O. Gostin, and Harold Hongju Koh (Oxford: Oxford University Press, 2003).

11. Peter Singer, "All Animals Are Equal" (1974); reprinted in *Ethics in Practice: An Anthology,* ed. Hugh LaFollette (Cambridge, Mass.: Blackwell, 1997), 124. Benn wrote his article in 1967.

12. Singer defines speciesism as "a prejudice or attitude of bias in favor of the interests of one's own species and against those of members of other species" (*Animal Liberation,* 6). I will discuss this concept at length in a later section.

13. Singer, "Animals," 124.

14. Ibid., 124–25.

15. Ibid., 125.

16. I realize that there is something odd about making this argument, since the question of how Singer defines the moral status of individuals with intellectual disabilities might be far more concerning than the use of an antiquated term (Benn's reference to imbeciles) in an argument that is actually arguing for the inclusion of persons with disabilities. (I thank Eva Kittay for pointing this out to me.) However, I still think this example is valuable insofar as it confirms that it is not problematized by many philosophers.

17. Vinit Haksar, *Equality, Liberty, and Perfectionism* (Oxford: Oxford University Press, 1979), 1.

18. Ibid., 69.

19. Ibid., 72.

20. Ibid., 74.

21. The 1959 AAMD classification manual was already using the term "mental retardation." See Rick Heber, *A Manual on Terminology and Classification in Mental Retardation* (American Association on Mental Deficiency, 1959). For more philosophical examples, see Paul Spicker, "Mental Handicap and Citizenship," *Journal of Applied Philosophy* 7, no. 2 (1990): 139–40.

22. Jeff McMahan, "Cognitive Disability, Misfortune, and Justice," *Philosophy and Public Affairs* 25, no. 1 (1996): 16–17.

23. Ibid., 26.

24. Paul Spicker, "Mental Handicap and Citizenship," *Journal of Applied Philosophy* 7, no. 2 (1990): 139–40.

25. This is similar to the marginalization of the female, relative to the androcentric norm in traditional Western philosophy.

26. See Goodley and Van Hove, eds., *Another Disability Studies Reader*; Elaine Castles, *"We're People First": The Social and Emotional Lives of Individuals with Mental Retardation* (Westport, Conn.: Praeger, 1996).

27. Luckasson, "Terminology," 52.

28. Paula Boddington and Tessa Podpadec, "Who Are the Mentally Handicapped?" *Journal of Applied Philosophy* 8, no. 2 (1991): 180.

29. Byrne, *Philosophical and Ethical Problems*, 14.

30. Eva Feder Kittay, "At the Margins of Moral Personhood," *Ethics* 116 (October 2005): 100–13, 126.

31. Ibid., 129.

32. For example, in one of the few collections of philosophical articles devoted to mental retardation, *Ethics and Mental Retardation*, only three of the twenty articles refer to the AAMR's definition of mental retardation or explicitly discuss the issue of definition. See Lawrence B. McCullough, "The World Gained and the World Lost: Labeling the Mentally Retarded"; Joseph Margolis, "Applying Moral Theory to the Retarded"; Loretta Kopelman, "Respect and the Retarded: Issues of Valuing and Labeling," in *Ethics and Mental Retardation*.

33. Jeffrie Murphy, "Rights and Borderline Cases," in *Ethics and Mental Retardation*, 12.

34. Ibid., 11.

35. Many firsthand testimonies refute this assumption, in addition to my own experiences working with children labeled "profoundly retarded" who were capable of making their wishes and decisions known.

36. Ibid., 11.

37. Stuart F. Spicker, "Person Ascriptions, Profound Disabilities, and Our Self-Imposed Duties: A Reply to Loretta Kopelman," in *Ethics and Mental Retardation*, 87.

38. Ibid., 87–88.

39. Ibid., 91.

40. Ibid., 97–98.

41. Boddington and Podpadec, "Who Are the Mentally Handicapped?" 181.

42. Stuart Spicker begins by acknowledging that it is a normative category but then proceeds to make statements suggesting that he views the mentally retarded as a pathological, qualitatively different kind best treated by doctors and psychologists.

43. Gould, *Mismeasure,* 24.

44. Ibid., 159.

45. Ibid., 155.

46. For instance, few acknowledge that in 75 percent of mild cases and 30–40 percent of more severe cases, no underlying cause is clearly identifiable. See note 19, chapter 1. For a fuller discussion of reification in philosophical arguments about mental retardation, see Carlson, "Mindful Subjects," chapter 5. This problem has also been discussed by a number of philosophers who adopt a critical disability stance. For examples, see Ron Amundson, "Against Normal Function" and "Biological Normality and the ADA," in *Americans with Disabilities,* ed. Leslie Francis and Anita Silvers (New York: Routledge, 2000); Silvers, "Formal Justice." Questions regarding the reification of intelligence have also emerged in bioethical discussions about enhancing intelligence.

47. McMahan's article is an example of dealing only with severe cases; see Daniel Wilker, "Paternalism and the Mildly Retarded," *Philosophy and Public Affairs* 8, no. 4 (1979) for the opposite end of the spectrum.

48. McCullough, "The World Gained," 89.

49. Boddington and Podpadec, "Who Are the Mentally Handicapped?" 183.

50. Byrne, *Philosophical and Ethical Problems,* 13.

51. For an interesting discussion of methodological issues surrounding the incorporation of these perspectives, see Rioux and Bach, eds., *Disability Is Not Measles.*

52. There are many other instances where philosophers have attempted to define quality of life according to some objective measures, and in doing so will engage with the question of disability and the extent to which it lowers an individual's quality of life. This has sparked a full discussion about the normative assumptions underlying such definitions and the dismissal of claims by persons with disabilities that they do, in fact, experience a high quality of life. For example, see *Quality of Life and Human Difference: Genetic Testing, Health Care, and Disability,* ed. David Wasserman, Jerome Bickenbach, and Robert Wachbroit (Cambridge: Cambridge University Press, 2005).

53. Robert M. Veatch, *The Foundations of Justice: Why the Retarded and the Rest of Us Have Claims to Equality* (New York: Oxford University Press, 1986), 197.

54. Jeffrie Murphy, "Do the Mentally Retarded Have a Right Not to Be Eaten?" in *Ethics and Mental Retardation.*

55. Jeff McMahan, *The Ethics of Killing* (New York: Oxford University Press, 2003), 230.

56. Eva Kittay presents a far more thorough and incisive critique of McMahan's work in "At the Margins of Moral Personhood," *Ethics* 116 (October 2005): 100–31.

57. Stiker, *History of Disability,* 1.

58. Byrne, *Philosophical and Ethical Problems,* 46.

59. Byrne, *Philosophical and Ethical Problems,* 48.

60. Byrne, *Philosophical and Ethical Problems,* viii.

61. This is indicative of the kind of humility that Eva Kittay calls for in her critique of McMahan. See "Ethics at the Margins."

62. Byrne, *Philosophical and Ethical Problems*, xi.

63. Kittay, *Love's Labor*, 173.

64. For other examples, see Sophia Wong, "At Home with Gender and Down Syndrome," *Hypatia* 17, no. 3 (Summer 2002): 89–117; Roger Gottleib, "The Tasks of Embodied Love: Moral Problems in Caring for Children with Disabilities," *Hypatia* 17, no. 3 (Summer 2002): 225–36; Hilde Lindemann Nelson, "What Child Is This?" *Hasting Center Report* 32, no. 6 (2002): 29–38.

65. Byrne is highly suspicious of the postmodern model of disability, and I do not necessarily share his concerns with a Foucauldian approach to the issue.

66. Wendell, *Rejected Body*, 73.

67. Mary Mahowald, "A Feminist Standpoint," in *Disability, Difference, Discrimination*, ed. Anita Silvers, David Wasserman, and Mary Mahowald (Lanham, Md.: Rowman & Littlefield, 1998), 217.

68. Ibid.

69. See note 16 in the introduction.

70. The danger of this is great, as evidenced by the sparse amount of work in disability studies and disability theory that actively addresses the concerns of this group and includes the voices of persons with intellectual disabilities.

71. Marianne Janack, "Standpoint Epistemology without the 'Standpoint'? An Examination of Epistemic Privilege and Epistemic Authority," *Hypatia* 12, no. 2 (Spring 1997): 135.

72. Ibid., 135.

73. Ibid., 137.

74. J. S. Reinders, "The Good Life for Citizens with Intellectual Disability," *Journal of Intellectual Disability Research* 46, no. 1 (2002): 5.

5. The Face of the Beast

The third epigraph is a description of Geraldo Rivera's visit to Willowbrook, which was aired that same evening. David Rothman and Sheila Rothman, *The Willowbrook Wars* (New Brunswick, N.J.: Aldine Transaction, 2005), 17.

1. David Rothman and Sheila Rothman, *The Willowbrook Wars* (New Brunswick, N.J.: Aldine Transaction, 2005), 23.

2. Ibid., 24.

3. For a full account of this, see Rothman and Rothman, *Willowbrook Wars*.

4. See Foucault, *Madness and Civilization;* Carlson, "The Human as Just an Other Animal," in *Phenomenology and the Non-Human Animal*, ed. Christian Lotz and Corinne Painter (Dordrecht: Springer, 2007), 117–33.

5. Boddington and Podpadec, "Who Are the Mentally Handicapped?" 177–90.

6. Ibid., 179.

7. Ibid.

8. Quantitative portraits of intellectual disability raise philosophical issues (e.g., the question of marginal persons; the problem of drawing the line between mild, mod-

erate, and severe cases). See Carlson, "Mindful Subjects." However, I find the portrayal of the intellectually disabled in philosophical discourse as *non*-persons and radically other a more pressing issue to address.

9. Hugh LaFollette, *Ethics in Practice: An Anthology* (Cambridge, Mass.: Blackwell, 1997), 692. Note the choice of the term "deficient" to refer to these individuals. The other appearance of this group in the index is under "mental defectives" followed by "*see* deficient humans" (p. 697).

10. Anthony Woozley, "The Rights of the Retarded," in *Ethics and Mental Retardation*, 51. He explains who the "many" are: "A person does not lack a sense of justice by being retarded—unless he is retarded enough; and surely plenty are retarded enough for that. . . . he does not have the comprehension which you must have to have a sense of justice" (50–51).

11. Jeff McMahan, "Cognitive Disability, Misfortune, and Justice," *Philosophy and Public Affairs* 25, no. 1 (1996): 3–35, 27.

12. Martha Nussbaum, *Frontiers of Justice: Disability, Nationality, Species Membership* (Cambridge, Mass.: Belknap, 2006), 192.

13. Nussbaum goes on to discuss the problems with drawing these connections in greater depth in her chapter on animals. Ibid., 363–65.

14. Jeffrie G. Murphy, "Do the Retarded Have a Right Not to Be Eaten? A Rejoinder to Joseph Margolis," in *Ethics and Mental Retardation*, 46.

15. Haksar, *Equality, Liberty, and Perfectionism*, 18.

16. McMahan, "Cognitive Disability," 32.

17. Jeff McMahan, *The Ethics of Killing: Problems at the Margins of Life* (New York: Oxford University Press, 2002), 228.

18. Ibid.

19. Spicker, "Mental Handicap and Citizenship," 139–51.

20. Peter Singer, *Animal Liberation* (London: Pimlico, 1995), 6.

21. Ibid., 9.

22. Ibid., 241.

23. The fact that the mild cases are never invoked will be discussed later.

24. Ibid., 16.

25. Ibid., 85.

26. Ibid., 17.

27. Ibid.

28. Singer has argued that infanticide, when decided by the parents, is acceptable in such cases. See Singer, *Should the Baby Live? The Problem of Handicapped Infants* (Oxford: Oxford University Press, 1985).

29. Singer, *Animal Liberation*, 18–19.

30. Ibid., 20.

31. Ibid.

32. Ibid., 20–21.

33. Ibid., 21.

34. I assume by this latter capacity Singer means some kind of reciprocal relationship, since "normal" humans can have relationships with animals and infants that are meaningful for the former, not the latter.

35. Singer, *Animal Liberation,* 239–40. Here again we see the problem of language. To equate the "permanently and profoundly retarded" with "human beings with severe and irreparable brain damage" gives the impression that there is some physical anomaly or process which has erased the individual's potential.

36. Psychologists point to the heterogeneity of this category and argue that even in cases with an identifiable genetic or biological cause, we still do not have the ability to accurately predict the severity of the cognitive impairment and the ways it will be manifested. See William E. MacClean Jr., *Ellis' Handbook of Mental Deficiency, Psychological Theory, and Research* (Mahwah, N.J.: Erlbaum, 1997), 14.

37. See James C. Harris, *Intellectual Disability: Understanding Its Development, Causes, Classification, Evaluation, and Treatment* (New York: Oxford University Press, 2005).

38. The depiction of this group as devoid of all potential for learning and development is both empirically misguided and, at a personal level, deeply disturbing. See Eva Kittay's response to McMahan, "At the Margins of Personhood."

39. John Gleason, "Theoretical Framework for What Persons with Severe and Profound Multiple Disabilities Do in Context," in *Disability Is Not Measles,* 249–50.

40. Singer, *Animal Liberation,* 18–19.

41. Ibid., 19.

42. Ibid.

43. Ibid., 85.

44. Of course, some would argue that it is a qualitatively different case because Grandma may have been a *once-competent person.* A comparative analysis of the substantial philosophical discourse surrounding dementia and intellectual disability could offer an important insight into this issue. For example, Bruce Jennings outlines a conception of "semantic agency" (to which I shall return later) in relation to dementia that may be useful in considering individuals who have severe congenital intellectual disabilities. See Bruce Jennings, "Freedom Fading: On Dementia, Best Interests, and Public Safety," *Georgia Law Review* 35 (2000–2001).

45. McMahan, "Cognitive Disability," 34.

46. This group is not the first to be accorded such status, and the work on otherness in relation to race, gender, ethnicity, and disability is too broad to mention here. Suffice it to say that Simone de Beauvoir's account of woman as other in *The Second Sex* (New York: Knopf, 1968) has been followed by a growing body of literature in feminism and postcolonial discourse on the processes of dehumanization which accompanies this position of otherness. See, for example, Linda Alcoff, "Philosophy and Racial Identity," *Radical Philosophy* 75 (January–February 1996).

47. Peter Singer, personal communication at the Cognitive Disability: A Challenge to Moral Philosophy conference, New York City, September 2008.

48. Kittay, "At the Margins of Personhood," 125.

49. Byrne, *Philosophical and Ethical Problems,* 51–52.

50. Young, *Justice,* 53.

51. Singer, *Animal Liberation,* 241.

52. Young, *Justice,* 58–59.

53. Byrne, *Philosophical and Ethical Problems,* 72.

54. Margolis, *Applying Moral Theory*, 33.

55. For a more recent example of how Singer does this, see his essay "Bridging the Gap," in *Writings on an Ethical Life* (New York: Harper Perennial, 2001).

56. Young, *Justice*, 46.

57. Given the wide range of abilities and experiences, it is questionable to what extent it even makes sense to speak about this as a unified group. In the context of theorizing oppression, however, I think it is justified.

58. Young, *Justice*, 43.

59. Ibid., 44.

60. It is important to note that this is not *necessarily* the case. See Castles, *"We're People First."*

61. Hacking, *Social Construction*, 370.

62. Young, *Justice*, 46.

63. I realize that part of what is at issue here is the question of what exactly it means to treat someone *as a human,* and thus critics of speciesism might find my statement problematic. However, it seems to me that to deny the moral relevance of *being human* is to risk closing off the possibility of having such discussions. I also want to clarify that the human beings about whom I am speaking here are existing beings who have been born (not fetuses, embryos, or future persons). The deeper metaphysical questions of what moral status anything human should have must be left aside for now.

64. Murphy, "Do the Mentally Retarded Have a Right Not to Be Eaten?" 46. Note the dualism between sentimentality and thought here.

65. Frank De Roose, "Ethics and Marginal Cases: The Rights of the Mentally Handicapped," *Journal of Applied Philosophy* 8, no. 2 (1991): 87–95, 87.

66. Murphy, "Do the Mentally Retarded Have a Right Not to Be Eaten?" 46.

67. There are many examples beyond Willowbrook. Geraldo Rivera also exposed Americans to the horrific conditions in another New York institution, Letchworth Village: "Virtually every patient in building Tau was undressed and there was shit everywhere; it looked and smelled like a poorly kept kennel. . . . The residents of Tau were young girls . . . most of them were literally smeared with feces—their roommates', their own. They looked like children who had been out making mudpies. My stomach still turns just thinking about it. But they were, after all, just little girls. And those little girls—just like your sister or daughter—wanted to be held and loved" (quoted in Trent, *Inventing the Feeble Mind*, 258). See also Burton Blatt and Fred Kaplan, *Christmas in Purgatory: Photographic Essay on Mental Retardation* (Syracuse, N.Y.: Human Policy Press, 1974).

68. Nussbaum makes a similar argument regarding the "kind of dignity relevant to a species." *Frontiers of Justice*, 351.

69. McMahan, *Ethics of Killing*, 232.

70. Ibid.

71. Ibid.

72. Ibid. For a fuller account of McMahan's views regarding species membership, see *Ethics of Killing*, 209–32.

73. Byrne, *Philosophical and Ethical Problems*, 69.

74. Kittay, *Love's Labor,* 173.

75. Recall the earlier discussion regarding why it is not necessary to view animal interests in conflict with the interests of persons with intellectual disabilities.

76. Kopelman, "Respect and the Retarded," 66.

77. Ibid., 67. For other examples of what it might mean to recognize membership in the human community as morally relevant, see Diamond, "Importance of Being Human"; Nussbaum, *Frontiers of Justice;* Kittay, *Love's Labor;* Byrne, *Philosophical and Ethical Problems.*

78. Cora Diamond, "The Importance of Being Human," in *Human Beings,* ed. D. Cockburn (Cambridge: Cambridge University Press, 1991), 35–62.

79. Diamond, "Importance of Being Human," 59. Hilde Lindemann has pointed to an important challenge to this position, namely, appeal to a *shared life* might sanction certain forms of racism or discrimination (by choosing to identify with a particular group's *shared* life). However, it seems that this is precisely what Diamond wants to challenge by grounding this notion of a shared fate in *simply* being human, by broadening our scope of moral consideration beyond particular groups or interests.

80. Ibid., 55.

81. Ibid., 56.

82. Ibid., 57.

83. For a variety of examples and approaches to this, see Nussbaum, *Frontiers of Justice;* MacIntyre, *Dependent Rational Animals;* Kittay, *Love's Labor.*

84. There is a significant body of literature from women of color and women with disabilities identifying the racism and ableism inherent in feminist literature.

85. Singer, *Animal Liberation,* 221.

86. MacIntyre, *Dependent Rational Animals,* 120.

87. Ibid., 8.

88. For a fuller discussion of MacIntyre's position and its implications for persons with intellectual disabilities, see Licia Carlson, "Rethinking Normalcy, Normalization, and Cognitive Disability," in *Science and Other Cultures: Issues in Philosophies of Science and Technologies,* ed. Sandra Harding and Robert Figueroa (New York: Routledge, 2003), 154–71.

89. See Kittay, *Love's Labor.*

90. MacIntyre, *Dependent Rational Animals,* 50.

91. See Lotz and Painter, eds., *Phenomenology and the Non-Human Animal;* Peter Atterton and Matthew Calarco, eds., *Animal Philosophy: Essential Readings in Continental Thought* (London: Continuum, 2005); Jami Weinstein, "Traces of the Beast: Becoming Nietzsche, Becoming Animal, and Faces of the Transhuman"; and Jennifer Hamm, "Circe's Truth: On the Way to Animals and Women," in *A Nietzschean Bestiary,* ed. Ralph R. Acampora and Christa Davis Acampora (Lanham, Md.: Rowman & Littlefield, 2004).

92. For a discussion of how Foucault traces this connection between madness and animality, see Licia Carlson, "The Human as Just an *Other* Animal"; Clare Palmer, "Madness and Animality in Michel Foucault's *Madness and Civilization,*" in *Animal Philosophy: Essential Readings in Continental Thought,* ed. Peter Atterton and Matthew

Calarco (London: Continuum, 2005), 72–84; Palmer, "Taming the Wild Profusion of Existing Things: A Study of Foucault, Power, and Human/Animal Relationships," *Environmental Ethics* 23 (Winter 2001): 339–58.

93. Foucault would be rightly suspicious of any attempt to lay claim to a universal conception of the *human*. Yet I read his texts as instances of resistance against certain mechanisms of dehumanization, as sites where the reader is forced to confront precisely what is at stake in disqualifying certain subjects, in making them into objects, in animalizing them. Of course the extent to which Foucault's methods can offer a philosophical basis on which to challenge forms of dehumanization and oppression is a subject of great debate, and to simply say that his texts are sites of resistance cannot resolve the issue without further discussion. For now, I simply want to make clear that I am not calling for a return to past incarnations of humanism, nor do I think that we should discount the promise of Foucault's work because he has critiqued them.

94. Wolf Wolfensberger, *The Principle of Normalization in Human Services* (Toronto: National Institute on Mental Retardation, 1972), 18–19.

95. Byrne, *Philosophical and Ethical Problems,* 67.

96. Foucault, *Madness and Civilization,* ix.

6. The Face of Suffering

The first epigraph is from Eric Cassel, *The Nature of Suffering and the Goals of Medicine* (Oxford: Oxford University Press, 2004). The second epigraph is from Elizabeth Spelman, *Fruits of Sorrow: Framing Our Attention to Suffering* (Boston: Beacon, 1997), 159. The third epigraph is from Steven Edwards, "Prevention of Disability on Grounds of Suffering," *Journal of Medical Ethics* 27, no. 6 (2001): 380–82.

1. There is a wide literature addressing this issue. Here are a few examples: Anita Silvers, "On Not Iterating Women's Disability: A Crossover Perspective on Genetic Dilemmas," in *Embodying Bioethics,* ed. Anne Donchin and Laura Purdy (Lanham, Md.: Rowman & Littlefield, 1999); Silvers, Wasserman, and Mahowald, eds., *Disability, Difference, Discrimination;* David Wasserman, Jerome Bickenbach, and David Wachbroit, eds., *Quality of Life and Human Difference: Genetic Testing, Health Care, and Disability* (Cambridge: Cambridge University Press, 2005); Steven Edwards, "Prevention of Disability on the Grounds of Suffering."

2. Spelman, *Fruits of Sorrow,* 159.

3. Deborah Kaplan, "Prenatal Screening and Its Impact on Persons with Disabilities," *Clinical Obstetrics and Gynecology* 36, no. 3 (1993): 605–12.

4. Bruce Jennings, "Technology and the Genetic Imaginary," *Prenatal Testing and Disability Rights,* ed. Adrienne Asch and Eric Parens (Washington, D.C.: Georgetown University Press, 2000), 137.

5. Ibid., 138.

6. I do not mean to suggest that this is the sole portrait of the "disabled fetus" in any of these fields. However, it is a dominant prototype that influences the moral conclusions that are drawn regarding the permissibility of prenatal testing and selective abortion. I point to this face of intellectual disability in order to challenge certain assumptions that lie behind it.

7. John Harris, "Is Gene Therapy a Form of Eugenics?" *Bioethics* 7, no. 2–3 (1993): 178–87. Steven Edwards critiques this definition in the context of intellectual disability and suffering in "Prevention of Disability on Grounds of Suffering."

8. Edwards, "Prevention of Disability," 381.

9. Ibid.

10. There are certain complexities regarding how one measures this, particularly in the case of persons with severe intellectual disabilities, a point to which I will return later in this chapter.

11. Pekka Louhiala, *Preventing Intellectual Disability: Ethical and Clinical Issues* (Cambridge: Cambridge University Press, 2004), 101.

12. Ibid., 116.

13. Silvers, "Formal Justice," 104.

14. See William M. Kane, Magdalena M. Avila, and Everett M. Rogers, "Community and Culture: World Views and Natural Affiliations as the Basis of Understanding, Trust, Assistance, and Support"; and Alexander J. Tymchuk, "Family Life: Experiences of People with Mild Cognitive Limitations," in *The Forgotten Generation: The Status and Challenges of Adults with Mild Cognitive Limitations,* ed. Alexander Tymchuk, K. Charlie Lakin, Ruth Luckasson (Baltimore: Paul H. Brookes, 2001); Goodley and Van Hove, *Another Disability Studies Reader.*

15. John R. McCartney and Vincent A. Campbell, "Confirmed Abuse Cases in Public Residential Facilities for Persons with Mental Retardation: A Multi-State Study," *Mental Retardation* 36, no. 6 (1998): 465–73.

16. For a few examples, see Goodley and Van Hove, *Another Disability Studies Reader;* Tymchuk, Lakin, Luckasson, eds., *The Forgotten Generation;* Castles, *"We're People First."*

17. For a discussion of concrete implications in the context of prenatal genetic screening, see Asch and Parens, *Prenatal Screening.*

18. Botkin, "Fetal Privacy and Confidentiality," *Hastings Center Report* 25, no. 5 (1995): 32–39.

19. Ibid., 37–38.

20. Ibid., 37.

21. Thomas E. Elkins and Douglas Brown, "Ethical Concerns and Future Direction in Maternal Screening for Down Syndrome," *Women's Health Issues* 5, no. 1 (1995): 15–20.

22. Hans Reinders, *The Future of the Disabled in Liberal Society* (Notre Dame, Ind.: University of Notre Dame Press, 2000), 173. For a first-person account of the complexities of addressing both a child's and parent's suffering in the context of intellectual disability, see Roger Gottleib, "The Tasks of Embodied Love: Moral Problems in Caring for Children with Disabilities," *Hypatia* 17, no. 3 (Summer 2002): 225–36.

23. Steven Edwards, "Prenatal Genetic Screening for ID," *Journal of Intellectual Disability Research* 47, no. 7 (2003): 526–32.

24. Elkins and Brown, "Ethical Concerns," 15.

25. See "Screen All Pregnancies, Some Doctors Say," *New York Times,* January 9, 2007. For a critical discussion of the effects of making genetic screening routine, see

Nancy Press, "Assessing the Expressive Character of Prenatal Testing: The Choices Made or the Choices Available?" in *Prenatal Testing and Disability Rights*. For an extensive discussion of the ethical questions surrounding eugenics and genetic testing, see Allen Buchanan, Dan W. Brock, Norman Daniels, and Daniel Wikler, *From Chance to Choice: Genetics and Justice* (Cambridge: Cambridge University Press, 2000).

26. I do not know how exactly this will affect our perceptions, though I would imagine that the medical model will become increasingly dominant, and persons with mental retardation may be viewed as avoidable genetic "accidents."

27. Though time does not permit here, an important epistemological project will be to trace how the association of these genetic abnormalities with mental retardation continues to transform and rearrange the boundaries of this heterogeneous classification.

28. Rayna Rapp, *Testing Women, Testing the Fetus: The Social Impact of Amniocentesis in America* (New York: Routledge, 2000), 89.

29. See Shelley Tremain, "Reproductive Freedom, Self-Regulation, and the Government of Impairment in Utero," *Hypatia* 21, no. 1 (2006): 35–53.

30. For example, see Kittay, *Love's Labor;* Barbara Hillyer, *Feminism and Disability.* A discussion that moves beyond the familial context and roots these questions firmly in the contexts of *women* with intellectual disabilities can be found in Cushing and Lewis's rich discussion of the relationships between caregivers and clients in the L'Arche community. See Pamela Cushing and Tanya Lewis, "Negotiating Mutuality and Agency in Care-giving Relationships with Women with Intellectual Disabilities," *Hypatia* 17, no. 3 (Summer 2002): 173–93.

31. Kittay, *Love's Labor.*

32. Barbara Katz Rothman, *The Tentative Pregnancy* (New York: Norton, 1986).

33. Rapp, *Testing Women,* 131.

34. See Annette Patterson and Martha Satz, "Genetic Counseling and the Disabled: Feminism Examines the Stance of Those Who Stand at the Gate," *Hypatia* 17, no. 3 (Summer 2002): 118–45; Nancy Press, "Assessing the Expressive Character of Prenatal Testing: The Choices Made or the Choices Made Available?"; and Barbara Bowles Biesecker and Lori Hamby, "What Difference the Disability Community Arguments Should Make for the Delivery of Prenatal Genetic Information," in *Prenatal Testing and Disability Rights*.

35. The most dramatic of these recently has been the Ashley X case, where a six-year-old girl was given growth attenuation treatment, which included the removal of her breast buds and sex organs, and large doses of hormones. This case provides a stunning example of the intersection of claims regarding both the child's and parents' suffering, gendered assumptions, and the need for a nuanced discussion of these connections. For a wonderfully rich, in-depth study of the ways in which the lives and discourses surrounding women with severe intellectual disabilities are gendered, see Kelley Johnson, *Deinstitutionalising Women: An Ethnographic Study of Institutional Closure* (Cambridge: University of Cambridge Press, 1998). See also Margaret Kennedy, "Sexual Abuse and Disabled Children," 116–34; and "Power in the House: Women with Learning Difficulties Organizing against Abuse," 135–42, in *Encounters with Strangers: Feminism and Disability,* ed. Jenny Morris (London: Women's Press, 1996), 116–34; Deborah Phillips, "Embodied Narratives: Control, Regulation, and Bodily Resistance

in the Life Course of Women with Learning Difficulties," in *Another Disability Studies Reader,* 135–50.

36. See Kelley Johnson et al., "The Possibility of Choice: Women with Intellectual Disabilities Talk about Having Children," in *Disability in the Life Course,* 206–18; Tim Booth and Wendy Booth, "Risk, Resilience, and Competence: Parents with Learning Difficulties and Their Children," in *Questions of Competence,* 76–101.

37. D. Wertz and John Fletcher, "Fatal Knowledge? Prenatal Diagnosis and Sex Selection," *Hastings Center Report* 19, no. 3 (1989): 21–27.

38. Adrienne Asch, "Can Aborting Imperfect Children Be Immoral?" in *Ethical Issues in Modern Medicine,* ed. John Arras and Bonnie Steinbock (Mountain View, Calif.: Mayfield, 1995), 387. For a similar argument regarding sex selection and disability, see Gregor Wolbring, "Where Do We Draw the Line? Surviving Eugenics in a Technological World," in Mark Priestly, *Disability in the Life Course: Global Perspectives* (Cambridge: Cambridge University Press, 2001), 38–49.

39. Kelley Johnson, speaking about the intellectually disabled women in a locked unit whose institutional life and journey through deinstitutionalization is the subject of her book *Deinstitutionalising Women,* 172–73.

40. C. F. Goodey, "Genetic Research into Intellectual Disability," *Journal of Intellectual Disability Research* 47, no. 7 (October 2003): 548–54.

41. Of course, there are philosophers who do have such knowledge. See the discussion of Kittay and Byrne in chapter 4 of this volume.

42. Goodey, "Genetic Research," 551.

43. Ibid., 552.

44. Ibid., 551–52.

45. McMahan, *Ethics of Killing,* 232.

46. It is important to note that even during this period, most children were still living at home with their families.

47. Laura Purdy, "Loving Future People," in *Reproduction, Ethics, and the Law: Feminist Perspectives,* ed. Joan Callahan (Bloomington: Indiana University Press, 1995), 308.

48. Ibid., 304.

49. Ibid., 309.

50. Silvers, "Formal Justice," 93.

51. Michael Bérubé captures this well in his depiction of his son Jamie's rich life. See *Life As We Know It: A Father, a Family, and an Exceptional Child* (New York: Pantheon, 1996).

52. In saying this, I realize that a seeming contradiction may arise. I wish to both emphasize and de-emphasize the fact that persons with mild and moderate intellectual disabilities suffer. However, I don't see the two as contradictory; in fact, I think that the copresence of these two important points (a challenge to the medical model's conflation of disability with suffering caused by the condition and the need to attend to social causes of suffering) highlights the complexity of this issue, and the need for a multifaceted discussion.

53. Bruce Jennings, "Freedom Fading: On Dementia, Best Interests, and Public Safety," *Georgia Law Review* 35 (2000–2001): 614. For a discussion of the relationship between

aging and intellectual disability, see Nancy Breitenbach, "Ageing with Intellectual Disabilities; Discovering Disability with Old Age: Same or Different?" in *Disability and the Life Course: Global Perspectives,* ed. Mark Priestly (Cambridge: Cambridge University Press, 2001), 231–39. Hilde Lindemann Nelson also speaks to the broad ways in which we confer personhood and contribute to the narrative identities of those with severe disabilities in "What Child Is This?" *Hastings Center Report* 32, no. 6 (2002): 29–38.

54. Spelman, *Fruits of Sorrow,* 70.

55. For examples of this, see the articles in Asch and Parens, *Disability Rights and Prenatal Testing;* Wasserman, Bickenbach, and Wachbroit, *Quality of Life and Human Difference.*

56. See Marsha Saxton, "Why Members of the Disabled Community Oppose Prenatal Testing"; and Adrienne Asch, "Why I Haven't Changed my Mind about Prenatal Diagnosis," in *Prenatal Testing and Disability Rights.*

57. Purdy, "Loving Future People," 311.

58. Ibid., 305.

59. Silvers, "Reconciling Equality to Difference," 37.

60. Jenny Morris, *Pride against Prejudice: Transforming Attitudes to Disability* (Philadelphia: New Society Publishers, 1991), 70.

61. For interesting discussions of this phenomenon in the context of facilitated communication and assessments of competence, see Nirmala Erevelles, "Signs of Reason," in *Foucault and the Government of Disability;* and Rapley, *Social Construction,* respectively.

62. See the discussion of Reinders in this chapter; for the discussion of "overly sentimental" portraits, see chap. 4.

63. McMahan, *Ethics of Killing,* 230.

64. Ibid., 230.

65. Edwards, "Prenatal Genetic Screening for ID," 382.

66. Reinders, *Future of the Disabled,* 205.

67. Louhiala, *Preventing Intellectual Disability,* 112.

68. Hauerwas, *Suffering Presence* (Notre Dame, Ind.: University of Notre Dame Press, 1986), 174.

69. Nelson's conception of personhood as a social practice raises interesting questions about the *necessity* of viewing the other in relation to myself in the construction of narrative identities and in recognizing a severely disabled individual as part of our human world. See "What Child Is This?"

Conclusion

The first epigraph is quoted in Gary Shapiro, *Archaeologies of Vision: Foucault and Nietzsche on Seeing and Saying* (Chicago: University of Chicago Press, 2003), 202–203. The second epigraph is from Linton, *Claiming Disability,* 152–53.

1. Foucault, "What Is Enlightenment?" 318.

2. Uma Narayan, *Dislocating Cultures* (New York: Routledge, 1997), 141.

3. The mechanisms through which these various reflections occur are complex, and I will not offer any account of how or why they happen. There is still far more work to be

done, and many theories that could assist in making sense of this (e.g. Goffman's account of stigma and other psychoanalytic and psychological theories, as well as philosophical theories of the self/other dynamic). I simply want to map out these various modes by which "the intellectually disabled" can serve as mirrors for the non-disabled.

4. MacIntyre, *Dependent Rational Animals*, 101.

5. Hauerwas, *Suffering Presence*, 174.

6. Hauerwas, *Suffering Presence*, 169.

7. Robert M. Veatch, *The Foundations of Justice: Why the Retarded and the Rest of Us Have Claims to Equality* (Oxford: Oxford University Press, 1986), 8–9.

8. MacIntyre, *Dependent Rational Animals*, 127–28.

9. Nussbaum, *Frontiers of Justice*, 190.

10. Linton, *Claiming Disability*, 13.

11. Narayan, *Dislocating Cultures*, 141.

12. Ibid., 141.

13. Benzaquen's *Wild Children* provides a fascinating account of how the "wild child" served as a mirror for various competing theories of human nature in the seventeenth and eighteenth centuries.

14. C. F. Goodey, "On Certainty, Reflexivity, and the Ethics of Genetic Research into Intellectual Disability," *Journal of Intellectual Disability Research* 47, no. 7 (2003): 550.

15. Bérubé, *Life As We Know It*, xvii. Though the quote above does not speak directly about philosophers, Bérubé has expressed concerns about this dissonance in hearing certain philosophical views. For his response to Singer, see "Equality, Freedom, and/or Justice for All: A Response to Nussbaum," in *Cognitive Disability and Its Challenge to Moral Philosophy,* ed. Eva Kitay and Licia Carlson (forthcoming).

16. Peter Singer, op-ed, *New York Times*, January 26, 2007.

17. Diamond, "Importance of Being Human," 35–62.

18. Byrne, *Philosophical and Ethical Problems*, 10.

19. Young, *Politics of Difference*, 53.

20. Jeff McMahan, "Cognitive Disability, Misfortune, and Justice," *Philosophy and Public Affairs* 25, no. 1 (1996): 3–35.

21. Mary Mahowald, "A Feminist Standpoint," in *Disability, Difference, Discrimination*, 229.

22. Tuana, "Speculum of Ignorance."

23. Ibid., 4–6.

24. Ibid., 10–13.

25. Ibid., 10.

26. Ibid., 9–10, 13–15, respectively.

27. Ibid., 9.

28. I don't see how Tuana would clarify the difference (if she intends one) between "groups deemed ignorant" and "constructed identities."

29. Ibid., 6–8.

30. Ibid., 15–16.

31. One cannot assume that those in close relation to the intellectually disabled will necessarily be in the best position to make decisions. This raises even more chal-

lenging epistemological and ethical problems that must be addressed in the context of claiming authority.

32. Nelson Goodman, *Ways of Worldmaking* (Indianapolis: Hackett, 1978), 3.

33. Ibid., 22.

34. Anita Silvers, "Reconciling Equality to Difference: Caring (F)or Justice for People with Disabilities," *Hypatia* 10, no. 1 (Winter 1995): 50.

35. Michel Foucault, "Structuralism and Post-structuralism," in *Michel Foucault: Aesthetics, Method, and Epistemology,* ed. Paul Rabinow (New York: New Press, 1998), 450.

36. Jacques Derrida, "Cogito and the History of Madness," in *Writing and Difference* (Chicago: University of Chicago Press, 1978), 33–34.

37. Michel Foucault, "Two Lectures," in *Power/Knowledge: Selected Interviews and Other Writings, 1972–1977,* ed. Colin Gordon (New York: Pantheon, 1980), 82.

38. See James I. Charlton, *Nothing about Us without Us* (Berkeley: University of California Press, 2000).

39. Michel Foucault, "Space, Knowledge, and Power," in *The Foucault Reader,* ed. Paul Rabinow (New York: Pantheon, 1984).

40. Maria Lugones, "'World'-Traveling and Loving Perception," in *Feminist Social Thought: A Reader,* ed. Diana Tietjens Meyer (New York: Routledge, 1997), 158–59.

41. There is interesting work in this vein. See David Michael Levin, *The Philosopher's Gaze: Modernity in the Shadows of Enlightenment* (Pittsburgh: Duquesne University Press, 2003); Gary Shapiro, *Archaeologies of Vision: Foucault and Nietzsche on Seeing and Saying* (Chicago: University of Chicago Press, 2003).

42. For Levinas, of course, the "face" is not meant literally. For some preliminary reflections on Levinas in the context of intellectual disability, see Licia Carlson, "The Human as Just an *Other* Animal," in *Phenomenology and the Non-Human Animal,* 117–33.

43. Bruce Jennings's work speaks to this (see chapter 6). Eve Kosofsky Sedgwick's book *Touching-Feeling: Affect, Pedagogy, Performativity* (Durham, N.C.: Duke University Press, 2003) is a rich exploration of these ideas. I also thank James Harris for pointing me to Ralph Harper's remarkable book, *On Presence: Variations and Reflections* (Baltimore: Johns Hopkins University Press, 2006).

44. Michel Foucault, "What Is Enlightenment?" in *Ethics: Subjectivity and Truth: Michel Foucault,* ed. Paul Rabinow (New York: New Press, 1997), 319.

Selected Bibliography

Adams, Mark. 1990. *The Wellborn Science: Eugenics in Germany, France, Brazil, and Russia*. Oxford: Oxford University Press.

Ainsworth, Patricia, and Pamela C. Baker. 2004. *Understanding Mental Retardation: A Resource for Parents, Caregivers, and Counselors*. Jackson: University of Mississippi Press.

Alcoff, Linda. 1996. "Philosophy and Racial Identity." *Radical Philosophy* 75 (January–February): 5–14.

American Psychiatric Association. 1994. *Diagnostic and Statistical Manual of Mental Disorders: DSM-IV*. Washington, D.C.: American Psychiatric Press.

Amundson, Ron. 2000a. "Biological Normality and the ADA." In *Americans with Disabilities*, ed. Leslie Francis and Anita Silvers. New York: Routledge.

———. 2000b. "Against Normal Function." *Studies in History and Philosophy of Biological and Biomedical Sciences* 31, no. 1: 33–53.

Asch, Adrienne, and Michelle Fine. 1988. "Shared Dreams: A Left Perspective on Disability Rights and Reproductive Rights." In *Women with Disabilities: Essays in Psychology, Policy, and Politics*, ed. Michelle Fine and Adrienne Asch, 297–305. Philadelphia: Temple University Press.

Asch, Adrienne, and Erik Parens, eds. 2000. *Prenatal Testing and Disability Rights*. Washington, D.C.: Georgetown University Press.

Baynton, Douglas. 1996. *Forbidden Signs: American Culture and the Campaign against Sign Language*. Chicago: University of Chicago Press.

Benzaquen, Adriana S. 2006. *Encounters with Wild Children: Temptation and Disappointment in the Study of Human Nature*. Montreal: McGill-Queen's University Press.

Bérubé, Michael. *Life As We Know It: A Father, a Family, and an Exceptional Child*. New York: Pantheon, 1996.

Binet, Alfred, and Theodore Simon. 1980. *The Development of Intelligence in Children*. Translated by Elizabeth Kite. Nashville, Tenn.: Williams.

————. 1905. "Upon the Necessity of Establishing a Scientific Diagnosis of Inferior States of Intelligence." In *The History of Mental Retardation: Collected Papers,* ed. Marvin Rosen, Gerald Clark, and Marvin Kivitz, 1:329–54. Baltimore: University Park Press.

Blatt, Burton. 1987. *The Conquest of Mental Retardation.* Austin, Tex.: Pro-ed.

Blatt, Burton, and Fred Kaplan. 1974. *Christmas in Purgatory: Photographic Essay on Mental Retardation.* Syracuse, N.Y.: Human Policy Press.

Block, Ned, and Gerald Dworkin, eds. 1976. *The IQ Controversy: Critical Readings.* New York: Pantheon.

Boddington, Paula, and Tessa Podpadec. 1991. "Who Are the Mentally Handicapped?" *Journal of Applied Philosophy* 8(2): 177–90.

Bogdan, Robert, and Steven J. Taylor. 1989. "Relationships with Severely Disabled People: The Social Construction of Humanness." *Social Problems* 36(2): 135–48.

————. 1982. *Inside Out: The Social Meaning of Mental Retardation.* Toronto: University of Toronto Press.

Borthwick, Chris. 1990. "Racism, IQ, and Down's Syndrome." *Disability and Society* 11(3): 403–10.

Bové, Paul. 1994a. "The End of Humanism: Michel Foucault and the Power of the Discipines." In *Michel Foucault: Critical Assessments,* ed. Barry Smart, 2:313–28. New York: Routledge.

————. 1994b. "Mendacious Innocents, or The Modern Genealogist As Conscientious Intellectual: Nietzsche, Foucault, Said." In *Michel Foucault: Critical Assessments,* ed. Barry Smart, 2:363–88. New York: Routledge.

Breitenbach, Nancy. 2001. "Aging with Intellectual Disabilities; Discovering Disability with Old Age: Same or Different?" In *Disability and the Life Course: Global Perspectives,* ed. Mark Priestly, 231–39. Cambridge: Cambridge University Press.

Bremner, Robert H. 1960. *American Philanthropy.* Chicago: University of Chicago Press.

Browne, Susan, Debra Conners, and Nanci Stern, eds. 1985. *With the Power of Each Breath: A Disabled Women's Anthology.* Pittsburgh: Cleis.

Buchanan, Allen, Dan W. Brock, Norman Daniels, and Daniel Wikler. 2000. *From Chance to Choice: Genetics and Justice.* Cambridge: Cambridge University Press.

Byrne, Peter. 2000. *Philosophical and Ethical Problems in Mental Handicap.* New York: St. Martin's.

Canguilhem, Georges. 1989. *The Normal and the Pathological.* Translated by Carolyn R. Fawcett. New York: Zone.

Caplan, Paula. 1989. *Don't Blame Mother: Mending the Mother-Daughter Relationship.* New York: Harper & Row.

Carlson, Licia. 2007. "The Human as Just an *Other* Animal: Madness, Disability, and Foucault's Bestiary." In *Phenomenology and the Non-Human Animal,* ed. Christian Lotz and Corinne Painter, 117–33. New York: Springer.

————. 2005. "Docile Bodies, Docile Minds: Foucauldian Reflections on Mental Retardation." In *Foucault and the Government of Disability,* ed. Shelley Tremain. Ann Arbor: University of Michigan Press, 2005.

————. 2003. "Rethinking Normalcy, Normalization, and Cognitive Disability." In *Science and Other Cultures: Issues in the Philosophy of Science and Technology,* ed. Sandra Harding and Robert Figueroa, 154–71. New York: Routledge.

———. 2002. "The Morality of Prenatal Testing and Selective Abortion: Clarifying the Expressivist Objection." In *Mutating Concepts, Evolving Disciplines: Genetics, Medicine, and Society,* ed. Lisa S. Parker and Rachel A. Ankeny, 191–213. Dordrecht: Kluwer.

———. 2001. "Cognitive Ableism and Disability Studies: Feminist Reflections on the History of Mental Retardation." *Hypatia,* special issue on feminism and disability, pt. 1, 16(4): 124–46.

———. 1998. "Mindful Subjects: Classification and Cognitive Disability." Ph.D. diss., University of Toronto.

Cassel, Eric. 2004. *The Nature of Suffering and the Goals of Medicine.* Oxford: Oxford University Press.

Castles, Elaine. 1996. *"We're People First": The Social and Emotional Lives of Individuals with Mental Retardation.* Westport, Conn.: Praeger.

Charlton, James I. 2000. *Nothing about Us without Us: Disability, Oppression, and Empowerment.* Berkeley: University of California Press.

Chesler, Ellen. 2007. *Woman of Valor: Margaret Sanger and the Birth Control Movement in America.* New York: Simon & Shuster.

Chesler, Phyllis. 1983. *Women and Madness.* New York: Avon.

Corker, Marian, and Tom Shakespeare. 2002. *Postmodernity/Disability: Embodying Disability Theory.* New York: Continuum.

Cushing, Pamela, and Tanya Lewis. 2002. "Negotiating Mutuality and Agency in Care Giving Relationships with Women with Intellectual Disabilities." *Hypatia* 17(3): 173–93.

Davis, Lennard J. 2002. *Bending Over Backwards: Essays on Disability and the Body.* New York: New York University Press.

Davis, Lennard J., ed. 1997. *The Disability Studies Reader.* New York: Routledge.

De Roose, Frank. 1991. "Ethics and Marginal Cases: The Rights of the Mentally Handicapped." *Journal of Applied Philosophy* 8(2): 87–95.

Derrida, Jacques. 1978. "Cogito and the History of Madness." In *Writing and Difference.* Chicago: University of Chicago Press.

Diamond, Cora. 1991. "The Importance of Being Human." In *Human Beings,* ed. David Cockburn, 35–62. Cambridge: Cambridge University Press.

Dix, Dorothea. 1843. "Memorial to the Legislature of Massachusetts, 1843." In *The History of Mental Retardation: Collected Papers, Volume I,* ed. Marvin Rosen, Gerald Clark, and Marvin Kivitz, 3–30. Baltimore: University Park Press.

Dowbiggin, Ian. 1991. *Inheriting Madness.* Berkeley: University of California Press.

Dreyfus, Hubert, and Paul Rabinow. 1983. *Michel Foucault: Beyond Structuralism and Hermeneutics.* 2nd ed. Chicago: University of Chicago Press.

Dwyer, Ellen. 2004. "The State and the Multiply Disadvantaged: The Case of Epilepsy." In *Mental Retardation in America,* ed. Steven Noll and James Trent. New York: New York University Press.

Dybwad, Gunnar, and Hank Bersani Jr., eds. 1996. *New Voices: Self-Advocacy by People with Disabilities.* Cambridge, Mass.: Brookline.

Edgerton, R. B. 1993. *The Cloak of Competence.* Berkeley: University of California Press.

————. 1970. "Mental Retardation in Non-Western Societies: Towards a Cross-Cultural Perspective on Incompetence." In *Socio-Cultural Aspects of Mental Retardation,* ed. H. C. Hayward. New York: Appleton-Century-Crofts.

Edwards, Steven. 2003. "Prenatal Genetic Screening for ID." *Journal of Intellectual Disability Research* 47(7): 526–32.

————. 2001. "Prevention of Disability on Grounds of Suffering." *Journal of Medical Ethics* 27(6): 380–82.

Ferguson, Philip M. 1994. *Abandoned to Their Fate: Social Policy and Practice toward Severely Retarded People in America, 1820–1920.* Philadelphia: Temple University Press.

————. 1987. "The Social Construction of Mental Retardation." *Social Policy* 18(1): 516.

Fernald, Walter E. 1893. "Description of American Institutions." In *The History of Mental Retardation: Collected Papers,* ed. Marvin Rosen, Gerald Clark, and Marvin Kivitz, 1:321–25. Baltimore: University Park Press.

Fine, Michelle, and Adrienne Asch, eds. 1988. *Women with Disabilities: Essays in Psychology, Culture, and Politics.* Philadelphia: Temple University Press.

Finger, Anne. 1988. "Claiming All of Our Bodies: Reproductive Rights and Disability." In *With the Power of Each Breath: A Disabled Women's Anthology,* ed. Susan Browne, Debra Connors, and Nanci Stern, 292–307. San Francisco: Cleis.

Foucault, Michel. 2008. *Psychiatric Power: Lectures at the Collège de France, 1973–1974,* ed. Jacques Lagrange and Arnold Davidson. Translated by Graham Burchell. London: Picador.

————. 2006. *History of Madness.* New York: Routledge.

————. 1999. "What Is Enlightenment?" In *Ethics: Subjectivity, and Truth: Michel Foucault,* ed. Paul Rabinow. New York: New Press.

————. 1998. "Structuralism and Post-structuralism." In *Michel Foucault: Aesthetics, Method, and Epistemology,* ed. Paul Rabinow. New York: New Press.

————. 1997. "The Masked Philosopher." In *Michel Foucault: Ethics: Subjectivity and Truth.* New York: New Press.

————. 1994. *The Birth of the Clinic: An Archaeology of Medical Perception.* Translated by A. M. Sheridan Smith. New York: Vintage.

————. 1991. "Discourse on Power." In *Remarks on Marx.* New York: Semiotext(e).

————. 1990. *The History of Sexuality.* Vol. 1, *An Introduction.* Translated by Robert Hurley. New York: Vintage.

————. 1984a. "Knowledge and Power." In *The Foucault Reader,* ed. Paul Rabinow. New York: Pantheon.

————. 1984b. "Polemics, Politics, and Problemizations: An Interview." In *The Foucault Reader,* ed. Paul Rabinow, 381–90. New York: Pantheon.

————. 1983. "Afterword: The Subject and Power." In *Michel Foucault: Beyond Structuralism and Hermeneutics,* ed. Hubert Dreyfus and Paul Rabinow, 208–26. Chicago: University of Chicago Press.

————. 1980. "Two Lectures." In *Power/Knowledge: Selected Interviews and Other Writings, 1972–1977,* ed. Colin Gordon, 78–108. New York: Pantheon.

————. 1979. *Discipline and Punish: The Birth of the Prison.* Translated by Alan Sheridan. New York: Vintage.

―――. 1972. *Archaeology of Knowledge.* Translated by A. M. Sheridan Smith. New York: Pantheon.

―――. 1965. *Madness and Civilization: A History of Insanity in the Age of Reason.* Translated by Richard Howard. New York: Pantheon.

Francis, Leslie, and Anita Silvers, eds. 2000. *Americans with Disabilities.* New York: Routledge.

Franks, Angela. 2005. *Margaret Sanger's Eugenic Legacy: The Control of Female Fertility.* Jefferson, N.C.: McFarland.

Goddard, Henry Herbert. 1913. "The Improvability of Feeble-Minded Children." In *The History of Mental Retardation: Collected Papers,* ed. Marvin Rosen, Gerald Clark, and Marvin Kivitz, 1:367–76. Baltimore: University Park Press.

―――. 1910. "Four Hundred Children Classified by the Binet Method." In *The History of Mental Retardation: Collected Papers,* ed. Marvin Rosen, Gerald Clark, and Marvin Kivitz, 1:355–66. Baltimore: University Park Press.

―――. [1912] 2000. *The Kallikak Family.* North Stratford, N.H.: Ayer.

Goodey, C. F. 2003a. "On Certainty, Reflexivity, and the Ethics of Genetic Research into Intellectual Disability." *Journal of Intellectual Disability Research* 47(7): 548–54.

―――. 2003b. "Genetic Research into Intellectual Disability." *Journal of Intellectual Disability Research* 47(7): 548–54.

Goodley, Dan, and Geert Van Hove. 2005. *Another Disability Studies Reader? People with Learning Difficulties and a Disabling World.* Antwerp-Apeldoorn: Garant.

Goodley, Dan, and Mark Rapley. 2002. "Changing the Subject: Postmodernity and People with 'Learning Difficulties.'" In *Disability/Postmodernity,* ed. Marian Corker and Tom Shakespeare. New York: Continuum.

Goffman, Erving. 1961. *Asylums: Essays on the Social Situation of Mental Patients and Other Inmates.* Garden City, N.Y.: Anchor.

Goldstein, Jan. 1987. *Console and Classify: The French Psychiatric Profession in the Nineteenth Century.* Cambridge: Cambridge University Press.

Goodman, Nelson. 1978. *Ways of Worlamaking.* Indianapolis: Hackett.

Gordon, Linda. 1976. *Woman's Body, Woman's Right: A Social History of Birth Control in America.* New York: Grossman.

Gottlieb, Roger. 2002. "The Tasks of Embodied Love: Moral Problems in Caring for Children with Disabilities." *Hypatia* 17(3): 225–36.

Gould, Stephen Jay. 1981. *The Mismeasure of Man.* New York: Norton.

Grob, Gerald. 1983. *Mental Illness and American Society, 1875–1940.* Princeton, N.J.: Princeton University Press.

Grossman, Herbert J., ed. 1983. *Classification in Mental Retardation.* Washington, D.C.: American Association on Mental Deficiency.

Gruen, Lori. 1993. "Animals." In *A Companion to Ethics,* ed. Peter Singer, 343–53. Cambridge, Mass.: Blackwell.

Gustafson, James. 1994. "The Johns Hopkins Case." In *Contemporary Issues in Bioethics,* ed. T. Beauchamp and L. Walters, 413–14. 4th ed. Belmont, Calif.: Wadsworth.

Hacking, Ian. 2004. *Historical Ontology.* Cambridge, Mass.: Harvard University Press.

―――. 1999. *The Social Construction of What?* Cambridge, Mass.: Harvard University Press.

————. 1994. "The Looping Effects of Human Kinds." In *Causal Cognition: A Multi-disciplinary Approach,* ed. Dan Sperber, David Premack, and Ann James Premack, 351–83. Oxford: Clarendon.

Haksar, Vinit. 1979. *Equality, Liberty, and Perfectionism.* Oxford: Oxford University Press.

Haller, Mark. 1963. *Eugenics: Hereditarian Attitudes in American Thought.* New Brunswick, N.J.: Rutgers University Press.

Harris, James. 2005. *Intellectual Disability: Understanding Its Development, Causes, Classification, Evaluation, and Treatment.* New York: Oxford University Press.

Harris, John. 1993. "Is Gene Therapy a Form of Eugenics?" *Bioethics* 7, no. 2–3: 178–87.

Hasain, Marouf A., Jr. 1996. *The Rhetoric of Eugenics in Anglo-American Thought.* Athens: University of Georgia Press.

Hauerwas, Stanley. 1986. *Suffering Presence.* Notre Dame, Ind.: University of Notre Dame Press.

Herr, Stanley, Lawrence O. Gostin, and Harold Hongju Koh, eds. 2003. *The Human Rights of Persons with Intellectual Disabilities: Different but Equal.* Oxford: Oxford University Press.

Herrnstein, Richard J., and Charles Murray. 1994. *The Bell Curve: Intelligence and Class Structure in American Life.* New York: Free Press.

Hillyer, Barbara. 1993. *Feminism and Disability.* Norman: University of Oklahoma Press.

Howe, Samuel Gridley. 1848. "On the Causes of Idiocy." In *The History of Mental Retardation: Collected Papers,* ed. Marvin Rosen, Gerald Clark, and Marvin Kivitz, 1:31–60. Baltimore: University Park Press.

Ireland, William W. 1882. "On the Diagnosis and Prognosis of Idiocy and Imbecility." In *The History of Mental Retardation: Collected Papers,* ed. Marvin Rosen, Gerald Clark, and Marvin Kivitz, 1:247–61. Baltimore: University Park Press.

Janack, Marianne. 1997. "Standpoint Epistemology without the 'Standpoint'? An Examination of Epistemic Privilege and Epistemic Authority." *Hypatia* 12(2): 125–39.

Jenkins, Richard, ed. 1998. *Questions of Competence: Culture, Classification, and Intellectual Disability.* Cambridge: Cambridge University Press.

Jennings, Bruce. 2000–2001. "Freedom Fading: On Dementia, Best Interests, and Public Safety." *Georgia Law Review* 35.

————. 2000. "Technology and the Genetic Imaginary." In *Prenatal Testing and Disability Rights,* ed. Adrienne Asche and Eric Parens. Washington, D.C.: Georgetown University Press.

Johnson, Kelley. 1998. *Deinstitutionalising Women: An Ethnographic Study of Institutional Closure.* Cambridge: University of Cambridge Press.

Johnson, Kelly, et al. 2002. "The Possibility of Choice: Women with Intellectual Disabilities Talk about Having Children." In *Disability in the Life Course Global Perspectives,* ed. Mark Priestly, 206–18. Cambridge: Cambridge University Press.

Kaplan, Deborah. 1993. "Prenatal Screening and Its Impact on Persons with Disabilities." *Clinical Obstetrics and Gynecology* 36(3): 605–12.

Kanner, Leo. 1964. *A History of the Care and Study of the Mentally Retarded.* Springfield, Ill.: Thomas.

Kerlin, Isaac N. 1891. "The Manual of Elwyn." In *The History of Mental Retardation: Collected Papers*, ed. Marvin Rosen, Gerald Clark, and Marvin Kivitz, 1:311–19. Baltimore: University Park Press.

———. 1889. "Moral Imbecility." In *The History of Mental Retardation: Collected Papers*, ed. Marvin Rosen, Gerald Clark, and Marvin Kivitz, 1:303–10. Baltimore: University Park Press.

———. 1880. "Our Household Pets." In *The History of Mental Retardation: Collected Papers*, ed. Marvin Rosen, Gerald Clark, and Marvin Kivitz, 1:283–91. Baltimore: University Park Press.

Kevles, Daniel. 1985. *In the Name of Eugenics*. New York: Knopf.

Khuse, Helga, and Peter Singer. 1985. *Should the Baby Live? The Problem of Handicapped Infants*. Oxford: Oxford University Press.

Kindred, Michael. 1984. "Legal Rights of Mentally Retarded Persons in Twentieth Century America." In *Ethics and Mental Retardation*, ed. L. Kopelman and J. C. Moskop, 185–208. Dordrecht: Reidel.

Kingsley, Jason, and Mitchell Levitz. 1994. *Count Us In: Growing Up with Down Syndrome*. New York: Harcourt Brace.

Kittay, Eva. 2005. "At the Margins of Moral Personhood." *Ethics* 116 (October): 100–13.

———. 2002. "When Caring Is Just and Justice Is Caring." In *The Subject of Care: Feminist Perspectives on Dependency*, ed. Eva Feder Kittay and Ellen K. Feder. Lanham, Md.: Rowman & Littlefield.

———. 1998. *Love's Labor: Essays on Women, Equality, and Dependency*. New York: Routledge.

Kleege, Georgina. 1999. *Sight Unseen*. New Haven, Conn.: Yale University Press.

Kopelman, Loretta. 1984. "Respect and the Retarded: Issues of Valuing and Labeling." In *Ethics and Mental Retardation*, ed. L. Kopelman and J. C. Moskop, 65–85. Dordrecht: Reidel.

Kopelman, Loretta, and John C. Moskop, eds. 1984. *Ethics and Mental Retardation*. Dordrecht: Reidel.

LaFollette, Hugh. 1997. *Ethics in Practice: An Anthology*. Cambridge, Mass.: Blackwell.

Lakoff, George. 1987. *Women, Fire, and Dangerous Things: What Categories Reveal about the Mind*. Chicago: University of Chicago Press.

Lane, Harlan. 1995. "Constructions of Deafness." *Disability and Society* 10(2): 171–89.

———. 1989. *When the Mind Hears: A History of the Deaf*. New York: Vintage.

Linton, Simi. 1998. *Claiming Disability: Knowledge and Identity*. New York: New York University Press.

Locke, John. 1900. *An Essay Concerning Human Understanding*. London: M'Corquodale.

Louhiala, Pekka. 2004. *Preventing Intellectual Disability: Ethical and Clinical Issues*. Cambridge: Cambridge University Press.

Luckasson, Ruth, et al. 1992. *Mental Retardation: Definition, Classification, and Systems of Supports*. 9th ed. Washington, D.C.: American Association on Mental Retardation.

Luckasson, Ruth, and A. Reeve. 2001. "Naming, Defining, and Classifying in Mental Retardation." *Mental Retardation* 39(1): 47–52.

Lugones, Maria. 1997. "'World'-Traveling and Loving Perception." In *Feminist Social Thought: A Reader,* ed. Diana Tietjens Meyer. New York: Routledge.

MacIntyre, Alisdair. 1999. *Dependent Rational Animals.* Chicago: Open Court.

Macklin, Ruth, and Willard Gaylin. 1981. *Mental Retardation and Sterilization: A Problem of Competency and Paternalism.* New York: Plenum.

MacLean, William E., Jr. 1997. *Ellis' Handbook of Mental Deficiency, Psychological Theory, and Research.* Mahwah, N.J.: Erlbaum.

Margolis, Joseph. 1984. "Applying Moral Theory to the Retarded." In *Ethics and Mental Retardation,* ed. L. Kopelman and J. C. Moskop, 19–35. Dordrecht: Reidel.

McCarthy, Kathleen, ed. 1990. *Lady Bountiful Revisited: Women, Philanthropy, and Power.* New Brunswick, N.J.: Rutgers University Press.

McCartney, John R., and Vincent A. Campbell. "Confirmed Abuse Cases in Public Residential Facilities for Persons with Mental Retardation: A Multi-State Study." *Mental Retardation* 36(6): 465–73.

McCullough, Lawrence B. 1984. "The World Gained and the World Lost: Labeling the Mentally Retarded." In *Ethics and Mental Retardation,* ed. L. Kopelman and J. C. Moskop, 99–118. Dordrecht: Reidel.

McMahan, Jeff. 2002. *The Ethics of Killing: Problems at the Margins of Life.* New York: Oxford University Press.

———. 1996. "Cognitive Disability, Misfortune, and Justice." *Philosophy and Public Affairs* 25(1): 3–35.

Mercer, Jane. 1973. *Labeling the Mentally Retarded: Clinical and Social Systems Perspectives on Mental Retardation.* Berkeley: University of California Press.

Morris, Jenny. 1991. *Pride and Prejudice: Transforming Attitudes to Disability.* Philadelphia: New Society Publishers.

Murphy, Jeffrie. 1984a. "Rights and Borderline Cases." In *Ethics and Mental Retardation,* ed. L. Kopelman and J. C. Moskop, 3–17. Dordrecht: Reidel.

———. 1984b. "Do the Retarded Have a Right Not to Be Eaten? A Rejoinder to Joseph Margolis." In *Ethics and Mental Retardation,* ed. L. Kopelman and J. Moskop, 43–46. Dordrecht: Reidel.

Narayan, Uma. 1997. *Dislocating Cultures.* New York: Routledge.

Nelson, Hilde Lindemann. 2002. "What Child Is This?" *Hastings Center Report* 32(6): 29–38.

Noll, Steven. 1995. *The Feeble-Minded in Our Midst: Institutions for the Mentally Retarded in the South, 1900–1940.* Chapel Hill: University of North Carolina Press.

Noll, Steven, and James Trent, eds. 2004. *Mental Retardation in America: A Historical Reader.* New York: New York University Press.

Nussbaum, Martha. 2006. *Frontiers of Justice: Disability, Nationality, Species Membership.* Cambridge, Mass.: Belknap.

Nye, Robert A. 1984. *Crime, Madness, and Politics in Modern France.* Princeton, N.J.: Princeton University Press.

Oliver, Michael. 1990. *The Politics of Disablement.* London: Macmillan.

Palmer, Clare. 2005. "Madness and Animality in Michel Foucault's *Madness and Civilization.*" In *Animal Philosophy: Essential Readings in Continental Thought,* ed. Peter Atterton and Matthew Calarco, 72–84. London: Continuum.

————. 2001. "Taming the Wild Profusion of Existing Things: A Study of Foucault, Power, and Human/Animal Relationships." *Environmental Ethics* 23 (Winter): 339–58.

Patterson, Annette, and Martha Satz. 2002. "Genetic Counseling and the Disabled: Feminism Examines the Stance of Those Who Stand at the Gate." *Hypatia* 17(3): 118–45.

Paul, Diane. 1995. *Controlling Human Heredity: 1865 to the Present.* New York: Humanity.

Pernick, Martin. 1996. *The Black Stork: Eugenics and the Death of "Defective" Babies in American Medicine and Motion Pictures.* New York: Oxford University Press.

Potter, Alonzo, et al. 1853. "Education of Idiots: An Appeal to the Citizens of Philadelphia." In *The History of Mental Retardation: Collected Papers,* ed. Marvin Rosen, Gerald Clark, and Marvin Kivitz, 1:61–67. Baltimore: University Park Press.

Potter, Howard, and Crystal McCollister. 1926. "A Resume of Parole Work at Letchworth Village." In *The History of Mental Retardation: Collected Papers,* ed. Marvin Rosen, Gerald Clark, and Marvin Kivitz, 2:127–43. Baltimore: University Park Press.

Priestly, Mark. 2001. *Disability in the Life Course: Global Perspectives.* Cambridge: Cambridge University Press.

Purdy, Laura. 1995. "Loving Future People." In *Reproduction, Ethics, and the Law: Feminist Perspectives,* ed. Joan C. Callahan, 300–327. Bloomington: Indiana University Press.

Rafter, Nicole Hahn. 1997. *Creating Born Criminals.* Chicago: University of Illinois Press.

————. 1988. *White Trash: The Eugenic Family Studies, 1877–1919.* Boston: Northeastern University Press.

Rapley, Mark. 2004. *The Social Construction of Intellectual Disability.* Cambridge: Cambridge University Press.

Rapp, Rayna. 2000. *Testing Women, Testing the Fetus: The Social Impact of Amniocentesis in America.* New York: Routledge.

————. 1990. "Constructing Amniocentesis: Maternal and Medical Discourses." In *Uncertain Terms: Negotiating Gender in American Culture,* ed. Faye Ginsburg and Anna Lonenhaupt Tsing. Boston: Beacon.

————. 1988. "Chromosomes and Communication: The Discourse of Genetic Counseling." *Medical Anthropology Quarterly* 2: 121–42.

Reilly, Philip R. 1991. *The Surgical Solution: A History of Involuntary Sterilization in the United States.* Baltimore: Johns Hopkins University Press.

Reinders, Hans. 2000. *The Future of the Disabled in Liberal Society.* Notre Dame, Ind.: University of Notre Dame Press.

Rhoden, Nancy K. 1994. "Treating Baby Doe: The Ethics of Uncertainty." In *Contemporary Issues in Bioethics,* 419–28. 4th ed. Belmont, Calif.: Wadsworth.

Rioux, Marsha, and Michael Bach. 1994. *Disability Is Not Measles.* North York: L'Institut Roeher.

Rose-Ackerman, Susan. 1982. "Mental Retardation and Society: The Ethics and Politics of Normalisation." *Ethics* 93: 81–101.

Rosen, Marvin, Gerald Clark, and Marvin Kivitz, eds. 1975. *The History of Mental Retardation: Collected Papers.* Vols. 1–2. Baltimore: University Park Press.

Rothenberg, Karen H., and Elizabeth J. Thomson, eds. 1994. *Women and Prenatal Testing: Facing the Challenges of Genetic Technology*. Columbus: Ohio State University Press.

Rothman, Barbara Katz. 1986. *The Tentative Pregnancy*. New York: Norton.

Rothman, David, and Sheila Rothman. 2005. *The Willowbrook Wars*. New Brunswick, N.J.: Aldine Transaction.

Rousseau, Jean-Jacques. 1979. *Emile, or On Education*. Translated by Allan Bloom. New York: Basic.

Safford, Philip L., and Elizabeth J. Safford. 1996. *A History of Childhood and Disability*. New York: Teachers College Press.

Sanger, Alexander. 2007. "Eugenics, Race, and Margaret Sanger." *Hypatia* 22(2): 210–17.

Sanger, Margaret. 1920. *Woman and the New Race*. New York: Brentano's.

Scheerenberger, R. C. 1987. *A History of Mental Retardation: A Quarter Century of Promise*. Baltimore: Brookes.

———. 1983. *A History of Mental Retardation*. Baltimore: Brookes.

Scott, Anne Firor. 1990. "Women's Voluntary Associations: From Charity to Reform." In *Lady Bountiful Revisited: Women, Philanthropy, and Power*, ed. Kathleen D. McCarthy. New Brunswick, N.J.: Rutgers University Press.

Sedgwick, Eve. 2003. *Touching-Feeling: Affect, Pedagogy, Performativity*. Durham, N.C.: Duke University Press.

Seguin, Edouard. 1910. *Idiocy and Its Treatment by the Physiological Method*. Albany, N.Y.: Brandow.

———. 1879. "Psycho-Physiological Training of an Idiotic Hand." In *The History of Mental Retardation: Collected Papers*, ed. Marvin Rosen, Gerald Clark, and Marvin Kivitz, 1:161–67. Baltimore: University Park Press.

———. 1864. "Origin of the Treatment and Training of Idiots." In *The History of Mental Retardation: Collected Papers*, ed. Marvin Rosen, Gerald Clark, and Marvin Kivitz, 1:151–59. Baltimore: University Park Press.

Shapiro, Joseph P. 1994. *No Pity: People with Disabilities Forging a New Civil Rights Movement*. New York: Times Books.

Showalter, Elaine. 1986. *The Female Malady: Women, Madness, and English Culture, 1830–1980*. New York: Pantheon.

Silvers, Anita. 1999. "On Not Iterating Women's Disability: A Crossover Perspective on Genetic Dilemmas." In *Embodying Bioethics*, ed. Anne Donchin and Laura Purdy, 177–202. Lanham, Md.: Rowman & Littlefield.

———. 1996. "(In)Equality, (Ab)Normality, and the Americans with Disabilities Act." *Journal of Medicine and Philosophy* 21: 209–24.

———. 1995. "Reconciling Equality to Difference: Caring (F)or Justice for People with Disabilities." *Hypatia* 10(1): 30–55.

Silvers, Anita, David Wasserman, and Mary Mahowald. 1998. *Disability, Difference, Discrimination*. Lanham, Md.: Rowman & Littlefield.

Singer, Peter. 1974. "All Animals Are Equal." In *Ethics in Practice: An Anthology*, ed. Hugh LaFollette, 116–26. Cambridge, Mass.: Blackwell.

Singer, Peter, ed. 2001. *Writings on an Ethical Life*. New York: Harper Perennial.

———. 1995. *Animal Liberation*. London: Pimlico.

———. 1993. *A Companion to Ethics*. Cambridge, Mass.: Blackwell.

Sloan, William, and Harvey A. Stevens. 1976. *A Century of Concern: A History of the American Association on Mental Deficiency, 1876–1976*. Washington, D.C.: American Association on Mental Deficiency.

Smith, Bonnie, and Beth Hutchison, eds. 2004. *Gendering Disability*. New Brunswick, N.J.: Rutgers University Press.

Smith, J. David. 1985. *Minds Made Feeble*. Rockville, Md.: Aspen Systems.

Spelman, Elizabeth. 1997. *Fruits of Sorrow: Framing Our Attention to Suffering*. Boston: Beacon.

———. 1988. *Inessential Woman: Problems of Exclusion in Feminist Thought*. Boston: Beacon.

Spicker, Paul. 1990. "Mental Handicap and Citizenship." *Journal of Applied Philosophy* 7(2): 139–51.

Spicker, Stuart F. 1984. "Person Ascriptions, Profound Disabilities, and Our Self-Imposed Duties: A Reply to Loretta Kopelman." In *Ethics and Mental Retardation*, ed. L. Kopelman and J. C. Moskop, 87–98. Dordrecht: Reidel.

Steinbock, Bonnie. 1994. "Reproductive Rights and Responsibilities." *Hastings Center Report* 24(3): 15–16.

Steinbock, Bonnie, and Ron McClamrock. 1994. "When Is Birth Unfair to the Child?" *Hastings Center Report* 24(6): 15–21.

Stewart, William Rhinelander. 1911. *The Philanthropic Work of Josephine Shaw Lowell*. New York: Macmillan.

Stiker, Henri. 1997. *A History of Disability*. Translated by William Sayers. Ann Arbor: University of Michigan Press.

Stroman, Duane. 1989. *Mental Retardation in Social Context*. Lanham, Md.: University Press of America.

Stubblefield, Anna. 2007. "'Beyond the Pale': Tainted Whiteness, Cognitive Disability, and Eugenic Sterilization." *Hypatia* 22(2): 162–81.

Talbot, Mabel. 1964. *Edouard Seguin: A Study of an Educational Approach to the Treatment of Mentally Defective Children*. New York: Columbia University Press.

Thiele, Beverly. 1986. "Vanishing Acts in Social and Political Thought: *Tricks of the Trade*." In *Feminist Challenges: Social and Political Theory*, ed. Carole Pateman and Elizabeth Grosz, 30–43. Boston: Northeastern University Press.

Thomson, Rosemarie Garland. 1997. *Extraordinary Bodies*. New York: Columbia University Press.

Tremain, Shelley. 2006. "Reproductive Freedom, Self-Regulation, and the Government of Impairment in Utero." *Hypatia* 21(1): 35–53.

———. 2005. *Foucault and the Government of Disability*. Ann Arbor: University of Michigan Press.

———. 2002. "The Subject of Impairment." In *Disability/Postmodernity*, ed. Marian Corker and Tom Shakespeare, 32–47. New York: Continuum.

Trent, James W., Jr. 1995. *Inventing the Feeble Mind: A History of Mental Retardation in the United States*. Berkeley: University of California Press.

Tuana, Nancy. 2006. "The Speculum of Ignorance." *Hypatia* 21(3): 1–19.

Tymchuk, Alexander K., Charlie Lakin, and Ruth Luckasson, eds. 2001. *The Forgotten Generation: The Status and Challenges of Adults with Mild Cognitive Limitations.* Baltimore: Brookes.

Tyor, Peter. 1977. "Denied the Power to Choose the Good: Sexuality and Mental Defect in American Medical Practice, 1850–1920." *Journal of Social History* 10: 472–89.

Tyor, Peter, and Leland Bell. 1984. *Caring for the Retarded in America.* Westport, Conn.: Greenwood.

Veatch, Robert. 1986. *The Foundations of Justice: Why the Retarded and the Rest of Us Have Claims to Equality.* New York: Oxford University Press.

Wasserman, David, Jerome Bickenbach, and David Wachbroit, eds. 2005. *Quality of Life and Human Difference: Genetic Testing, Health Care, and Disability.* Cambridge: Cambridge University Press.

Waugh, Joan. 1997. *Unsentimental Reformer: The Life of Josephine Shaw Lowell.* Cambridge, Mass.: Harvard University Press.

Weir, Robert. 1994. "Selective Nontreatment of Handicapped Newborns." In *Contemporary Issues in Bioethics,* ed. T. Beauchamp and L. Walters, 414–18. 4th ed. Belmont, Calif.: Wadsworth.

Wendell, Susan. 1996. *The Rejected Body: Feminist Philosophical Reflections on Disability.* New York: Routledge.

———. 1989. "Toward a Feminist Theory of Disability." *Hypatia* 4(2): 104–24.

Wertz, Dorothy, and John Fletcher. 1989. "Fatal Knowledge? Prenatal Diagnosis and Sex Selection." *Hastings Center Report* 19(3): 21–27.

Wilbur, Charles T. 1888. "Institutions for the Feeble-Minded." In *The History of Mental Retardation: Collected Papers,* ed. Marvin Rosen, Gerald Clark, and Marvin Kivitz, 1:293–301. Baltimore: University Park Press.

Wilker, Daniel. 1979. "Paternalism and the Mildly Retarded." *Philosophy and Public Affairs* 8(4): 63–87.

Williams, Paul, and Bonnie Shoultz. 1982. *We Can Speak For Ourselves: Self Advocacy by Mentally Handicapped People.* London: Souvenir.

Wolbring, Gregor. 2001. "Where Do We Draw the Line? Surviving Eugenics in a Technological World." In *Disability in the Life Course: Global Perspectives,* ed. Mark Priestly, 38–49. Cambridge: Cambridge University Press.

Wolfensberger, Wolf. 1976. "The Origin and Nature of our Institutional Models." In *Changing Patterns in Residential Services for the Mentally Retarded,* ed. Robert Kugel and Ann Shearer, 35–82. Washington, D.C.: President's Committee on Mental Retardation.

———. 1972. *The Principle of Normalization in Human Services.* Toronto: National Institute on Mental Retardation.

Wong, Sophia. 2002. "At Home with Gender and Down Syndrome." *Hypatia* 17, no. 3 (Summer): 89–117.

Woozley, Anthony D. 1984. "The Rights of the Retarded." In *Ethics and Mental Retardation,* ed. L. Kopelman and J. C. Moskop, 47–56. Dordrecht: Reidel.

World Health Organization. 1994. *ICD-10: International Statistical Classification of Diseases and Related Health Problems.* Geneva: World Health Organization.

Young, Iris Marion. 2002. "Lived Body vs. Gender: Reflections on Social Structure and Subjectivity." *Ratio*, December 4.

———. 1990. *Justice and the Politics of Difference*. Princeton, N.J.: Princeton University Press.

Zola, Irving Kenneth. 1993. "Self, Identity, and the Naming Question: Reflections on the Language of Disability." *Social Science and Medicine* 36(2): 167–73.

———. 1972. "Medicine as an Institution of Social Control." *Sociological Review* 20: 487–504.

Index

Licia Carlson has written numerous articles on philosophy and disability and is the co-editor of *Cognitive Disability and Its Challenge to Moral Philosophy.* She is an assistant professor of philosophy at Providence College.